A Benevolent Dictator

Restoring America to Primacy and Prosperity in One Year

Marlin H. Thompson

ISBN-13: 978-1500320850
ISBN-10: 1500320854

CONTENTS

ACKNOWLEDGMENTS

My daughter Tammy for her invaluable work in designing the cover, proofreading, arranging the chapters and bibliography, and adapting the layout for Kindle Direct Publishing.

Ed and Tony for their encouragement and support.

Gerry for alerting me to Kindle Direct Publishing.

Bo, Carleen, Dale, Deborah, Jeanine, Joann, and Sarah for reviewing and critiquing the book.

Rush Limbaugh, Mark Levin, Herman Cain, Laura Ingraham, Mark Steyn, Dr Michael Savage, and Glenn Beck on radio, and a host of television personalities on Fox News Network for delivering a consistent conservative message.

Chip, Greg, and the Roanoke Tea Party for enumerating the core principles of liberty and exposing the ideologies and voting records of local, state, and federal politicians.

Barack for inspiring me to write another chapter every time I heard him speak.

FORWARD

On 02/05/2008, I authored an online post "Benevolent Dictators Make Good Government". Examples are King David -Israel - (1010 BC –970 B.C.) in ancient times and General Douglas McArthur - Japan (1945 –1952) in modern times. I started musing about what I would do if I were absolute dictator of the United States for one year to fast track our country back to a position of primacy and prosperity. I have submitted a series of posts online to PA Pundits (many controversial) about what solutions I would put forward to solve the major issues facing our nation. I want to thank Ed and Tony for the opportunity to express my opinions without editorial censorship. Prominent conservative Americans that I respect, and who I believe would best implement the tenants of this book are Dr. Ben Carson, Businessman Donald Trump, Senator Ted Cruz,, Governor Sarah Palin, Governor Mike Huckabee, and Governor Scott Walker.

Top conservative economists I respect who would help restore our nation to fiscal health are Dr. Thomas Sowell, Arthur Laffer, Dr. Walter E. Williams, and the television personalities at the Fox Business Network.

A former governor of Wisconsin had it right when he reportedly said, "The only three things I want the Federal Government to do for me are deliver my mail, keep any enemies out of my front yard, and stay out of my life."

Once upon a time, there was a charismatic and eloquent young leader who decided his nation needed a change, and he was the one to implement it. The people were receptive and ready for a change. He spoke passionately when denouncing the existing government system, and the press loved him. Nobody questioned what he believed in or who his friends were. He would help the poor and bring free medical care and education to all. He would bring justice and equality. He said, "I am for hope and change, and will bring you both." Nobody bothered to ask about the change, so by the time the executioner's guns went silent, all guns had been confiscated. When everyone was finally equal, they were equally poor, hungry, and miserable. Their free education was worthless. When the change was fully implemented, the country had been reduced to Third World status. More than one million people fled in small boats and rafts. The charismatic young leader was Fidel Castro. The nation was Cuba. In 2008, the citizens of the United States also fell for a charismatic, eloquent young leader who promised hope and change without asking, "What change, and how much will it cost us?" As Sarah Palin so eloquently asked, "How's that Hopey Changey thing working out for you?" Those words are not part of the Obama administration vocabulary in the second term.

Alexander Tytler, in his 1770 book, Cycle of Democracy, wrote, "A democracy cannot exist as a permanent form of government. It can only exist until the voters discover they can vote themselves largesse from the public treasury. From that moment on, the majority always votes for the candidates promising them the most benefits from the treasury, with the result that a democracy always collapses over loose fiscal responsibility, always followed by a dictatorship. The average of the world's great civilizations before they decline has been 200 years. Nations have progressed in this sequence:

From bondage to spiritual faith
From spiritual faith to great courage
From courage to liberty
From liberty to abundance
From abundance to selfishness
From selfishness to complacency
From complacency to apathy
From apathy to dependency
From dependency back again to bondage."

The United States has outlasted the average by 35 years, but with over 200 federal programs that foster dependency and nearly half of adults getting a monthly "entitlement" check, we are now on the road to bondage. Americans are becoming increasingly addicted to government, and politicians are the dealers of the drug named "dependency". Let's hope and pray we get a benevolent dictator.

The clam is a bivalve mollusk that lives out its entire life on sand in shallow coastal waters of the earth's oceans, and is totally dependent on its environment. It is a filter-feeding animal, and to obtain food, the clam merely opens its shell and lets nutrient filled water flow in. When disturbed, the clam ejects a spurt of water and withdraws to safer depths in the sand. The clam is known to Americans only as a source of food, but can also be viewed as a classic emblem or mascot for the welfare state. The eagle is a diurnal bird of prey that must leave the roost every morning in all kinds of weather to find and capture fish, birds, or small animals to feed itself and its family. It has to hunt each waking hour and use its keen eyes, strength, and superb aerial skills to avoid starvation. The eagle is known to Americans as our national symbol and a representation of freedom, independence, courage, and power. For fifty years, our national Congress under Democratic leadership enacted laws that consolidated power in Washington, D.C., by promising handouts to all segments of society, financed with confiscatory taxes and deficit spending. If these liberal proponents for the failed policies of dependency, secularism, entitlement, class envy, and income redistribution manage to permanently impose their agenda on the United States of America, it would be appropriate that we change our national symbol from the eagle to the clam. Clams are much easier to control than eagles, and when the majority of voting Americans are getting monthly checks from the federal government, the liberals will have achieved the goal of a perpetual welfare state. Then we can all be "happy as clams".

An Aesop Fable illustrates the Law of Compensation. A lean, hungry, half-starved wolf happened one moonlit night to meet a jolly, plump, well-fed dog. The wolf said, "You look extremely well. I have never seen such a happy well groomed dog. How come you live so much better than I? I spend al my time hunting for food and yet I am about to perish with hunger". The dog replied, "You could live as well as me" "How is that?" asked the wolf. "Why," said the dog, "I only have to guard the house at night." "I am having a hard time of it living in the woods. A warm roof and a belly full of food would be good," said the wolf. The dog said, "Follow me." The wolf spied a mark around the dog's neck. "What is it?" "It's nothing," said the dog. "I am tied up with a chain in the daytime. At night I am turned loose and go where I please. My owner brings me table scraps left by the family. Come along, now." "No," replied the wolf, "You can keep your happiness. Liberty is for me." Lesson: Capitalism is freedom. Socialism is slavery. Almost half of all Americans have become addicted to entitlements and do not understand the Law of Compensation. They are sacrificing liberty for financial gain. When you take the king's bread, (welfare, unemployment, food stamps, disability benefits), you do the king's bidding. Do not accept President Obama's table scraps and chain.

Throughout the 6,000 years of man's recorded history, there have been many heads of state, military commanders, philosophers, writers, and poets who exhibited eloquence and charisma. Some used these abilities for good and some for evil. Jesus Christ was the most eloquent man who ever lived, and his words are recited millions of times every week throughout the world for the good of mankind. A well known story from Germany in the year 1284 was the Pied Piper of Hamelin. This mysterious figure claimed to be a rat catcher, and for a sum of money he would rid the city of all rats and mice. The citizens struck a deal with him. He took a small fife from his pocket, began to blow on it, and rats and mice came from every house and gathered around him. He led them to the river Weser, walked into the water, and the animals following him fell in and drowned. Freed of their plague, the citizens refused to pay him, and he left bitter and angry. He returned on June 26, Saint Paul's Day, now dressed in a hunter's costume. When he sounded his fife this time, all the children of the town over 4 years old (130 in all), followed him into the water to their deaths. To this day, the residents of Hamelin record their proclamations according to the years and days since the loss of their children. Billy Graham is an example of using eloquence and charisma for good. Known as the preacher to presidents, in his 50 years of preaching the Gospel to millions of people all over the world, he recognized the power of the words in his sermons. He reportedly said that when he asked people to come forward and accept Christ at the end of each crusade, if instead he asked them to walk off the back of the stadium wall, some would do it -to almost certain injury or death. When Barack Obama was elected president of the United States, would he use his rhetorical skills to become a Pied Piper or a Billy Graham? In the 2008 election, he used platitudes and inane words like "hope" and "change" without any explanation. This was sufficient for the American people in selecting a person for the most powerful position in the world? In 2012, he had no in-depth questioning of his anti-capitalist anti-military socialist ideology. He thinks government has all the answers. He is no Billy Graham. Is he a Pied Piper?

In the Holy Bible, Romans 13:1 says, "Let every person be subject to governing authorities. For there is no authority except from God, and those that exist have been instituted by God." This meant that on January 20, 2009, God wanted Barack Obama to be the leader of the free world. In the book of Jeremiah in the Old Testament, God also appointed a man be ruler of the entire known world. His name was Nebuchadrezzer, who ascended to the throne of Babylon in 605 B.C., and in March 587 B.C., he conquered Judah and Jerusalem. Three times in the book of Jeremiah, Jeremiah calls Nebuchadrezzer "The Servant of the Lord", declaring that he was an instrument to bring divine judgment on Judah. God gave him the power and authority to subjugate all kingdoms and nations. Is God using Barack Obama to bring divine judgment on the United States for taking God out of our schools and courts, with laws permitting same-sex marriage and destruction of the unborn? The book of Daniel, Chapter 4, expands on the role of Nebuchadrezzer in world history. He was feeling secure and completely free from apprehension. His wars were over; his kingdom was tranquil and prosperous beyond his fondest dreams. He had built a magnificent city; gathered about him the wealth and luxuries of the world and now he was preparing to while away the remainder of his life enjoying it all. Then came the fearsome dreams so familiar in Scripture. He was relying on his old advisors to interpret them, and they were failing; so he turned to Belteshazzar (Daniel), the chief-of-staff of his advisors. The king was still a polytheist during this time, but he felt that the gods could somehow dwell with men, at least with Daniel. God showed him an angel (he called a watcher) in his dreams, who was to mete out the punishment because of his arrogance. The Holy ones in heaven demanded the braggart's hide. The message was that "He (God) arranges kingdom affairs however He wishes, and makes leaders out of losers." Daniel had to tell King Nebuchadrezzer that his dreams meant he had one year to repent of his pride or he was to be dethroned. Telling the most powerful man on the planet (and your employer) that he is going to be fired is not the most enviable work that a prophet could have. Daniel was troubled and unable to speak. The king noted how upset Daniel was over having to interpret the dreams. Perhaps the blow was softened some as Daniel recited the greatness of Nebuchadrezzer in the dream picture. Daniel was a man who would not violate his conscience at the king's command; but neither would he be disloyal to the king when it was not a matter of conscience. The most important part of Daniel's revelation is the focus or purpose of the king's insanity. The intent of the matter is to give mankind, specifically this heathen king and his subjects, and the covenant people of God, a proof that the fortunes of kings and empires are in the hand of Jehovah. When he went on one of his bragging sprees, heaven had heard enough and the axe fell. He may have been giving some visiting royalty a tour at the time. God caused him to become insane, and he was sent to the fields alone to join the lowly oxen and forage for his food. Scripture says his body was wet with dew that may have indicated a lack of clothing. His hair and nails grew long, and there were no manicures. Seven years passed. His mind returned, he knew who was in charge of the earth, and it wasn't him. He would look up to God and not down for grass. Nebuchadrezzer understood armies, and he knew that God was commander-in-chief in heaven and earth, and He is beyond questioning. His power and dominion were acknowledged. God will only put up with so much arrogance and narcessism, and if He decides to intervene directly in the affairs of the United States in President Obama's second term, I wonder what salad dressing the president would like with his grass.

Uncertainty. This word is heard every day on television and radio news. The Webster Collegiate Dictionary defines uncertainty as doubt, dubiety, skepticism, suspicion, and mistrust. It means a lack of sureness about someone or something. There will likely be no economic recovery or significant private sector job creation while President Obama is in office. Businesses and investors are sitting on 16 trillion dollars (13 trillion offshore) because they question what the Democrats and the administration will do to them next. By how much will taxes be raised? Will the unsustainable spending continue? Will China continue to buy our debt? Will the Federal Government keep hiring employees? Will hundreds of new regulations be imposed on industry? Will cap and trade be enacted and raise energy prices? What industries will be taken over after banks, auto companies, and healthcare? Will they enact laws to give amnesty to illegal aliens? How much will ObamaCare cut Medicare and Medicaid? Will card check be passed so employees can easily unionize? Will public sector union pension plans be bailed out? Will Israel be forced to make an unacceptable peace with the Palestinians? Will troops be withdrawn from Afghanistan in 2014? Will the budget for the military be eviscerated?

There have been about 1 billion seconds since Ronald Reagan was elected President and about 1 billion minutes since Jesus Christ was on earth as a man. The federal government spends 1 billion dollars of our tax money every 2 hours, or $4.5 trillion a year, with most of it going to social programs never envisioned by the framers of the Constitution. These programs are supposed to help the "poor" by redistribution of wealth - taking money from productive citizens and giving it to those who contribute nothing. Government debt began the 20th Century at about 20 percent of GDP. It peaked above 45 percent as a result of World War I and above 70 percent in the depths of the Great Depression. Debt has reached 100 percent of GDP twice in the 20th century - during World War II and since Obama was elected President in 2008. With a projected deficit of $1.23 trillion in 2013, we need, we need to cut the Federal Government budget this year by $2 Trillion. I would balance the budget now, not in 2025, by cutting the non-military federal work force by 50% (laying off 1,375,000 employees) and eliminating most Federal Executive departments. If the tenants of this book were implemented, there would be full employment and the United States would again be the symbol of hope for the world. No politician on the horizon has the guts to propose these concepts, they're just whistling past the graveyard, but if we don't do something radical, we are doomed. It has been said, "We get the government we deserve." Pogo was right. "We have met the enemy, and he is us."

- Marlin H. Thompson

1 THE CONSTITUTION

I would issue an order that the United States Constitution is not a 'living' document and is to be left as the framers wrote it, except for amendments that would have to go through the normal ratification process. As noted in subsequent posts, as dictator, I would repeal the Sixteenth Amendment to institute the Fair Tax, modify the Seventeenth Amendment to eliminate the direct election of Senators and change the length of term and interpret the Fourteenth amendment regarding citizenship. Finally, I would issue an order that the Tenth Amendment, The powers not delegated to the United States by the Constitution, nor prohibited by it to the States, are reserved to the States respectively, or to the people, will be strictly enforced. This Amendment provides that powers not granted to the federal government nor prohibited to the states by the Constitution are reserved, respectively, to the states or the people. This would markedly limit the intrusion and overreach of the Federal government into the lives of American citizens. I would interpret the Tenth Amendment to permit state nullification of laws pertaining to powers not specifically delegated to the Federal Government.

Here are quotes from some of our nation's leaders about the Constitution:

"We the people are the rightful masters of both Congress and the courts, not to overthrow the Constitution but to overthrow the men who pervert the Constitution." - Abraham Lincoln

"The Constitution only gives people the right to pursue happiness. You have to catch it yourself." - Benjamin Franklin

"Firearms are second only to the Constitution in importance; they are the peoples' liberty's teeth." - George Washington

"The United States Constitution has proved itself the most marvelously elastic compilation of rules of government ever written." - Franklin D. Roosevelt

"Our constitution protects aliens, drunks and U.S. Senators." - Will Rogers

"Our Constitution was made only for a moral and religious people. It is wholly inadequate to the government of any other." - John Adams

"The framers of our Constitution meant we were to have freedom of religion, not freedom from religion." - Billy Graham

"The Constitution preserves the advantage of being armed that Americans possess over the people of almost every other nation where the governments are afraid to trust the people with arms." - James Madison

"It is the genius of our Constitution that under its shelter of enduring institutions and rooted principles there is ample room for the rich fertility of American political invention." - Lyndon B. Johnson

"If there is any principle of the Constitution that more imperatively calls for attachment than any other it is the principle of free thought, not free thought for those who agree with us but freedom for the thought that we hate." - Oliver Wendell Holmes

"The Constitution and the laws are supreme and the Union indissoluble." - Andrew Jackson

"Let it be borne on the flag under which we rally in every exigency, that we have one country, one Constitution, one destiny." - Daniel Webster

"To live under the American Constitution is the greatest political privilege that was ever accorded to the human race." - Calvin Coolidge

The House of Representatives intended to read the U.S. Constitution in its entirety when the House convened to open its 112th session. Who would be against that? Ezra Klein, a famously liberal Washington Post blogger, explained that the 'gimmick' of reading the Constitution on the floor was ultimately silly because the Constitution was written "more than one hundred years ago and is, therefore, too confusing for anyone to understand." If that is the case, so is the Bible, notwithstanding the multitude of modern translations. Meanwhile, the GOP's promise to require that every piece of legislation contain a clause citing the constitutional authority for it has sparked a riot of incredulity. A writer for U.S. News & World Report says the idea is "just plain wacky". Delaware Senatorial candidate Christine O'Donnell declared that the litmus test by which I cast my vote for every piece of legislation will be "whether or not it is Constitutional." Dahlia Lithwick, Slate magazine's legal editor, responded, "How weird is that?" I thought. "Isn't it a court's job to determine whether or not something is, in fact, Constitutional? And, isn't that sort of provided for in, well, the Constitution?" Actually, it IS part of their job description. Each member of Congress, as well as the U.S. President, the Supreme Court and other public offices are sworn to "support and defend" the venerable document. The court's job in relation to the Constitution is to make sure that the legislative bodies do their job.

Ever since the Progressive era began, American liberals have been deeply troubled by the idea that the Constitution can prevent the government from doing anything the forces of progress desire. The annoying thing is, they used to be honest about this. Woodrow Wilson openly expressed his contempt for fidelity to the Constitution, preferring a 'living' Constitution that social planners could rewrite at a glance to fit the changing times. After his sinister court-packing scheme failed, FDR openly said we needed to supplant the "inadequate" Bill of Rights with a 'second' or 'economic' Bill of Rights.

In recent years, liberals have retreated from admitting that the Constitution is inconvenient to arguing that it is either simply irrelevant or infinitely malleable. President Obama writes in *The Audacity of Hope* that the Constitution is not "static but rather a living document, and must be read in the context of an ever-changing world." On its face, this is not altogether implausible. In reality, what the living Constitution crowd means is that when push comes to shove, "we're going to do what we think is best and figure out the Constitutional arguments later, if at all."

The 111th Congress was of the "living" Constitution mentality. "Are you serious?" said Nancy Pelosi, responding to a question over the constitutionality of the healthcare reform bill. James Clyburn (S-SC) infamously declared that "there's nothing in the Constitution that says that the federal government has anything to do with most of the stuff we do." Phil Hare, (D-IL), once told a town hall meeting on healthcare reform, "I don't worry about the Constitution". Reading the Constitution at the opening of the 112th session is symbolic signaling the priorities of the new Congress. If they actually do it, it would be quite a break from the past. Don't forget that every principle of the U.S. Constitution will be repudiated, so it isn't likely that they will.[1]

You have to love the "progressives" among us. You know them -all those great guys and gals who really think they are part of an elite intelligentsia. These "progressives" and neo-hippies, formerly known as "liberals", are still trying to figure out what they want to be when they grow up. Meanwhile they're doing their best to pull another fast one by trying to convince us that they are no longer left-wing liberals. Gee, I wonder why? Maybe it's because these self-anointed, liberal elitists really do think we're that dumb. Nice try. Included among their leaders is a group of members from the U.S. Senate. These characters and their followers are asking us to believe that the more than 200 year old U. S. Constitution is a "living" document subject to the whims and fads of what they would have us believe is "enlightened" thinking. Somehow it escapes them that the reason why our Constitution has survived so long is because of its clarity, and the fact that it cannot be changed without satisfying some significant requirements. So just what is it that these politicians and their "progressive" friends are trying to sell us? Not much. Except for anything that they believe will buy them a few votes, it seems they actually believe that the Constitution is nothing more than a piece of paper, which it is - provided you don't read it. They really think the Constitution can be changed by means in violation of the required procedures clearly spelled out!

Let's apply their logic to our everyday lives. Most of us have at one time or another entered into some form of contract. Contracts specify the terms and obligations of those who sign the contract. In other words, a contract binds us to its terms and conditions. It could be a car rental contract, or apartment rental, a bank loan, or your own mortgage. Suppose that one fine day you awaken and decide that you aren't terribly pleased with one of the provisions of the contract. What do you do? Just ignore it, tear it up or violate one or more of the specific conditions that you agreed to by signing the contract? What do you think would happen? You get the point. However, every contract contains provisions that specify the terms under which the contract could be changed or amended. It's what makes contracts work and the glue that keeps an organized society operating while avoiding open warfare any time some dim bulb decides he or she wants out of a contract. In other words it's a document that relies on the integrity of those who signed the contract. For some reason the so-called progressives seem to have real trouble with this concept.

That's probably at the heart of the on-going campaign of progressive/liberal politicians and their loyal followers to periodically attempt to change the Constitution while ignoring the quite specific methods required to make such changes, all of which are clearly spelled out in that "living" document. But hey, should progressives be required to abide by the terms and conditions of any contract? Especially the contract we call the Constitution? Make no mistake…the Constitution is a contract that was signed by those leaders of the time that spelled out the terms and conditions of our form of government, including the rights and obligations of both the government and the governed.

In addition, the Constitution provided for possible changes that might be desirable in the future, which are called Amendments. In the process, it clearly specified the manner and method of making changes so the governed, you and I, were always included in the process. Amazing -it has worked for more than 200 years! But lately those charming progressives, virtually all of whom are educated quite beyond their intelligence, have decided that the contract that created our form of government is a "living" document, and subject to be changed by a process that does not resemble those requirements spelled out in the document. They actually believe that they need only find a friendly, sympathetic judge who happens to agree with whatever position they are currently promoting, and that judge can issue an edict proclaiming their position as legal. Obviously the edict may be challenged and taken all the way up to the Supreme Court for a final decision. However, can someone show us the language in the Constitution that gives the judicial branch of government the right, ability or power to effectively change the language and meaning of the Constitution, while ignoring the specific requirements to make any changes to the document? For all the elite progressives and neo-hippies among us here's the challenge. Please share with us your knowledge of that precise language in what you call a "living" document that permits and provides for making changes in direct conflict with the provisions required by that document, which is nothing if not a contract. And while you're at it, please let us know where the phrase "separation of church and state" appears in the Constitution, and just when the phrase "freedom *of* religion" was changed to "freedom *from* religion." As soon as our progressive, elitist friends share their superior knowledge with the rest of us, we can continue the discussion. We're waiting.

The Tenth Amendment has been the most violated of any amendment. The amendment is similar to an earlier provision of the Articles of Confederation, "Each state retains its sovereignty, freedom, and independence, and every power, jurisdiction, and right, which is not by this Confederation expressly delegated to the United States, in Congress assembled. After the Constitution was ratified, some wanted to add a similar amendment limiting the federal government to powers "expressly" delegated, which would have denied implied powers. However, the word "expressly" ultimately did not appear in the Tenth Amendment as ratified, and therefore the Tenth Amendment did not reject the powers implied by the Necessary and Proper Clause. When he introduced the Tenth Amendment in Congress, James Madison explained that many states were anxious to ratify this amendment, despite critics who deemed the amendment superfluous or unnecessary: "I find, from looking into the amendments proposed by the State conventions, that several are particularly anxious that it should be declared in the Constitution, that the powers not therein delegated should be reserved to the several States. Perhaps words which may define this more precisely than the whole of the instrument now does, may be considered as superfluous. I admit they may be deemed unnecessary: but there can be no harm in making such a declaration, if gentlemen will allow that the fact is as stated. I am sure I understand it so, and do therefore propose it." The states decided to ratify the Tenth Amendment and thus declined to signal that there are non-enumerated powers in addition to non-enumerated rights. The amendment rendered unambiguous what had previously been at most a mere suggestion or implication.

Nullification, in United States constitutional history, is a legal theory that a state has the right to nullify, or invalidate, any federal law which that state has deemed unconstitutional. The theory of nullification has never been legally upheld; rather, the Supreme Court has rejected it. The theory of nullification is based on a view that the States formed the Union by an agreement (or "compact") among the States, and that as creators of the federal government, the States have the final authority to determine the limits of the power of that government. Under this, the compact theory, the States and not the federal courts are the ultimate interpreters of the extent of the federal government's power. Under this theory, the States therefore may reject, or nullify, federal laws that the States believe are beyond the federal government's constitutional powers. The related idea of interposition is a theory that a state has the right and the duty to "interpose" itself when the federal government enacts laws that the state believes to be unconstitutional. Thomas Jefferson and James Madison set forth the theories of nullification and interposition in the Kentucky and Virginia Resolutions in 1798.

Why would Americans elect a President who believes the Constitution is a hindrance to the implementation of his agenda? Barack Obama wrote "The Constitution allows for many things, but what it does not allow is the most revealing. The so-called Founders did not allow for economic freedom. While political freedom is supposedly a cornerstone of the document, the distribution of wealth is not even mentioned." Obama is running roughshod over the Constitution, legal scholars say, by disregarding it, changing laws outside the legislative process, and extending federal power in unprecedented ways. The president has "profound disdain for the Constitution," said David Rivkin, a lawyer at the Baker Hostetler law firm in Washington, DC. "Across a whole host of policy areas, President Obama and other high officials in his administration have pushed the envelope more than anything attempted before," said Ilya Shapiro, a constitutional expert at the Cato Institute. Under the president's judicial philosophy, legislation ideally "streamlines government action" so it can "grow and experiment," all while overcoming barriers like the checks and balances built into the Constitution, said Charles Kesler, a professor of government and constitutional scholar at Claremont McKenna College. He said the president's judicial philosophy requires taking a structurally inflexible document that views political power as potentially dangerous—and thus divides it between three coequal branches—and changing it to "concentrate political power." Multiple experts cited the Obama administration's willingness to disregard laws for the sake of his policy goals as evidence that the president is disregarding the Constitution.

1. http://www.usatoday.com/news/opinion/forum/2011-01-04-column04_ST_N.htm?csp=Dailybriefing

2 WORSHIP

I would issue an order that there will be freedom of worship, but that does not mean freedom *from* worship. I will also state that we are not a nation of secular humanists, as today's liberals would have us believe - but a Judeo-Christian nation as acknowledged by the founders, and that Judeo-Christian symbols such as the Ten Commandments can be freely displayed without any interference from the ACLU or any other organization.

No one can deny that many of the founding fathers were men of deep religious convictions and their faith in Jesus Christ. Of the 56 men who signed the Declaration of Independence, nearly half (24) held Seminary or Bible school degrees. These quotes of the founding fathers will give an overview of the strong moral and spiritual certainty that helped form the foundations of our nation and our government.

"While we are zealously performing the duties of good citizens and soldiers, we certainly must not be inattentive to the higher duties of religion. To the distinguished character of Patriot, it should be our highest glory to add the more distinguished character of Christian." - George Washington

"Suppose a nation in some distant region should take the Bible for their only law book, and every member should regulate his precepts by the precepts there exhibited! Every member would be obliged in conscience to temperance, frugality, and industry; to justice, kindness, and charity toward his fellow men; and to piety, love, and reverence toward Almighty God." - John Adams

"God who gave us life gave us liberty. And can the liberties of a nation be thought secure when we have removed their only firm basis, a conviction that these liberties are of

the Gift of God and that they are not to be violated but by His wrath?" - Thomas Jefferson

"Resistance to tyranny becomes the Christian and social duty of each individual. Continue steadfast and, with a proper sense of your dependence on God, nobly defend those rights that heaven gave, and no man can take from us." - John Hancock

"Here is my Creed. I believe in one God, the Creator of the Universe. That He governs it by His Providence. That He ought to be worshipped. That the most acceptable service we render to Him is in doing good to His other children. That the soul of man is immortal." - Benjamin Franklin

"Cursed be all that learning that is contrary to the cross of Christ." - James Madison

"When we view the blessings with which our country has been favored, those which we now enjoy, and the means which we possess of handing them down unimpaired to our latest posterity, our attention is irresistibly drawn to the source from whence they flow. Let us then, unite in offering our most grateful acknowledgement for these blessings to the Divine Author of All Good." - James Monroe

"It cannot be emphasized too strongly or too often that this great nation was founded, not by religionists, but by Christians; not on religions, but on the gospel of Jesus Christ. For this very reason peoples of other faiths have been afforded asylum, prosperity, and freedom of worship here. The Bible is worth more than all the other books that were ever printed." - Patrick Henry

Christianity as a religion was an offshoot of Judaism. It has been said that Judaism does not need Christianity to explain its existence, but Christianity needs Judaism both to explain its existence and what it believes. Hence, Christianity has also been termed historically as the Judeo-Christian faith. In the early years of the Christian faith, Christianity was regarded as just another sect of Judaism (Acts 28:22) known as the sect of the Nazarenes. The early disciples and the twelve Apostles were all Jewish. Judeo-Christian Values in America have a basis in the Declaration of Independence.

"We hold these truths to be self-evident, that all men are created equal, that they are endowed by their Creator with certain unalienable rights, that among these are life, liberty and the pursuit of happiness."

Since the pursuit of happiness, as Sigmund Freud surmised, is tied to human love and to creative work and play, the principles of American

Judeo-Christian Values can rightly be summarized as the honoring of God-given Life, Liberty and Creativity. This seed of American social justice was then fleshed out in the U.S. Constitution through reason and common sense, unencumbered by the dysfunctional religious and secular traditions, and laws of Old Europe.

Our Founding Fathers separated church from state, but they wisely did not separate God from state. They acknowledged God as the source of our rights. In fact, they were careful to place Biblical morality directly into our founding documents and laws and into our values and culture precisely to help prevent a future of totalitarian or tyrannical rule in America. The combination of keeping Judeo-Christian religious morality in the state, as opposed to the church itself and, additionally, setting up our laws based on reason and common sense has contributed to the American Character, and to what is known as "American Exceptionalism."

Our Founding Fathers were religious in a new way, the Judeo-Christian way, and they were the liberals of their day by deducing that our political and human rights come from a power higher than human government. However, they were conservative in Biblical morality. There was and still is a connection between God and Liberty. He is the author of it. It is ironic that American Conservatives are now the champion of this our most liberal founding principle. It is also an irony that most American Conservatives are wholly unaware of their connection with the liberal founding ideas of this great republic. It is also an irony that many American Liberals have turned a blind eye to the required connection between God and Liberty. As Thomas Jefferson and John Adams noted, Liberty cannot survive among men without its Divine connection.

In Judeo-Christian America one finds the idea of equality before God and the law but not government-forced economic equality. Modern European culture has stressed the value of economic equality rather than Liberty, and their governments unjustly enforce the principle. This has led to the failed European inventions of Socialism and Communism. Socialists in America have been lured into this failed European idea of social justice.

Socialism is a failure in that it unjustly suppresses human creativity by excessively taxing away its rewards and by foolishly giving economic reward to many who, even though mentally and physically able, fail to honor their Divine privilege and duty to work creatively. Thus, Socialism is a dual insult to God-given creativity. Communism was much worse in that it also dishonored the sacredness of human life and liberty. Communism was the inevitable result of separating not just church from state, but separating

God from state. Communism dishonored God's gifts of Life, Liberty and Creativity.

European cultures have frequently been tied to authoritarian and totalitarian systems dating back to the Roman Empire. Even European Christianity was, for a time, contaminated by its links to authoritarian rule. American Judeo-Christian Culture, on the other hand, has been linked to honoring Life, Liberty and Creativity from the outset deriving its wisdom from the lights of reason, common sense, and both the Hebrew Bible and New Testament Christian Bible.

Thomas Jefferson, and as far as I can tell, the great majority of our Founding Fathers explicitly put God into the national life of the United States, precisely by putting the Creator into the Declaration of Independence. It is important that American Liberty has something to do with God. That is something for students to know and discuss even if they are not particularly religious.

This does not represent some form of tyranny of the religious majority or an injustice. It was, in fact, the wisdom of our Founding Fathers to stand in opposition to tyranny and injustice by acknowledging the source of our rights -- those rights originating from God rather than from King George III, or for that matter from the Soviet or Chinese Politburo, or a courthouse, or a legislature. It should be self-evident that if our sacred human rights are derived from government, they can also be removed by government.

America is a melting pot of diverse people including Christians, Jews, Muslims, Buddhists and Atheists. From the Judeo-Christian perspective all these people are made in God's image. We have in America a multi-ethnic society, and that is good. What is unhealthy for America is for it to become Balkanized, which is very likely to happen with the atrophy of Judeo-Christian American Culture and Values.

Worse yet would be for America to adopt the toxic values which exist in some parts of the world and which are endemic in some foreign cultures. The values of Fascism, Nazism, Communism or Totalitarian Islamic Sharia Law, for example, must never metastasize in our American Culture, which traditionally has been Judeo-Christian. These Judeo-Christian values have been with us from the beginning, and they have made us strong and successful. These values should be kept central to the American spirit and culture even as we have become more multi-ethnic. Honoring foreign cultures is desirable, but we should never tolerate the values of violence, coercion, totalitarianism, supreme racism, bigotry or intolerance - values which are sadly endemic in some foreign cultures.

We must recognize that our culture is also worth preserving.[1]

Radical Islam is one of the greatest threats to the Judeo-Christian character of our nation and the entire Western world. Does Islamic law, Sharia, have a place in American courts? There is a movement in a lot of state legislatures to ban Islamic law, Sharia, and its application in domestic courts, state and federal. It's one of those national issues that for now is not before the U.S. Supreme Court, but almost inevitably will be before the justices somewhere down the line, even if just in the petition stage. "Sharia Law is Islamic law. It is based on two principal sources, the Koran and the teachings of Mohammed, and is often a consideration in family issue cases involving U.S. Muslims. But its precepts apply to all aspects of life, and its severest critics allege it is a factor in some acts of terror. Legislators in at least 32 of the 50 U.S. states introduced bills from 2010 to 2012 to limit consideration of foreign or religious laws in state court decisions, the Pew Forum on Religion and Public Life reports. During those two years, Arizona, Kansas, Louisiana, Oklahoma, South Dakota and Tennessee enacted such bills. In Oklahoma, the law explicitly banned judicial consideration of Islamic law, or Sharia. The ban was approved by the voters. The ballot measure read: "This measure amends the State Constitution. It changes a section that deals with the courts of this state. It would amend Article 7, Section 1. It makes courts rely on federal and state law when deciding cases. It forbids courts from considering or using international law. It forbids courts from considering or using Sharia Law. In 2010, in a challenge brought by Muneer Awad of the Council of American-Islamic Relations, a federal judge struck down the law as unconstitutional, saying it violated the rights of Muslims. A federal appeals court upheld the ruling, and the law was never implemented.

The Pentagon has consulted the virulently anti-Christian atheist Mickey Weinstein to develop new policies on "religious tolerance," including a policy for court-martialing military chaplains who share the Christian Gospel during spiritual counseling of American troops. In May, 2013, a statement from the Pentagon confirmed that not only will military chaplains be court martialed, any soldier who engages in "religious proselytizing" (i.e., who shares the Christian faith with another) will also be subjected to court martial and "non-judicial punishments". "Christians in the U.S. military are being persecuted and prosecuted. Here are two examples of Christian servicemen being coerced. Technical Sgt. Layne Wilson, a 27-year veteran of the Utah Air National Guard wrote a private email to a chaplain at West

Point, stating his unhappiness about a "gay" wedding in West Point's Cadet Chapel. The Commandant of Cadets notified the Utah Air National Guard, that led to Wilson being reprimanded for conduct inconsistent with the United States Air Force, which had brought disgrace and discredit upon the Air National Guard. Master Sgt. Nathan Sommers, a 25-year military veteran, a decorated soloist with the U.S. Army Band, and a Christian conservative said he was facing discrimination and persecution because of his conservative political and religious beliefs, His troubles began last year when he was confronted about having pro-Republican and anti-Obama bumper stickers on his personal vehicle. The stickers read: "Political Dissent is NOT Racism," and "NOBAMA," He was told, "As a Soldier you must be cognizant of the fact that your statements can be perceived by the general public and other service members to be of a nature bordering on disrespect to the President of the United States."

1. http:/www.americanthinker.com/2007/10/judeochristian_values.html

3 EXECUTIVE BRANCH

I would issue an order and reorganize the Federal Government to have five Secretaries reporting to the President -State, Defense, Homeland, Treasury, and Justice, with a Chief of Staff reporting to the VP. All other federal domestic departments could be downgraded or eliminated, saving hundreds of billions of dollars a year - without significant consequences. All the Czars and recess appointments offices will be closed. We can no longer take a scalpel to the Federal Government and attendant budget. We need to take a chain saw to both. I would also issue an order that, except for the Defense Department and State Department, there would be total patronage in the Executive Branch. When there is a change of administration, all employees would submit their resignations and be interviewed for possible rehire. This would break the tenure of lifetime career "civil servants" who are now immune from changes in top elected officials. Finally, I would issue an order that the President will have line-item veto authority to selectively veto individual measures in any bill. Most governors have that authority now.

Because they deal with matters of life and death, the military has a more effective and rational organization chart than any corporate or political body. After the basic unit of the squad (9 to 10 individuals), all other levels through the Secretary of Defense -Platoon, Company, Battalion, Brigade, Division, Corps, Army, and Joint Chiefs of Staff -have 5 sections, with 4 active and 1 support. No officer has more than 5 persons reporting to him or her, an optimum organizational structure. This is the way the entire Executive branch should be organized.

To show how the U.S. Federal Government has grown out of control, President Barack Obama has 32 persons reporting directly to him. It is impossible to properly supervise the duties of this many people. There are 15 Cabinet Secretaries, 7 other Cabinet-level posts, (including Vice President) and 10 Czars immune from Congressional confirmation. Average pay for these individuals is about $160,000 per year and most have extensive staffs.

Cabinet and Cabinet level posts are:

Secretary of State ($16.4 Billion -18,900 employees)
Secretary of the Treasury ($19.6 Billion -115,900 employees)
Secretary of Defense ($757 Billion -3,000,000 employees with 1,591,000 in uniform)
Attorney General Justice Department ($46.2 Billion -112,600 employees)
Secretary of the Interior ($90 Billion -71,450 employees)
Secretary of Agriculture ($134.1 Billion -109,800 employees)
Secretary of Commerce ($15.80 Billion -43,900 employees)
Secretary of Labor ($140 Billion -17,500 Employees)
Secretary of Health and Human Services ($879 Billion -67,000 employees)
Secretary of Education ($45.4 Billion -4,500 employees)
Secretary of Housing and Urban Development ($40.50 Billion -10,600 employees)
Secretary of Transportation ($73.2 Billion -58,600 employees)
Secretary of Energy ($24.10 Billion -109,000 employees)
Secretary of Veterans Affairs ($97.70 Billion -235,000 employees)
Secretary of Homeland Security ($40,00 Billion -208,000 employees)
Administrator of the Environmental Protection Agency ($8.70 Billion - 17,500 employees)
Office of the President, to include Vice President, White House Chief of Staff
Director of the Office of Management and Budget, Trade Representative, Ambassador to the United nations, and Chair of the Council of Economic Advisors ($1.00 Billion -1,725 employees)

Independent agencies have another 884,700 employees with an unknown budget, bringing the total executive branch work force to 2,750,000 employees. Since becoming President, Barack Obama has added 200,000 hires to the domestic federal rolls and the Bureau of Labor statistics show that federal employees in the public sector made an average of $67,691 in 2008, while private sector workers in the same occupations made $60,046. The Government data also shows that federal workers received benefits valued at $40,785 compared to benefits valued at $9,882 for private sector workers, for a total of 70% more pay and benefits than the private sector.

In 2012, Czars appointed by President Obama are Afghanistan Czar, AIDS Czar, Auto Recovery Czar, Border Czar, California Water Czar, Car Czar, Central Region Czar, Climate Specialist Czar, Domestic Violence Czar, Drug Czar, Economic Czar, Energy and Environment Czar, Eurasian Energy Czar, Faith Based Czar, Great Lakes Czar, Green Jobs Czar, Guantanamo Closure Czar, Health Czar, Information Czar, International Climate Czar, Mideast Peace Czar, Pay Czar, Regulatory Czar, Southwest Asia Czar, Science Czar, Stimulus Accountability Czar, Sudan Czar, TARP Czar, Terrorism Czar, Technology Czar, Urban Affairs Czar, Weapons Czar, and WMD policy Czar. Most of these were not confirmed by the Senate, and it's a way for Obama to bypass Congress. The total budget for these 'positions' is about $50 Million. Obama saw something else in the position of "czar": a means of overcoming the limitations of the system of checks and balances that would enable him to carry out programs under the radar and without oversight by Congress -- or anyone else either. The czars were tailor-made for Obama's community organizer method of government. A more fitting example of the perils of subverting the constitutional order could not have been devised. Obama has applied the concept of czar with alacrity unknown to previous administrations. He began with 32, shortly expanded to 39, and thereafter to the mid-40s. The numbers have shifted but have always remained within that range. How many are there now? That's difficult to say. So opaque is the cloak of bureaucratic secrecy surrounding these positions that there is no complete, accurate, and up-to-date list of Obama czars active in 2013. The administration has played a consistent game of three-card monte all down the line, abolishing some positions only to reestablish them under other names, consolidating some into a single position while spinning off others, and every other conceivable bureaucratic trick. What have the Obama czars accomplished? We don't know.

In 2013, the budget for the Executive Branch was $3.8 Trillion (Including Defense), with the Defense budget $757 Billion, leaving $2.793 Trillion for the other departments. Total receipts to the treasury are $2.9 trillion revenue, leaving a deficit of $901 billion. If budgets for the Legislative, Judiciary, and off-budget expenses are included, the total budget is $3.99 Trillion with a deficit of $1.83 Trillion.

Government jobs do not create wealth. Our politicians must understand the concept that profits employ while taxes destroy. More federal jobs lead to wealth destruction compared with private sector jobs that create wealth.

"If you put the federal government in charge of the Sahara Desert, in five years, there'd be a shortage of sand." - Milton Friedman.

"Everyone is entitled to his own opinion, but not his own facts." - Daniel Patrick Moynihan.

I will cut the non-military federal work force by 50% and lay off 1,375,000 employees. The Interior Department, Agriculture Department, Labor Department, Health and Human Services Department, Education Department, Housing and Urban Development Department, Transportation Department, Energy Department, and Environmental Protection Agency will be eliminated and necessary functions and personnel will be merged into the Homeland Department. With these Departments gone, so will the myriad of regulations they have created with unfunded mandates on the private sector. As will be noted in subsequent posts, I will privatize Social Security and Medicare, so they will not be the Entitlement nightmare they now pose for the budget. The Commerce Department, Trade Representative, and the Ambassador to the United Nations will be eliminated and key personnel merged into the State Department. The Homeland Security Department will be eliminated and needed employees transferred to the Justice Department. The Office of Veterans Affairs will be merged into the Defense Department. The Office of Management and Budget and the Council of Economic Advisors will be incorporated into the Treasury Department. Independent agencies will be eliminated and their 884,700 employees.

The good news is that proponents of limited government are fired up and fighting for freedom. Obama's statist proposals on everything from healthcare to taxes have reinvigorated the leave-us-alone coalition. The bad news is that this rebirth of activism is not stopping the march to collectivism. The burden of government is much larger today than it was when Obama took office. Federal government spending is now consuming about 25% of GDP. This must be reduced to 10% if we are to survive. The really bad news is that the burden of federal spending is projected to rise to at least 45% of GDP in coming decades because of an aging population and programs such as Medicare, Medicaid, and Social Security.

The only way to prevent this is to reform the entire government and institute the FairTax system. I will demonstrate in subsequent chapters of this book how the entitlements can be made sustainable. Even if we stop the rest of Obama's agenda, we are doomed because of entitlement programs to become a European-style welfare state. Is there a way to save America from becoming another Greece? What is our best strategy to prevent the left from creating a society where a majority of adults live off the state and consistently vote to rape and pillage the productive minority? There are no sure-fire answers to these questions, but part of the solution is that we need to make it more difficult for the statists to treat private sector workers, investors, and entrepreneurs as ATM machines to finance redistribution of wealth. This is why tax competition (FairTax) is a powerful tool for constraining government.

Unfortunately, high-tax nations have figured out that tax competition is a threat and want to interfere with the right of low-tax jurisdictions to maintain good policy. This campaign to undermine fiscal sovereignty is usually characterized as an attack on so-called tax havens, but that is just the first step. International bureaucracies such as the Paris-based Organization for Economic Cooperation and Development favor 'global governance' policies. Other bureaucracies, including the United Nations and European Commission, favor rules to benefit high tax nations such as France and Germany. If international bureaucracies succeed in creating an 'OPEC for Politicians', our chances of thwarting big government drop from slim to none.[1]

1. http://cdn.breitbart.com/Big-Government/2010/03/24/Can-We-Constrain-Bloated-and-Oppressive-Government

4 LEGISLATIVE BRANCH

I would issue an order and reorganize the Legislative Branch to have mandatory term limits of eight years for both Senators and House members. Senators will have two four-year terms, like the Presidency, with 25% term rotation every two years, and the House having four two-year terms. I would repeal the Seventeenth Amendment to the Constitution concerning election of Senators and revert back to the original Article 1 Section 3, modified to read, "The Senate of the United States shall be composed of two Senators from each state, (chosen by the Legislature) thereof for four years and each Senator shall have one vote." I would also issue an order that no law can have more than 4,400 words, which is the number of words in the Constitution. For each new law enacted, an existing law has to be repealed. This would make Congress think about priorities and choose concise verbiage before they generate new legislation, not leaving it up to Federal Executive departments to create unfunded mandates and regulations. As I state in the Chapter "Lawyers", I would not allow any lawyer to run for national elective office. Further, Congress would not be allowed to have any paid consultants, contractors, or lobbyists when generating legislation.

"Giving money and power to government is like giving whiskey and car keys to teenage boys." - P.J. O'Rourke

"We hang petty thieves and appoint the great ones to public office." - Aesop, Greek slave & fable author

"Those who are too smart to engage in politics are punished by being governed by those who are dumber." - Plato, ancient Greek Philosopher

"Politicians are the same all over. They promise to build a bridge even where there is no river." - Nikita Khrushchev, Russian Soviet politician

"When I was a boy I was told that anybody could become President; I'm beginning to believe it." - Quoted in 'Clarence Darrow for the Defense' by Irving Stone

"Politicians are people who, when they see light at the end of the tunnel, go out and buy some more tunnel." - John Quinton, American actor/writer

"Politics is the gentle art of getting votes from the poor and campaign funds from the rich, by promising to protect each from the other." - Oscar Ameringer, "the Mark Twain of American Socialism"

"I offered my opponents a deal: "If they stop telling lies about me, I will stop telling the truth about them." - Adlai Stevenson, campaign speech, 1952

"A politician is a fellow who will lay down your life for his country." - Texas Guinan. 19th century American businessman

"I have come to the conclusion that politics is too serious a matter to be left to the politicians." - Charles de Gaulle, French general & politician

"Instead of giving a politician the keys to the city, it might be better to change the locks." - Doug Larson (English middle-distance runner who won gold medals at the 1924 Olympic Games in Paris , 1902-1981)

"Politicians are like diapers; they need to be changed often and for the same reason. Suppose you were an idiot. And suppose you were a member of Congress. But then I repeat myself. There is no distinctly native-American criminal class, save Congress. No man's life, liberty, or property is safe while the legislature is in session." - Mark Twain

"In my many years I have come to a conclusion that one useless man is a shame, two is a law firm, and three or more is a Congress." - John Adams

"Our Constitution protects aliens, drunks and U.S. Senators." - Will Rogers

"The government is like a baby's alimentary canal, with a happy appetite at one end and no responsibility at the other." - Ronald Reagan

"Talk is cheap, except when Congress does it." -Anonymous

The only tool Congress has to perform its duties is through words. On September 4, 2009, I authored a post published at papundits.com entitled

"Words Mean Things", and some of these thoughts are appropriate for this post.

"The written and spoken word is how we communicate as human beings. Words mean things. In the Oxford English dictionary, the recognized authority on the English language, there are about 615,000 different words, with iterations to 1 million.

With the controversy about HR 3200, the house version of health reform, here are some interesting facts about words:

The Declaration of Independence has 1,340 words.
The United States Constitution has 4,400 words.
The Magna Carta, that British Great Charter of Freedom, has 4,500 words.
Lincoln's Gettysburg Address has 256 words.
The King James Bible has 783,000 words.
There are obscure books with over 2,000,000 words, but two well-known books with high word count are Tolstoy's War and Peace, with 560,000 words and Ayn Rand's Atlas Shrugged, with 645,000 words.
HR 3200 has 211,000 words
The IRS Tax Code has 3,700,000 words

The Legislative branch of the Federal Government has 29,930 employees, with 10,710 employed by the House of Representatives and 6,820 by the Senate. This means each House member has an average staff of 26, while each Senator has an average staff of 67 persons. Non-legislative agencies add another 12,400 employees. Base pay for each rank and file Representative and Senator is $174,000, with majority and minority leaders paid $193,400. The Speaker of the House paid $223,500. The budget for members is about $80 Million. Average pay for staffers and other agency personnel is about $60,000, for a total of $1.80 Billion. Therefore the Legislative branch budget is about $2.60 Billion. This is insignificant compared to the budget appropriations for the Executive branch departments.

Congress is out-of-touch. If Americans want more responsive government out of Washington - and less government - it's time to end the tyranny of the professional politician. The House and Senate need citizen-legislators. But don't expect representatives and senators to voluntarily enact fundamental reforms. Paychecks, status, power, and influence aren't easily surrendered. That's why as a voter and taxpayer, as dictator I would insist that Congress change. With an annual U.S. median household income of about $46,300 ($67,300 for dual earners), it's not surprising that many

Americans see congressional salaries as outrageous. The notion still floats around that Members of Congress are fellow citizens who sacrifice time from their real careers to serve their country. But for too many Members of Congress, that's not the case, and it hasn't been since at least the early 1970's. The U.S. House is supposed to be the legislative chamber closest to the people, but the 435 members of the House are representing larger and larger numbers of constituents (approximately 715,000 constituents per representative) and full-time employment and life in Washington removes representatives from the day-to-day lives of their fellow citizens.

The nation is afflicted in two ways, first by liberal or progressive ideology and second by professional politicians. Progressivism, that gained impetus in the early 20th Century, is the rationale for big government. Big government is a full-time operation and has given rise to full-time overseers. This development didn't happen overnight, but it happened. Those who defend a full-time Congress argue it's necessary to counterbalance a powerful presidency and to ride herd on the 2.75 million non-military federal bureaucrats. Clearly, longer term, liberalism needs to be marginalized to weaken the foundations of big government. Conservatives have been engaged in doing so since the 1950's. Events now may be helping facilitate liberalism's decline.

Congressional reform means opening up Congress to inspired non-lawyer amateurs - citizens who would opt to serve the nation if not forced from their communities to serve full-time in Washington, D.C. The good news is that most congressional reforms don't require constitutional amendments. The Constitution grants Congress the power to regulate itself in many important aspects.[1]

There is a growing argument for making Congress part-time, separating "professional" from "politician" and changing mindsets among federal legislators. A simple premise is that a legislator's job is to legislate. Undoubtedly, congressional liberals legislate a lot because they want more government, more taxpayer dollars flowing to their constituencies and to the special interests that support them. (Republicans aren't above those considerations, either.)

There are also non-ideological reasons why, in modern times, Congress after Congress produces so many laws. It's job justification. If a lawmaker isn't producing law, then how can the lawmaker make the strongest case to voters that he or she is doing their job? Oversight is pretty mundane stuff. New projects or programs, new or expanded benefits, are sales points when incumbent legislators seek to be rehired every two or six years. And when candidates want office, they typically advance a laundry list of legislative solutions. As Herman Cain said, "There's too much regulation, legislation, and taxation." Congressional staffers are mostly full-time employees. Not all of them are engaged in constituent services, i.e., helping your Aunt Mimi with her Medicare benefits. Senior staffers are involved in researching and drafting legislation. To cut the output of laws means reducing congressional staff sizes and operating budgets. To paraphrase an old line from retired Senator Fritz Hollings (D–SC), "The trouble with America, there's too much legislatin' going on out dere." America needs less Congress and a Congress closer to home.

At the 1787 Constitutional Convention, delegates linked the Senate class measure to the debate on term lengths. On June 25, Nathaniel Gorham suggested a four-year Senate term with one-fourth of the senators elected each year. This is the same plan I would order for Senate elections. Here is the reason I want to repeal the Seventeenth Amendment, ratified in 1913. The framers of the Constitution did not intend Senators to be elected by a popular vote of the people. The men who wrote this document knew from their experiences with England that too much power centrally located meant the loss of individual freedoms. Therefore, they constructed the Constitution under the framework of Federalism, which is the division of power between a central governing authority and smaller constituent political units - in our case, states. Integrally woven into this plan of Federalism were two divergent methods for filling Congressional seats. Representatives were elected by a popular vote of the people, and Senators were elected by the state legislature. This provided a separate voice in Federal government for both the populace as a group and the states as a whole and maintained the checks and balances of accountability that infuse our system of government. Each body of Congress would answer to a different set of constituents, and therefore be less likely to make the same mistakes or be corrupted by the same methods.

The Founders thought it was necessary for states to have their own representation and for the people to have their own as well. The Senate's actions had to be concurrent with most of the states since the Senate answered to the state legislatures. Having each state select their own representatives allowed for each state to be more independent. Not only does the Senate protect the states and their rights against the people, it also protects them against the federal government and making it dependent upon those states. The Senate has the power not to approve of presidential nominees if it thinks they are inappropriate. Since the state governments founded the federal government, it is only necessary that the executive branch should cater to the states opinions.

The opinion of the Founders was that it was both the people and the states who created this new government. The role of the House was to protect the people, and the role of the Senate was to protect the states. This original viewpoint changed in the years that followed the creation of the Constitution. It is now common belief that it was only the people who established the current government - not the states and people. The original intentions of the Founding Fathers in concern to the Senate were to protect the states' rights from the tyranny of the people and federal government. When the Seventeenth Amendment was passed, it destroyed those intentions and the change damaged the original concept. The Senate is now just a miniature House of Representatives with a set number of representatives. Before, the Senate was not compelled by popular issues of the day but was focused on the states' rights. Now, since they are popularly elected, the Senate acts with the intention of winning the popular vote. Senators do what the people want. They no longer protect the states' rights. There are no checks and balances.

1. http://www.americanthinker.com/2011/04/radically_reform_congress.html

5 ELECTIONS

I would issue an order that in district and state elections, only persons living within a jurisdiction would be permitted to contribute to candidate's political campaigns. This will prevent national PAC's and other carpetbagger entities from swaying the outcome of elections. I would issue an order that all states require each voter to present personal, acceptable identification to include photo identification, a proof of residency, a name that confirms to the poll list, a non-driver ID, proof of U.S. citizenship or a U.S. Passport Certificate of naturalization issued not more than 2 years before the election. If Native American, an ID card issued by a federally recognized Indian tribe. I would issue an order that there will be no absentee voting (except for members of the military or the foreign service in other countries) and no early voting. All voting must be done by electric voting machines with a paper record. Any disputed elections will be settled by the Legislature of the state where the election was held. Every precinct must have poll workers specifically trained to recognize voter fraud and voter intimidation. I would also issue an order that the Federal Government cannot restrict freedom of speech by limiting campaign contributions from any donor, but there must be complete transparency in who donated to a candidate. I would issue an order that national political campaigns could only start on the first Tuesday after the first Monday of November one year before the date of federal elections. No politician could campaign, hold fund raising rallies, or buy any print, television, or other media promotions before that date. Also, I would issue an order that the first Tuesday after the first Monday in May, six months before a national election, will be the day that all primary elections will be held in every state.

In a Democratic society, your vote counts. In a Feudal society, your Count votes.

It has been formally certified that Osama bin Laden is dead, because he has registered as a Democrat to vote in Chicago.

"It's not the people who vote that count. It's the people who count the votes." -Josef Stalin

Democrats are the most disturbed about strict voter identification. When a voter ID bill passed in Rhode Island, longtime opponents were stunned. How could this happen in one of the country's most Democratic and liberal states? Why did Democratic leaders and black legislators support it? And why did Governor Chafee sign it? Some say black politicians were trying to protect themselves from Hispanics' growing political power. Two longtime black legislators were defeated by Hispanics in the 2010 elections. Some cite illegal immigration as a driving force. Some say voter ID is simply essential. Whatever the reason, people are still seething. That includes many within the minority community, who chide Chafee for saying he was compelled by concerns from the "minority community" about voter fraud. "Many organizations are deeply troubled by the governor's erroneous comments that the legislation had the support of the minority community. In fact, there is not one organization from the minority community that supported this bill," said Steven Brown, executive director of the Rhode Island Affiliate of the American Civil Liberties Union. "Rather, groups like the NAACP and the R.I. Commission for Human Rights were among the strongest opponents of the legislation. In addition, groups that represent other vulnerable minority populations — such as the homeless, the poor and people with disabilities — also uniformly objected to the legislation and its potential impact on the right to vote."[1]

Election fraud can take many forms, but the two that are most in the public eye happen on opposite sides of the polling booth. On one side, an election can be fraudulent because of issues surrounding the voter - the casting of the vote. For example, supporters of photo ID legislation argue that without it, there's no proof that a voter is who they say they are and really entitled to vote. This is commonly known as "voter fraud." On the other side, an election can be fraudulent because the votes "counted" were not the votes "cast." This argument examines the voting and counting mechanisms. Some call this "vote fraud" and it is the primary impetus for a "paper trail" for electronic voting systems. Another issue of concern is voter intimidation -- actions designed to influence a vote, either to not vote at all or to vote a certain way. A 2003 report, Securing the Vote - An Analysis of Election Fraud, reaches the "overall conclusion that the incidence of election fraud in the United States is low and that fraud has had a minimal impact on electoral outcomes." Nevertheless, in recent elections accusations of voter fraud have become central to the political messaging of both Democrats and Republicans.[2]

How Democrats Steal Elections -Top Ten Traditional Methods of Vote Fraud [3]

Over-Voting In Democrat strongholds like St. Louis, Philadelphia and Detroit, some precincts had 100% of their registered voters voting, with 99% of the ballots going to Gore. Clearly, multiple voting resulted in extra tallies for Gore in the 2000 election.

Dead Voters This classic Democratic method of vote fraud goes all the way back to 1960 in Chicago and Dallas. The 2000 election was no exception. In Miami-Dade County, for example, some of the 144 ineligible votes (those that officials actually admitted to) were cast by dead people, including a Haitian-American who's been deceased since 1977

Mystery Voters These "voters" cast votes, but are not even registered to vote. In heavily Democratic Broward County, for example, more than 400 ballots were cast by non-registered voters.

Military ballots Many of these votes were disqualified for the most mundane and trivial reasons. At least 1,527 valid military ballots were discarded in Florida by Democratic vote counters.

Criminals Felons are a natural Democratic voter and they're protected on voter rolls across the country. In Florida at least 445 ex-convicts - including rapists and murderers -- voted illegally on November 7th. Nearly all of them were registered Democrats.

Illegal aliens These voters have long been a core liberal constituency, especially in California. In Orange County in 1996, Rep. Bob Dornan had his congressional seat stolen from him when thousands of illegal aliens voted for Loretta Sanchez

Vote-buying Purchasing votes has long been a traditional scheme by Democrats, and not just with money. In the 2000 election in Milwaukee, Wisconsin, Democratic workers initiate a "smokes-for-votes" campaign in which they paid dozens of homeless men with cigarettes if they cast ballots for Al Gore. Ben Cooper, 64, the former mayor of the tiny coal town of Appalachia, VA, who prosecutors say masterminded a scheme to buy votes with beer, cigarettes and even pork rinds, pleaded guilty to 243 felonies, including vote-rigging and corruption.

Phantom Voters These voters don't really exist, but their ballots do. In the 1996 Louisiana Senate race, GOP candidate Woody Jenkins had the election stolen from him when he discovered that 7,454 actual votes were cast but had no paper trail to authenticate them

Dimpled chads Those infamous punch-cards were a ballot bonanza for Al Gore. Democratic poll workers in Palm Beach, Dade and Broward counties tampered and manipulated thousands of ineligible ballots and counted them for Gore, even though no clear vote could be discerned.

Absentee ballots Normally it's assumed that Republicans benefit from absentee ballots. But in the case of Miami's 1997 mayoral election, hundreds of absentee ballots were made for sale or sent out to non-Miami residents. Fraud was so extensive in the race that the final results were overturned in court.

In 2012, the Democrats stole the election by the use of the most feared agency in the U.S. government, the IRS. Remember all the headlines during the election, wondering what happened to the Tea Party, the liberal crowing that it had gone silent? In February 2012, NPR asked, "Strong in 2010, Where Is the Tea Party Now?" - "what's most striking about the movement this election has been its notable absence." Mother Jones, "The Tea Party is Dead." ." ABC: "What Happened to the Tea Party?" New York Times, June 2012: "The Movement Has Fizzled Out." Remember how odd it was hear conservative pundits saying, 'our voters would crawl over broken glass to vote against Obama', while pollsters correctly predicted that Republican turnout would be nowhere near what it was in 2010? Remember 2010, when the Tea Party grassroots roared? Remember 2012, when the Tea Party was missing? Obama lost Democrat votes in the 2012 election. He won because Republicans stayed home. Democrats got their vote out, we didn't. The contrast between Republican turnout in 2010 and 2012 can be summed up in two words: Tea Party. Now we know the answer to all those questions about what happened to the Tea Party. It was busy being abused and silenced by the Obama Administration IRS. The original scandal erupted in early May when a Treasury Department inspector general revealed that nonprofit tea party, conservative, and religious groups had been singled out for special scrutiny by the IRS for their tax-exempt applications between 2010 and through the 2012 presidential election. During the period, the IRS agents placed groups with words like "tea party and "patriot" in their names on a "be on the lookout" — or BOLO — list for additional screening of its applications for tax-exempt status. The 501(c)(4) status allows groups to keep their donors private. The Internal Revenue Service is still targeting tea party and conservative groups in their applications for tax-exempt status, a full three months after the scandal first erupted. "The IRS is still targeting tea party cases," an aide to Rep. Dave Camp, chairman of the House Ways and Means Committee, told The Washington Examiner. Lois Lerner, who oversaw the IRS division that targeted the groups, is still on administrative leave. In May, she invoked her Fifth Amendment right to avoid self-incrimination, refusing to testify before the House Oversight and Government Reform Committee, which is investigating the matter. Twenty-five groups have since sued the IRS and the Obama administration in federal court over the additional scrutiny.

In the 2008 presidential election, Republicans charged that ACORN (Association of Community Organizations for Reform Now) fraudulently registered voters. The GOP also simultaneously tried to link then Senator Barack Obama to ACORN. Obama's campaign did pay an ACORN affiliate - Citizens Services Inc. - $800,000 to conduct "get-out-the-vote" projects during the 2008 primary; in August 2008 the Obama campaign amended its Federal Election Commission reports to record this expenditure. In addition, the ACORN political action committee endorsed Obama for president. The Election Assistance Commission, formed by the Help America Vote Act of 2002, is charged with "identifying, deterring, and investigating voting fraud in elections for Federal office" as well as "identifying, deterring, and investigating methods of voter intimidation."[4]

The U.S. House of Representatives, in September 2006, passed a bill that would require voters to show a valid photo identification in federal elections. This is a much more stringent bar than set by Congress with in 2000 with HAVA, the Help America Vote Act.

In 2007, before the election, there was a scathing documentary by Citizens United about Hillary Clinton. The film became the center of a huge legal battle over the free-speech-stifling McCain- Feingold campaign finance scheme. Parts of the law were struck down by the Supreme Court when the Wisconsin Right to Life group challenged advertising provisions in 2007. The law took an even bigger hit as a majority of the United States Supreme Court sided with Citizens United: In a stunning reversal of the nation's federal campaign finance laws, the Supreme Court ruled 5-4 that as an exercise of free speech, corporations, labor unions and other groups can directly spend on political campaigns. Siding with filmmakers of "Hillary: The Movie," who were challenged by the Federal Election Commission on their sources of cash to pay for the film, the court overturned a 20-year-old ruling that banned corporate and labor money. The decision threatens similar limits imposed by 24 states. The justices also struck down part of the landmark McCain-Feingold campaign finance bill that barred union- and corporate-paid issue ads in the closing days of election campaigns.

Justice Anthony Kennedy wrote the main opinion, which reads in part that there is "no basis for allowing the government to limit corporate independent expenditures. There is no basis for the proposition that, in the political speech context, the government may impose restrictions on certain disfavored speakers." he wrote. "The government may regulate corporate speech through disclaimer and disclosure requirements, but it may not suppress that speech altogether." Dissenters included Justices John Paul Stevens, Ruth Bader Ginsburg, Stephen Breyer and Sonia Sotomayor. "The notion that the First Amendment dictated the ruling is, in my judgment, profoundly misguided." Stevens wrote for the others. "In the context of election to public office, the distinction between corporate and human speakers is significant. Although they make enormous contributions to our society, corporations are not actually members of it." he added. The ruling is sure to send a jolt to political campaigns throughout the country that are gearing up for the 2010 midterm elections. It will also impact the 2012 presidential race and federal elections to come. This certainly is constitutionally correct. Unions will benefit from the ruling and spend more money, but sunlight is the best disinfectant. Also, Public Sector Unions will not exist, since I ordered that they be eliminated. Full, transparent, accessible disclosure is the ultimate campaign finance reform. As for viewing the decision through the "political plus" lens, the Constitution matters more than electoral consequences. Too bad more in Washington don't see it that way.[5]

With the black-robed justices of the Supreme Court sitting not far away, President Obama took aim at the recent court decision that said corporations could spend as much as they wanted to sway voters in federal elections. "Last week, the Supreme Court reversed a century of law to open the floodgates for special interests - including foreign companies - to spend without limit in our elections." Obama said. "Well, I don't think American elections should be bankrolled by America's most powerful interests, and worse, by foreign entities. They should be decided by the American people, and that's why I'm urging Democrats and Republicans to pass a bill that helps to right this wrong." Justice Alito mouthed, "Not true." The court's ruling overturned a century-old restriction. In a 5-4 decision led by the court's conservative bloc, the justices said that corporations had the same right to free speech as individuals, and for that reason the government could not stop corporations from spending to help their favored candidates. Many analysts predict the ruling will benefit Republicans in next fall's elections.[6]

Often the legislation our politicians pass is designed less to solve problems than to protect the politicians from defeat in our never-ending election campaigns. They are, in short, too frightened of us to govern. Americans do not merely have elections on the first Tuesday after the first Monday of November in every year divisible by four. They have elections on the first Tuesday after the first Monday of November in every year divisible by two. In addition, five states have elections in odd-numbered years. Indeed, there is no year in the United States - ever - when a major statewide election is not being held somewhere. To this catalogue of general elections has of course to be added an equally long catalogue of primary elections (for example, forty-three presidential primaries last year). Moreover, not only do elections occur very frequently in the United States but the number of jobs legally required to be filled by them is enormous. It has been estimated that no fewer than half a million elective offices are filled or waiting to be filled in the United States today. U.S. elected officials in many cases have very short terms of office and face the prospect of being defeated in primary elections They have to run for office more as individuals than as standard-bearers for their party and have to continually raise large sums of money in order to finance their own election campaigns. Some of these factors operate in other countries. There is no other country, however, in which all of them operate, and operate simultaneously. The cumulative consequences are both pervasive and profound.

To a visitor to America's shores, the never-ending campaign presents a largely unfamiliar spectacle. In other countries election campaigns have both beginnings and ends, and there are even periods, often prolonged periods, when no campaigns take place at all. When the Founding Fathers decided on such a short term of office for House members, they were setting a precedent that has been followed by no other major democratic country. In Great Britain, France, Italy, and Canada the constitutional or legal maximum for the duration of the lower house of the national legislature is five years. In Germany and Japan the equivalent term is four years. Only in Australia and New Zealand, whose institutions are in some limited respects modeled on those of the United States, are the legal maximums as short as three years. In having two-year terms the United States stands alone. Other features of American elections are also unfamiliar. In few countries do elections and campaigns cost as much as they do in the United States. Official campaigns are usually brief in most of the countries. In Australia, federal election campaigns are traditionally approximately six weeks and voting is compulsory for all Australian citizens above the age of eighteen. In France, the President's campaign only lasts for the two weeks preceding the first ballot and, if necessary, the week between the two ballots, while in the case of elections to the National Assembly, the campaign opens twenty days before the date of the first ballot. In the United Kingdom, the campaign period is typically five to six weeks. In Israel, it lasts 101 days prior to the date when the Knesset election takes place as scheduled, four years from the day on which the previous Knesset was elected. Early elections may result in a different duration. However, in Germany, federal law does not contain provisions limiting the duration of election campaigns.[7]

1. Parts of this are taken from an article on the Providence Journal's website which is no longer available on their website. A copy of that article can be viewed here: http://www.freerepublic.com/focus/f-news/2747634/posts

2. http://uspolitics.about.com/od/elections/i/election_fraud.htm

3. http://www.conservativeaction.org/resources.php3?nameid=votefraud

4. http://uspolitics.about.com/od/elections/i/election_fraud.htm

5. http://michellemalkin.com/2010/01/21/supreme-court-decimates-mccain-feingold-campaign-finance-law/

6. http://latimesblogs.latimes.com/washington/2010/01/obamas-state-of-the-union-address-criticism-of-the-supreme-court-campaign-finance-ruling.html

7. http://www.theatlantic.com/past/docs/issues/97jan/scared/scared.htm

6 JUDICIARY

I would issue an order to amend Article III, Section 1 of the U.S. Constitution to read "The judges, both of the supreme and inferior Courts shall hold their Offices during good behavior for a maximum tenure of 16 years". I would also issue an order that only the Supreme Court of a state or the Supreme Court of the United States can stay a law passed by a state or federal legislative body or a referendum voted on by the citizens. This would prevent some low-level activist federal judge from overturning or staying legally-enacted laws or ballot initiatives affirmed by the voters. I would also issue an order that no opinion rendered by any court can have more than 4,400 words, the number of words in the Constitution. Lastly, I would issue an order that any ruling issued by the United States Supreme Court can be overturned by a 2/3 vote of the United States Senate and House of Representatives.

The Judicial branch of the Federal Government has 33,750 employees, with 480 employed by the United States Supreme Court and 33,270 by the other federal courts. This means each Supreme Court justice has an average staff of 53. There are (1) Chief Justice of the United States $203,000, (8) Associate Justices of the Supreme Court $194,300, Judges, (687) U.S. Courts of Appeal $167,600, Judges, U.S. and Court of Appeals for the Armed Services $167,600, (2,615) Judges, U.S. District Courts #158,100, Judges, United States Court of Federal Claims $158,100, and (9) Judges, United States Court of International Trade $158,100. There are an additional (324) judges in the following: Judges, Tax Court of the United States $158,100, Judges, U.S. Court of Appeals for Veterans Claims $158,100, Bankruptcy Judges $145,500, Magistrate Judges $145,500. This adds up to a total of 3,492 total appointments, and 29,780 staffers interns, clerks, and other personnel (8 average for each judge).. At an average pay of

$160,000 for judicial appointments, totaling $560 Million and $60,000 for each staff member, totaling $1.8 Billion this totals to about $2.4 Billion. This is miniscule compared to the budget appropriations for the Executive branch departments.

Near the end of his lengthy Supreme Court career, Justice Thurgood Marshall used to joke that in order to hang onto his judicial power until a Democratic president was in office to appoint his successor, "I've instructed my clerks that if I should die they should have me stuffed - and continue to cast my votes." Jokes aside, the life tenure granted to justices by the Constitution has suddenly come under critical scrutiny because it has added to the rancor of recent battles over appointments to the U.S. Supreme Court. Democrats opposed to the confirmation of John Roberts as chief justice complained bitterly that at age 50, Roberts could impose his conservative values on the court for 30 years or more. When the Constitution was being drafted, it seemed to make sense to protect the independence of all federal judges by giving them life tenure. Almost no other government, however, goes that far. Only Rhode Island appoints state Supreme Court justices for life, and every other major democratic nation has age or term limits for judges. For the first 180 years under the U.S. Constitution, life tenure for Supreme Court justices created few problems. But two changes in the country have made lifetime appointments an anachronism. One is the increasing life expectancy of Americans, and the other is the vastly expanded power that the justices wield. From 1789, the year the Supreme Court was created, to 1970, the average justice served 15 years and retired at 68. Since 1970, though, the average tenure has climbed to more than 25 years, and the average age at retirement or death to almost 80. As the justices have hung on longer, incidents of decrepitude have increased. Chief Justice William Rehnquist was unable to show up for several court arguments before his death at age 80. The longer tenures have come at a time when the court has been exerting expanded power over multiple areas of American life. The increased power tends to entice the justices to stay on and limits the president's ability to reshape the court through new appointments. Judges understandably tend not to favor term limits. At his hearings, Alito said he favored either a very long term or no limit at all.[1]

Activist judges have been a plague on American liberty for decades. Many of their rulings, based more on political ideology and political agendas than on the rule of law and the actual provisions of the United States Constitution, are undermining and destroying the reserved powers of the states under the Tenth Amendment to the Constitution and the guarantee of a Constitutional Republic form of government to each and every state under Article IV of the Constitution. Activist judges are destroying state autonomy and local self-government and are a threat to individual liberty. For example, the United States Supreme Court has used its powers to, in effect, overturn the abortion laws of all 50 states. After the Roe v. Wade decision, states, under threat of further legal action, were forced to rewrite their laws to fit the decision of the activist majority on the Supreme Court. In Alabama, Judge Roy Moore was forced to remove the Ten Commandments from the State Supreme Court grounds because a federal judge declared the monument to be in violation of the Establishment Clause of the First Amendment to the U.S. Constitution and therefore an unconstitutional attempt to establish a state religion. Now, there is a looming danger that federal judges with political agendas will use their bench powers to overturn voter-approved ballot measures and state legislative efforts regarding such public policy issues as the legal definition of marriage.

So great is the power of activist judges that local public school boards are literally banning everything from voluntary prayer in schools to wearing a tee shirt with a Christian message, doing so for fear federal courts will take action against school officials. Across the nation, the outrageous spectacle of local communities banned from displaying nativity scenes during the Christmas season is all too common. Activist judges have declared themselves the power over state legislatures, school boards, and city and county councils. Prayer in public places, personal privacy, and now marriage laws are under siege from federal courts. Courts, in turn, are responding to a battery of lawsuits filed by such predatory Liberal Leftist activist groups as the American Civil Liberties Union (ACLU); in so responding, the courts are making the ACLU more powerful than locally elected officials. All of this is in pursuit of a radical agenda of political centralization, statist public policy, and social engineering profoundly hostile to constitutional democracy and individual liberty. Americans have long wanted something done about this situation. The answer now comes from Congressman Ron Paul (Republican - Texas). He has introduced the "We the People" Act (H.R. 5739). The *We the People Act* forbids federal courts, including the U.S. Supreme Court, from adjudicating cases concerning state laws and polices relating to religious liberties or "privacy," including cases involving sexual practices, sexual orientation, or human reproduction. The *We the People Act* also protects the traditional definition of marriage from judicial activism by ensuring the Supreme Court cannot abuse the equal protection clause to redefine marriage.[2]

Article V of our Constitution, provides that our Constitution can only be changed by the people and their representatives. It takes two thirds of both houses of our federal legislature, or two thirds of the legislatures of the states to commence an amendment. It then must be approved by three fourths of the legislatures of the states or by conventions in three fourths of the states - thus providing for strong federal weighting. Yet liberal Supreme Court justices have often usurped this sole right of the people and their representatives, and unlawfully changed our Constitution to their own liking - often by bare majorities of the Court. "Legislating from the bench" is another way of describing when a court overreaches Article III in the Constitution, Separation of Powers authority, and creates law. The court's job is to interpret the Constitution and apply law (either from Congress, the Constitution, or common law) to the facts of the case at hand. If Congress passes a law that violates a Constitutional right, it is the Court's job to overturn the law as soon as it becomes a relevant case or controversy before them. In other words, the Court may not overturn an unconstitutional law until it is made an issue before them (somebody suing as a result of the law, etc.). If Congress passes a law that does not violate the Constitution, the Court has no right to overturn the law, even if they are against the law itself. Their only job in that instance is to take the law and apply it to the present issue. Sometimes however, Courts will impose their own opinions and beliefs onto the law, rather than simply determining what was meant by the law. In these cases, the Court is said to be "legislating from the bench." Sometimes this is called acting as a super-legislature. Courts determined they had a right to "Judicial Review" in a case called Marbury v. Madison, and since then, the level of this review (referred to as Judicial Activism when the Court is being too aggressive, and Judicial Restraint when they are being too passive) has been constantly criticized by whomever is being negatively impacted by a particular decision. The Constitution is the ultimate law. No laws are able to violate this document. After the Constitution there is Federal Law, created by Congress. No State laws may violate Federal Laws, which in turn can't violate the Constitution. Some relevant cases on this issue may be: Marbury v. Madison, Brown v. Board of Education (I and II), Dred Scott, Roe v. Wade, McCulloch v. Maryland, Lochner v. New York, and Korematsu v. United States.

There are many domestic enemies within America. Some of these have very deep pockets. These enemies are attempting to destroy America by nullifying our Constitution, by disobeying our nation's laws, by taking away individual liberties, and by buying the silence of the media. Although it's the same deep pockets that own those media outlets that remain silent while America falls. Our Constitution is the law of America. It holds in it the power to stop all of the corruption being committed by our politicians. However; since 1920, a progressive movement of corrupt politicians, Judges, and lawyers somehow forced case law down America's throat and did away with Constitutional law. And now, we currently have new groups belonging to the same corrupt Progressive movement of Socialists and Communists, along with crooked politicians and activist Judges hell bent on destroying our great nation. Groups like, The Apollo Alliance (started by Joel Rogers, a big money socialist), The American Center for Progress (led by Henry Cisneros, former Clinton cabinet member, who also employs Van Jones, a self-avowed communist and former Obama administration green jobs czar), Green for All (an environmental socialist group), CCX (Chicago Climate Exchange) a 10 trillion dollar a year carbon trading business, with investors like Fannie Mae, Al Gore, and Goldman Sachs, S.E.I.U. (Service Employees International Union), led by Andy Stern, AFL-CIO (led by Richard Trumpka, Acorn (voter fraud) led by Bertha Lewis, and The Joyce Foundation (a liberal/progressive financer of many social justice groups).

Within weeks of swearing his oath to preserve, protect, and defend the Constitution, Obama began his campaign to amass his army of IRS agents, and he continued that campaign with his landmark ObamaCare legislation. Even while the right hand was vociferously professing that the individual mandate in his ObamaCare leviathan was not a tax, the left hand was building up the IRS by another 16,500 agents. But, the slight of hand came to a halt last week when the Supreme Court rejected the individual mandate as a gross violation of our Constitution under the Commerce Clause, then relabeled the same violation a tax and gave it a free pass. Thus, the Supreme Court has given the Federal government unrestrained power to force its citizens to do anything it capriciously commands under the guise of a tax, and Obama has gloriously found his way to circumvent the Constitution. His army is the IRS and his ammunition is money. Our Founding Fathers framed our Constitution to protect not only our right to liberty, but also our property, for the two are as "sacred as the Laws of God" and cannot be separated.

"The moment the idea is admitted into society that property is not as sacred as the laws of God, and that there is not a force of law and public justice to protect it, anarchy and tyranny commence. If 'Thou shalt not covet' and 'Thou shalt not steal' were not commandments of Heaven, they must be made inviolable precepts in every society before it can be civilized or made free." - John Adams.

Of course, there was no IRS when our Constitution was written, because as the Supreme Court ruled in 1894 in Pollock v. Farmers' Loan & Trust Company, the Federal government did not have the authority or power under the U.S. Constitution to directly tax an individual's personal income. But, in 1913, that changed with the Sixteenth Amendment. Here we are one hundred years later with an incomprehensible debt crisis, an economy teetering on the brink of disaster, high unemployment, and the largest tax increase in history is about to roll across America with the implementation of ObamaCare...after the massive tax increase coming January, 2013. The unalienable rights of humanity held sacred and protected by our Constitution have been taxed and regulated into extinction. Sovereignty of the individual was judicially replaced with sovereignty of the unrestrained Federal government. There's a reason so many Americans are leaving. When our individual liberty and property are no longer revered as sacred as the Laws of God, American citizenship has no value. Sen. Marco Rubio proposed a constitutional amendment to negate Obamacare's individual mandate because "we want to make it abundantly clear that it is unconstitutional." "The Supreme Court ruled that under Obamacare, the individual mandate that basically says if you don't buy health insurance, you're going to be punished with a tax or a fine -- they argued that it was legal,". "That Congress could pass a law that basically makes you buy something by punishing you through a tax, that while they can't force you to buy insurance, they can force you to pay a tax for not buying insurance." In upholding Obamacare last year, the nation's highest court ruled that the individual mandate, which requires individuals to purchase health insurance starting in 2014 regardless of their ability, was constitutional under the government's taxing authority. Rubio's proposed "Right to Refuse" legislation would make it unconstitutional for Congress to enact a law that imposes a tax on citizens who fail to buy goods or services that Congress has deemed mandatory.

Judges think everyone should get a trial, even enemies of America. If there were no trials, judges would be just guys or gals in black robes, and there aren't enough gospel choirs in America to absorb them all. A basic problem is that our Constitution has no curb for activist judges, except impeachment, which they obviously do not fear. There is nothing in our Constitution that states how a law or a constitutional provision should be interpreted by the courts. The courts, and particularly the United States Supreme Court, make their own rules for interpretation. Our early Supreme Court justices developed rules for interpretation that determined the meaning for a provision of our Constitution to be what was intended by those who formed and ratified it. Later liberal justices left those long accepted rules, and began substituting their own personal views thereby clanging our Constitution from what was intended by those forming and enacting it to what they thought it should be. This judicial misbehavior by liberal judges has imposed completely erroneous meanings that must now be followed because by the Court's own interpretations these decisions are now controlling.

1. http://www.usatoday.com/news/opinion/editorials/2006-01-15-graham-edit_x.htm

2. http://www.proconservative.net/PCVol8Is151DeWeeseActivistJudges.shtml

7 TAXATION

I would issue an order to repeal the Sixteenth Amendment to the Constitution and institute the Fair Tax. This would do more to revive the economy than any single act. First of all, about $13 Trillion of United States off-shore money that companies have moved to avoid the 35% U.S. tax would immediately come back home and create millions of jobs. Also, the 46% of Americans that pay no taxes would become taxpayers. Illegal aliens and foreign tourists would pay taxes. The monthly "prebate" to every family would protect low income persons from being penalized. The "underground" economy would disappear and become transparent because every purchase would be taxed. The IRS would be gone, as would thousands of tax accountants. Only politicians would be hurt, because it would take away 90% of their power. The power to tax is the power to destroy. The FairTax has been called the most thoroughly researched tax reform plan in recent history. It is also the most unfairly demonized. Scholarly research tells us that the FairTax rate of 23 percent on a total taxable consumption base of $11.244 trillion will generate $2.586 trillion dollars, $358 billion more than the taxes it replaces.

"I contend that for a nation to try to tax itself into prosperity is like a man standing in a bucket and trying to lift himself up by the handle." - Winston Churchill.

"A government that robs Peter to pay Paul can always depend on the support of Paul." - George Bernard Shaw

"Giving money and power to government is like giving whiskey and car keys to teenage boys." - P.J. O'Rourke

"The only difference between a tax man and a taxidermist is that the taxidermist

leaves the skin." - Mark Twain

"A government big enough to give you everything you want, is strong enough to take everything you have." - Gerald Ford

"The moment the idea is admitted into society that property is not as sacred as the laws of God, and that there is not a force of law and public justice to protect it, anarchy and tyranny commence. If 'Thou shalt not covet' and 'Thou shalt not steal' were not commandments of Heaven, they must be made inviolable precepts in every society before it can be civilized or made free." - John Adams

The IRS: Obama's Powerful Army of Punishment and Fear. Every empire needs its army. The Romans had their Legions. Obama has his IRS. Two months ago, Eduardo Saverin, co-founder of Facebook, put a spotlight on a growing trend in our country. The number of Americans giving up their U.S. citizenship has exploded. In 2008, 235 Americans gave up their citizenship. In 2011, that number was 1,780. That is an absolutely stunning 700+ percent increase in the volume of expatriation since Barack Obama took office. Travel back through almost four years of Obama's tenure of tyranny to reform our country into something abhorrently unrecognizable and we begin with his attack on the global banks. At the same time he was busy subjugating America's dignity to the dictators of the underworld, Obama launched his campaign of threat and retribution to offshore banks doing business with America's citizens, along with the largest organization safeguarding their banking privacy. After Obama's aggressive campaign of Chicago-style bullying and extortion, Americans who have no connection with criminal wrongdoing are no longer afforded any financial privacy outside the boundaries of the United States, and even the most innocently affected now live in fear of financial ruin for the slightest misstep. This was not an issue of going after money launderers or tax evaders. This was a ruthless and brutal attempt by Obama's IRS to confiscate the wealth of innocent U.S. citizens, many of whom are living and working abroad. And, of course, this scheme to shake the planet for every last U.S. coin that escaped the clutches of a Socialist administration demanded a massive increase in the size of its IRS by 800 more agents. Two years later, Obama would need 5,000 more.

A New York asset law firm explains, banking secrecy was codified as statutory law (and in some cases, written into the constitution) of certain countries. Other countries observed long traditions and cultures of financial secrecy. Although Switzerland signed a Mutual Legal Assistance Treaty (MLAT) with the US back in the 1990's, that treaty allowed for secrecy to be breached and information shared only for criminal investigations, not the mere failure to report income in a foreign bank account. Thus, Americans with accounts in Switzerland were able to rely on Swiss banking secrecy, as long as they were not connected with criminal activities. No longer. Offshore banking secrecy has been significantly eroded. Now, in all countries, failure to report a foreign account or income in that account constitutes criminal activity and will give rise to exchange of banking information with the IRS. The IRS has sued UBS, criminally and civilly, claiming that UBS conspired and even encouraged Americans to hide income in secret UBS accounts. In February, 2009, UBS settled the criminal charges, paid a large fine and handed the IRS the names of hundreds of Americans with UBS accounts. The IRS is now investigating and prosecuting these account holders. In the civil lawsuit, the US has subpoenaed the names of some 52,000 Americans with undeclared UBS accounts. One IRS tactic is to issue "John Doe" summonses, which seek information on an entire class of unknown account holders, rather than an individual taxpayer already known to have a foreign bank account.- Domestically, President Obama and Senators Levin and Baucus have each introduced proposed legislation targeting foreign accounts and Americans who own them. President Obama's legislation seeks to increase the IRS budget and manpower to pursue undeclared money offshore, including hiring 800 IRS special agents to investigate foreign accounts.

Within weeks of swearing his oath to preserve, protect, and defend the Constitution, Obama began his campaign to amass his army of IRS agents, and he continued that campaign with his landmark ObamaCare legislation. Even while the right hand was vociferously professing that the individual mandate in his ObamaCare leviathan was not a tax, the left hand was building up the IRS by another 16,500 agents. But, the slight of hand came to a halt last week when the Supreme Court rejected the individual mandate as a gross violation of our Constitution under the Commerce Clause, then relabeled the same violation a tax and gave it a free pass. Thus, the Supreme Court has given the Federal government unrestrained power to force its citizens to do anything it capriciously commands under the guise of a tax, and Obama has gloriously found his way to circumvent the Constitution. His army is the IRS and his ammunition is money. Our Founding Fathers framed our Constitution to protect not only our right to liberty, but also our property, for the two are as "sacred as the Laws of God" and cannot be separated.

Of course, there was no IRS when our Constitution was written, because as the Supreme Court ruled in 1894 in Pollock v. Farmers' Loan & Trust Company, the Federal government did not have the authority or power under the U.S. Constitution to directly tax an individual's personal income. But, in 1913, that changed with the Sixteenth Amendment. Here we are one hundred years later with an incomprehensible debt crisis, an economy teetering on the brink of disaster, high unemployment, and the largest tax increase in history is about to roll across America with the implementation of ObamaCare...after the massive tax increase coming January, 2013. The unalienable rights of humanity held sacred and protected by our Constitution have been taxed and regulated into extinction. And after last week, sovereignty of the individual was judicially replaced with sovereignty of the unrestrained Federal government. There's a reason so many Americans are leaving. When our individual liberty and property are no longer revered as sacred as the Laws of God, American citizenship has no value.

The FairTax is a major tax reform proposal for the federal government of the United States that would replace all federal taxes on personal and corporate income with a single broad national consumption tax on retail sales. The FairTax Act (HR 25/S 13) would apply a tax once at the point of purchase on all new goods and services for personal consumption. The proposal also calls for a monthly payment to all family households of lawful U.S. residents as an advance rebate, or "prebate", of tax on purchases up to the poverty level. First introduced into the United States Congress in 1999, a number of congressional committees have heard testimony on the bill. However, it has not moved from committee and has yet to have any effect on the tax system. In recent years, a tax reform movement has formed behind the FairTax proposal. Increased support was created after talk radio personality Neal Boortz and Georgia Congressman John Linder published The FairTax Book in 2005 and additional visibility was gained in the 2008 presidential campaign.

The sales tax rate, as defined in the legislation for the first year, is 23% of the total payment including the tax ($23 of every $100 spent in total - calculated similar to income taxes). This would be equivalent to a 30% traditional U.S. sales tax ($23 on top of every $77 spent - $100 total). The rate would then be automatically adjusted annually based on federal receipts in the previous fiscal year. With the rebate taken into consideration, the FairTax would be progressive on consumption, but would also be regressive on income at higher income levels (as consumption falls as a percentage of income). Supporters contend that the plan would decrease tax burdens by broadening the tax base, effectively taxing wealth, and increasing purchasing power.

The plan's supporters believe that a consumption tax would have a positive effect on savings and investment, that it would ease tax compliance, and that the tax would result in increased economic growth, incentives for international business to locate in the U.S., and increased U.S. competitiveness in international trade. The plan is expected to increase cost transparency for funding the federal government, and supporters believe it would have positive effects on civil liberties, the environment, and advantages with taxing illegal activity and illegal immigrants.

The FairTax Act is designed to replace all federal income taxes (including the alternative minimum tax, corporate income taxes, and capital gains taxes), payroll taxes (including Social Security and Medicare taxes), social, gift taxes, and estate taxes with a national retail sales tax. The legislation would remove the Internal Revenue Service (after three years), and establish an Excise Tax Bureau and a Sales Tax Bureau in the Department of the Treasury. The states are granted the primary authority for the collection of sales tax revenues and the remittance of such revenues to the Treasury. The plan was created by Americans for Fair Taxation, an advocacy group formed to change the tax system. The group states that, together with economists, it developed the plan and the name "FairTax", based on interviews, polls, and focus groups of the general public. Since the term "fair" is subjective, the name of the plan has been criticized as deceptive marketing by some, while being touted as true to its name by others. The FairTax legislation has been introduced in the House by Georgia Republican John Linder (1999–2010) and Rob Woodall (2011), while being introduced in the Senate by Georgia Republican Saxby Chambliss.

Linder first introduced the FairTax Act (HR 2525) on July 14, 1999 to the 106th United States Congress and has reintroduced a substantially similar bill in each subsequent session of Congress. The bill attracted a total of 56 House and Senate co-sponsors in the 108th Congress (HR 25/S 1493), 61 in the 109th Congress (HR 25/S 25), 76 in the 110th Congress (HR 25/S 1025), 69 in the 111th United States Congress (HR 25/S 296), and 67 in the 112th United States Congress (HR 25/S 13). Former Speaker of the House Dennis Hastert (Republican) has co-sponsored the bill but it has not received support from the Democrat leadership, which still controls the Senate. Democrat Representative Collin Peterson of Minnesota and Democrat Senator Zell Miller of Georgia co-sponsored and introduced the bill in the 108th Congress, but Peterson is no longer co-sponsoring the bill, and Miller has left the Senate after serving in the 109th-111th Congresses.

Representative Dan Boren has been the only Democrat to co-sponsor the bill. A number of congressional committees have heard testimony on the FairTax, but it has not moved from committee since its introduction in

1999. The legislation was also discussed with President George W. Bush and his Secretary of the Treasury Henry M. Paulson. To become law, the bill will need to be included in a final version of tax legislation from the U.S. House Committee on Ways and Means, pass both the House and the Senate, and finally be signed by the President. In 2005, President Bush established an advisory panel on tax reform that examined several national sales tax variants including aspects of the FairTax and noted several concerns. These included uncertainties as to the revenue that would be generated, and difficulties of enforcement and administration, which made this type of tax undesirable to recommend in their final report. The panel did not examine the FairTax as proposed in the legislation. The FairTax received visibility in the 2008 presidential election on the issue of taxes and the IRS, with several candidates supporting the bill. A poll in 2009 by Rasmussen Reports found that 43% of Americans would support a national sales tax replacement, with 38% opposed to the idea. The sales tax was viewed as more fair by 52% of Republicans, 44% of Democrats, and 49% of unaffiliated voters. President Barack Obama does not support the bill, arguing for more progressive changes to the income and payroll tax systems.

The tax would be levied on all United States retail sales for personal consumption on new goods and services. During the first year of implementation, the FairTax legislation would apply a 23% federal retail sales tax on the total transaction value of a purchase; in other words, consumers pay to the government 23 cents of every dollar spent in total (sometimes called tax inclusive). The equivalent assessed tax rate is 30% if the FairTax is applied to the pre-tax price of a good like traditional U.S. state sales taxes (sometimes called tax-exclusive). After the first year of implementation, this rate is automatically adjusted annually using a predefined formula reflecting actual federal receipts in the previous fiscal year. The effective tax rate for any household would be variable due to the fixed monthly tax rebates that are used to "untax" purchases up to the poverty level.

The tax would be levied once at the final retail sale for personal consumption on new goods and services. Goods would be considered "used" and not taxable if a consumer already owns it before the FairTax takes effect or if the FairTax has been paid previously on the goods, which may be different than the item being sold previously. Exports and intermediate business transactions would not be taxed, nor would savings, investments, or education tuition expenses as they would be considered an investment (rather than final consumption). Personal services such as healthcare, legal services, financial services, and auto repairs would be subject to the FairTax, as would renting apartments and other real property. In comparison, the current system taxes income prior to purchasing such personal services. State sales taxes generally exempt certain goods and services in an effort to reduce the tax burden on low-income families. The FairTax would use a monthly "prebate" system instead of the common state exclusions. The FairTax would apply to Internet purchases and would tax retail international purchases (such as a boat or car) that are imported to the United States (collected by the U.S. Customs and Border Protection).

A household's effective tax rate on consumption would vary with the annual expenditures on taxable items and fixed monthly tax rebates. The rebates would have the greatest effect at low spending levels, where they could lower a household's effective rate to zero or below. The lowest effective tax rate under the FairTax could be negative due to the rebate for households with annual spending amounts below poverty level spending for a specified household size. At higher spending levels, the rebate has less impact, and a household's effective tax rate would approach 23% of total spending. For example, a household of three persons spending $30,000 a year on taxable items would devote about 6% of total spending to the FairTax after the rebate. A household spending $125,000 on taxable items would spend around 19% on the FairTax. Buying or otherwise receiving items and services not subject to federal taxation can contribute towards a lower effective tax rate. The total amount of spending and the proportion of spending allocated to taxable items would determine a household's effective tax rate on consumption. If a rate is calculated on income, instead of the tax base, the percentage could exceed the statutory tax rate in a given year.

8 FEDERAL BUDGET

I would issue an order that the federal budget would be balanced immediately with a balanced budget Amendment to the Constitution. As stated in Chapter 3 (Executive Branch), I would cut the non-military federal work force by 50% and lay off 1,375,000 employees. To accomplish this, I would eliminate and/or consolidate most cabinet level departments. I would also issue an order that Congress and the President would have to pass an annual budget on time or none of them would receive a paycheck. There would be no 840 days without a national budget. The words "invest" and "investment" or "stimulus" will not be permitted in any oral or written discussion of the budget because they are code words for increasing taxes and deficit spending.

We need to elect representatives who have the courage to cut taxes and slash domestic spending. A retired sailor reportedly said he resents hearing about the Obama administration spending money like a drunken sailor. He said, "As a former drunken sailor, when I ran out of money, I quit drinking and spending. They don't."

"One of the great tragedies of life is the murder of a beautiful theory by a gang of brutal facts." -Benjamin Franklin.

President Obama and the Congress have just run into the gang of brutal facts. They are called Standard and Poor's and Moody's. Maybe when Standard and Poor's downgraded the United State's AAA credit rating got their attention. With the bill to raise the national debt ceiling passed, Congress has passed the buck again by creating a 12-person committee to determine the next round of cuts and taxes. It has been said, "For God so loved the world that He didn't send a committee."

The outstanding public debt as of 19 Oct 2013 at 02:08:25 AM GMT is $17.0 trillion. The estimated population of the United States is 316,839,934 so each citizen's share of this debt is $53,875 or $138,240 for every household. This amounts to 100% of the U.S. gross domestic product or 526% of annual federal revenues. The National Debt has continued to increase an average of $1.82 billion per day since September 30, 2012! Publicly traded companies are legally required to account for "explicit" and "implicit" future obligations such as employee pensions and retirement benefits. The federal budget, which is the "federal government's primary financial planning and control tool," is not bound by this rule. In 2013, there is a $3.8 trillion budget with $2.9 trillion in revenue and a $901 billion deficit. We can't spend ourselves into prosperity. Moody's is now considering downgrading the United States AAA credit rating, and China is threatening to stop buying our debt. Also, there is a move to eliminate the dollar as the standard for world currency. No nation, empire, or civilization is "too big to fail", and we are no exception. From the chronicles of world history, where are the Roman Empire, the Medo-Persian Empire, the Ottoman Empire, and the British Empire? American philosopher George Santayana (1863-1952) reportedly said, "Those who cannot remember the past are condemned to repeat it." Mystery writer Rita Mae Brown, in her novel Sudden Death, wrote, "The definition of insanity is doing the same thing over and over and expecting different results." Draw your own conclusions about our national politicians.

At the close of the federal government's 2012 fiscal year (September 30, 2012), the federal government had roughly: $7.5 trillion in liabilities that are not accounted for in the national debt, such as federal employee retirement benefits, accounts payable, and environmental/disposal liabilities. $21.6 trillion in obligations for current Social Security participants above and beyond projected revenues from their payroll and benefit taxes, certain transfers from the general fund of the U.S. Treasury, and assets of the Social Security trust fund. $27.0 trillion in obligations for current Medicare participants above and beyond projected revenues from their payroll taxes, benefit taxes, premium payments, and assets of the Medicare trust fund. The figures above are determined in a manner that approximates how publicly traded companies are required to calculate their liabilities and obligations. The obligations for Social Security and Medicare represent how much money must be immediately placed in interest-bearing investments to cover the projected shortfalls between dedicated revenues and expenditures for all current participants in these programs (both taxpayers and beneficiaries). Combining the figures above with the national debt and subtracting the value of federal assets, the federal government had about $67.7 trillion in debts, liabilities, and unfinanced obligations for current

Social Security and Medicare participants at the close of its 2012 fiscal year.

This $67.7 trillion shortfall is 105% of the combined net worth of all U.S. households and nonprofit organizations, including all assets in savings, real estate, corporate stocks, private businesses, and consumer durable goods such as automobiles. This shortfall equates to: $215,311 for every person living in the U.S. or $559,331 for every household in the U.S. or 428% of the U.S. gross domestic product or 2,513% of annual federal revenues.

The unprecedented, improbable and indeed almost unimaginable global financial crisis has virtually put an end to the comfortable notion that American and Western capitalism would dominate the world economy. In turn, the financial meltdown threatening another Great Depression has been the rationale for a phenomenal expansion of government spending to prop up demand and fend off economic disaster. As a result, the deficit quadrupled from $459 billion in 2008 to $1.83 Trillion in 2011. It has gone from 3.2% of gross domestic product to 13.1%, twice the post-World War II record of 6% in 1983 under President Reagan. What's more, the debt surge is unlike the one that accompanied WWII in that it will not be temporary. The nonpartisan Congressional Budget Office reckons that the deficit will run for a decade and will still exceed $1.2 Trillion in 2019. By that time, the United States will have more than doubled its national debt, to over $20 trillion. Then, after 2019, we get another turn of the screw as the peak waves of baby boomers move into their retirement years and costs soar for the major entitlements, Social Security and Medicare. Here are the numbers for 2011: Mandatory Spending $2.173 trillion (+14.9%), Social Security $695 billion (+4.9%) Medicare $453 billion (+6.6%) Medicaid $290 billion (+12.0%) Interest on National Debt $164 billion (+18.0%) Other Mandatory Programs $571 billion (+58.6%)

At 41% of GDP in 2008, the accumulated federal debt will rise to 82% by 2019. One out of every six dollars spent then by the feds will go to interest, compared with 1 in 12 dollars in 2010. These out-year budgets will require an increase in everyone's income taxes, raising federal income taxes an average of $11,000 for families, a hike of 55% per household - a political impossibility. The Government Accountability Office estimates that by 2040, interest payments will absorb 30% of all revenues and entitlements will consume the rest, leaving nothing for defense, education or veterans' pensions. If the economy would grow quickly, we might hope to pay down this debt. No such luck. The GDP trajectory is gloomy, and on top of that, the demands of special interest groups threaten to reduce growth even more. Just look at the medical world, which pushes expensive treatments at government expense for its benefit. American attitudes and behavior have undergone a substantial change. We are saving more and paying down debt. We are transforming our society from a consumer culture to a culture of thrift. In a recent Wall Street Journal/NBC News Poll, Americans were asked which economic issue facing the country concerns them the most. Deficit reduction ruled over healthcare. Half were prepared to defer spending or to spend less, even if it meant extending the recession. [1]

How much money does it take for governments of sovereign nations to do their job? Different countries obviously have different answers. Countries run by social democratic or socialist parties will spend lavishly on cradle-to-grave social systems. On the other hand, citizens in non-socialist countries have more choice over how to spend their money. When Americans think of countries with really big governments, they probably think of Sweden or France or Finland. Most of Europe is thought to have much larger governments than the United States. Unfortunately, this isn't true anymore. Even after adjusting for differences in the cost of living and taking into account how many people live in the country, total U.S. government spending - at all levels of government - accounts for more real resources per capita than 95 percent of the countries in the world. In fact, 166 out of 175 countries have governments that spend less money than the United States. Our government spends 276 percent more than is spent by the average government of another country around the world. That comes out to about $17,400 per person living in the United States - almost $70,000 for a family of four.

Sweden's famous "welfare state" spends only about 8.6 percent more per capita than the United States - probably a much smaller difference than most would have guessed. France spends virtually the same amount as the U.S., just 1.6 percent more. Meanwhile, Finland spends 6 percent less. Countries such as Germany, Italy, and the U.K. don't even come close to the U.S. And our neighbor Canada spends 14 percent less per capita than the United States. Japan spends 32 percent less. Two of the eight countries where governments spend more than our government likely do so because the government owns the country's oil wealth (Qatar and Norway). Looking at government spending alone isn't a perfect way to compare countries. For example, while the Swedish government rewards parents with a check for each additional child a family has, the United States uses the tax credits and the tax code to accomplish the same goal. That would make federal government's expenditures look relatively smaller even though the end result is the same. Americans spend more on national defense than most other countries, but the differences in defense expenditures are relatively minor so that comparing non-defense government expenditures doesn't make that much difference. The federal government's per capita government expenditures still exceeds that of 93 percent of other countries. With the new trillion dollar health law signed by President Obama, the U.S. total spending and rank is guaranteed to go up further. The federal government has control over more resources per capita than virtually any other country in the world. The government decides from whom the money is taken, who gets it, and how that money can be spent. Of course, the money also pays for the enforcement of all the regulations and laws that tell us what to do. That is a huge amount of government control over people's lives. Think about just how much more freedom the average family of four would have if they, not the government, got to determine how that $70,000 was spent. That is one reason we need the FairTax.[2]

1. http://www.nydailynews.com/opinion/drowning-debt-obama-spending-borrowing-leaves-u-s-gasping-air-article-1.395796

2. http://www.foxnews.com/opinion/2010/04/08/john-lott-federal-government-socialism-size-capita-spending-sweden-france-qatar/

9 REGULATIONS

I would issue an order that the Environmental Protection Agency (EPA) and the Occupational Safety and Health Administration (OSHA) are eliminated and all regulations issued by these bureaucracies are null and void. These two organizations are classic examples of government run amuck, and have done more to stifle growth and entrepreneurship than any other agencies. That faceless un-elected bureaucrats can cause so many problems for the American private business sector is unconscionable. I will list graphic examples of their overreaching regulations (especially under the Obama administration). Federal regulations are now costing private industry about $2 Trillion a year, more than the money paid in Federal income taxes.

You are an entrepreneur who accumulates enough capital to start a business. On the day of your opening, two men in dark blue suits come into your office.

One of them says, "Congratulations on your new business. We are your partners."

You say, "I have all the resources and don't need any partners."

He replies, "You don't have any choice. We are not providing you with any capital or labor. We will, however, give you a set of regulations that tell you what products you can produce and how much (and how often) you pay your employees. To cover our expenses for supplying these rules, we are demanding roughly half of whatever profits you make each year. You also have to pay us about 12% of whatever you decide to pay your employees and furnish sufficient insurance and healthcare for them. If you cheat us on any of these fees or orders, you can be fined or jailed."

In a panic, you ask, "Who are you?"

One of the men says, "We are with the United States government. These are the conditions we give to new businesses."

And the geniuses in Washington wonder why there are no new jobs.

The growth of federal regulations over the past six decades has cut U.S. economic growth by an average of 2 percentage points per year, according to a new study in the Journal of Economic Growth. As a result, the average American household receives about $277,000 less annually than it would have gotten in the absence of six decades of accumulated regulations—a median household income of $330,000 instead of the $53,000 we get now. The researchers, economists John Dawson of Appalachian State University and John Seater of North Carolina State, constructed an index of federal regulations by tracking the growth in the number of pages in the Code of Federal Regulations since 1949. The number of pages, they note, has increased six-fold from 19,335 in 1949 to 134,261 in 2005. (As of 2011, the number of pages had risen to 169,301.) Regulations also affect the allocation of labor and capital—by, say, raising the costs of new hires or encouraging investment in favored technologies. Overall, they calculate, if regulation had remained at the same level as in 1949, current GDP would have been $53.9 trillion instead of $15.1 in 2011. In other words, current U.S. GDP in 2011 was $38.8 trillion less than it might have been. GDP growth would have averaged 2 percent higher annually, yielding a rate of about 5.2 percent over the period between 1949 and 2011. Compounded, that yields a total GDP in 2005 dollars of approximately $43 trillion, or $49 trillion in 2011 dollars, which is in the same ballpark as the $53.9 trillion figure calculated by Dawson and Seater. Compounding that growth rate from the real 1949 GDP of $1.8 trillion to now would have yielded a total GDP in 2013 of around $31 trillion. Considerably lower than the $54 trillion estimated by Dawson and Seater, but nevertheless about double the size of our current GDP. All this means that the opportunity costs of regulation—that is, the benefits that could have been gained if an alternative course of action had been pursued—are much higher than the costs of compliance. Dawson and Seater have calculated that if the regulatory burden had remained the same as it was in 1949, the U.S. economy would be about $38 trillion bigger than it currently is. Whatever the benefits of regulation, an average household income of $330,000 per year would buy a lot in the way of health care, schooling, art, housing, environmental protection, and other amenities. Mancur Olson, argued in

The Rise and Fall of Nations (1982) that economic stagnation and even decline set in when powerful special-interest lobbies—crony capitalists if you will—capture a country's regulatory system and use it to block competitors, making the economy ever less efficient. The growing burden of regulation could some day turn economic growth negative, but in a note Dawson and Seater suggest that in the long run that will "not be tolerated by society." Let's hope that they are right.

Businesses and jobs are always on the minds of politicians. Sen. Pat Toomey (R -PA) went to Cambria County to discuss what needs to be fixed with government regulations. He toured McQuaide Trucking Co. in Richland Township, and found out what's hurting them and businesses similar to theirs. He said, "The voters and Congress made it perfectly clear that we don't want cap and trade." Rex McQuaide said in 2009, the EPA put more regulations on their truck engines and cost them $17,000 more per engine. They also talked about the cost of fuel becoming a problem for drivers and trucking companies. McQuaide said, "When you have prices go up 30 to 35 percent in a short period of time, that's a significant issue for somebody in the trucking business." Toomey said it's time for America to end its dependency on foreign oil and help eliminate the pain at the pump. He said there could be drilling in Alaska - offshore and onshore - but we chose not to do it. "That's ridiculous." he said.

Congressman Mike Coffman (R-CO), chairman of the Oversight Investigations and Regulations Subcommittee for the Small Business Committee of the U.S. House of Representatives, listened to small-business owners from Colorado cry foul over Environmental Protection Agency (EPA) regulations that they say are destroying their ability to grow and create jobs. "In the midst of a recession, it really defies all common sense that the EPA would move forward with instituting some 30 new costly regulations, without taking into account the job losses they will create," Coffman said. "The EPA's complete disregard for the Regulatory Flexibility Act, a federal law designed to protect small businesses from unnecessary federal regulations, is also extremely troubling." Coffman called the hearing to determine if the EPA is complying with the Regulatory Flexibility Act, which is intended to protect small businesses from severe government regulations by forcing federal agencies to account for the economic burdens the regulations impose on small business. Currently, un-elected bureaucrats at the EPA are attempting to implement a scheme to regulate everything from greenhouse gases to fuel additives. Glenn Johnston, vice president of regulatory affairs for Gevo Inc., an advanced biofuels company located in Englewood, Colorado, said the EPA regulations in the Clean Air Act are blocking his company from providing a bio-based alternative to petroleum-based fuels. "Gevo and the Advanced Biofuels industry in general believe that the EPA should review its regulatory regime and to the extent possible should assure that biofuels other than ethanol have equal and unfettered access to the market," Johnston said. Johnston says provisions in the Clean Air Act would prohibit the use of isobutanol, a fuel source made from renewable raw materials that could be used as an alternative to gasoline in combustion engines. Gevo is working to develop the fuel, which would lessen our dependency on foreign oil. Coffman's subcommittee also heard testimony from John Ward, chairman of Citizens for Recycling First in Broomfield, Colorado. Ward said that the EPA, through the Resources Conservation and Recovery Act, is hindering the ability to recycle coal ash, a byproduct of burning coal. Currently, almost half of America's energy is generated from coal and in 2009, 135 million tons of coal ash was produced as a result. It is possible to recycle coal ash to make concrete and cement. "In the Agency's single-minded quest to gain more enforcement authority over the disposal of coal ash, EPA appears resolved to ignore the negative impacts of its actions on an entire recycling industry and the small businesses that comprise it," Ward said. "If the EPA succeeds in getting the regulations it wants, our nation will end up putting hundreds of millions of tons more material into landfills rather than safely recycling it -hardly a 'green' result." Coffman said he hopes the hearing will compel the Obama administration to review the negative effects EPA regulations are having on small business growth.[1]

Sen. James Inhofe (R–OK) has issued a report that examines the effects on state and local governments of several federal water regulations that the Obama EPA is, or will shortly be, implementing: new water quality criteria in Total Maximum Daily Load (TMDL) and numeric nutrient criteria for geographic locations, new storm-water rules, and the new Pesticide General Permit (PGP). These rules carry with them significant unfunded mandates that will cost state and local governments tens, if not hundreds, of billions of dollars. These new rules are not the outcome of legislation or rigorous scientific findings, but the direct result of a number of lawsuits by environmentalists, and the benefits do not outweigh the costs. As this report shows, these new rules will cause a lot of economic pain for state and local governments, without any guarantee of water quality improvement. States and municipalities are suffering because this administration is cranking out expensive unfunded mandates at a breakneck pace.

Richard Fisher, President of the Federal Reserve Bank of Dallas, said: "Before the recent mid-term election, most all of my business contacts claimed that taxes, regulatory burdens and the lack of understanding in Washington were disincentives for private-sector job creation and were inhibiting the expansion of their payrolls. They felt stymied by a Congress and an executive branch that have appeared to them to be unaware of, if not outright opposed to, what fires the entrepreneurial spirit. Many felt that opportunities for earning a better and more secure return on investment are larger elsewhere than here at home. It is a sad day when investors have more confidence in China and Brazil than in the United States, but that is the climate that Barack Obama's startling economic ignorance has created."

The incandescent bulb lit up America and came to symbolize a great idea. Now on the cusp of a federal ban, Thomas Edison's invention has become a symbol for personal liberty. Perhaps no issue better illuminates the transformation of the right from Big Government conservatism to Tea Party activism. With many consumers griping about the cost and type of light of the substitute bulb, populists have won the ear of some once-staunch ban supporters. Recently, Rep. Fred Upton, (R–MI) vowed to reverse the very ban on incandescent bulbs that he helped pass. But after five months as chairman of the House Energy and Commerce Committee, he had yet to hold a hearing. "This is a violation of (Upton's) promise," said Jennifer Stefano, co-chairwoman of the Loyal Opposition, Pennsylvania's largest Tea Party group. "The time is now for him to go back and do what he said he was going to do. The government never should have intruded in this matter." The Energy Bill of 2007 phases out incandescent bulbs, with the 100-watt banned in January 2012. The ban hits the 75-watt bulb in January 2013, and 60- and 40- watt bulbs in January '14.[2]

President Obama's pick to serve as the assistant secretary of the Occupational Safety and Health Administration is an "aggressively anti-business" proponent of junk science who should not be confirmed by the Senate, his critics say. Dr. David Michaels, a research professor and interim chairman in the Department of Environmental and Occupational Health at George Washington University's School of Public Health and Health Services, was nominated on July 28, 2010, to become OSHA's next assistant secretary. He was confirmed and serves under Labor Secretary Hilda Solis. Michaels was also the chief architect of an initiative to compensate Department of Energy nuclear weapons workers who developed cancer or lung disease as a result of their exposure to radiation, beryllium and other life-threatening hazards. Since 2000, the Energy Employees Occupational Illness Compensation Program has doled out more than $4.5 billion in benefits to those workers and their relatives. Second Amendment advocates are up in arms, too, saying they expect Michaels to seek stricter gun control in the workplace as an issue of public health. "It's one of the scariest appointments the new administration has made." said James Copland, director of the Manhattan Institute's Center for Legal Policy, which argues that the country's litigation system adversely affects innovation and safety.

"One would expect this administration would pick some folks relatively left of center, relatively pro-labor, that's to be understood." Copland said. "Michaels has associated himself throughout his career with junk science claims that are pushed by the plaintiff's bar and have seen a significant rise in the percentage of expert testimony excluded from the courtroom, an increase in successful motions for summary judgments, 90 percent of which "came down" against plaintiffs. "Michaels is closely associated with trial lawyers, so they're going to try to overturn this." said Steven Milloy, founder of junkscience.com. "That's his mission. Our concern is that he's going to take this mission and somehow implement it at OSHA." Milloy said, Trial lawyers would love him. He has a junk science agenda. The standards of science at OSHA under Michaels will be extremely low. If nothing else, he will promulgate junk science-based workplace regulation."

Michaels' critics say he could keep safe products off the market, much like silicone breast implants that sank Dow Corning Corp. into bankruptcy after it agreed in 1998 to pay women $3.2 Billion to settle their claims. A year later, however, an independent panel of 13 scientists convened by the Institute of Medicine concluded that silicone breast implants do not cause any major diseases. Copland said Michaels was tapped to head OSHA because of his support of "activist regulation through litigation" that often proves beneficial to plaintiff attorneys who frequently have Democrat ties. His supporters also dismiss claims that Michaels is an "anti-gun zealot," as he was described in a Sept. 7 Washington Times editorial that urged the Senate to deny his confirmation. In 2007, while writing on a failed bill that would have allowed workers to bring guns into company parking lots, Michaels predicted that the National Rifle Association "will no doubt be back, pushing legislation that stands in the way of preventing gun violence." "Thankfully, the NRA's legislation failed." Michaels wrote. Hans Bader, a senior attorney and counsel for special projects at the Competitive Enterprise Institute said he expects "a lot more restrictions" on real or perceived workplace hazards if Michaels is confirmed. "If you view guns as a public health hazard, that may have implications for people's ability to possess firearms at the workplace." Bader said. "It raises the possibility that by overzealous regulations he'll be undermining rather than advancing workplace safety."[3]

The Small Business Administration opposition (SBA) says the new OSHA rule on ergonomics (carpal tunnel) will cost up to $18 billion a year - several times higher than the OSHA estimated impact - without a proven benefit. Small businesses are creating most of America's new jobs, and 79 percent of the membership of the National Federation of Independent Business opposes the rule. There is already a market-oriented workplace safety program in existence in every state and community. It's called workers' comp insurance. Safe workplaces pay lower rates. Unsafe workplaces pay higher rates. Every employer in America reads the handwriting on the wall. As a result, workplaces are safer than ever. Employers' workplace safety improvement is due to two other factors. Aside from workers' comp, employers have a human interest and a business interest in safe workplaces. The human interest is that they know their employees and their families by name. The business interest is that in a tight labor market, lost workdays due to injury, cost big money in lost productivity. Of course, there's always room for improvement - the good news is that employers are doing it on their own, without more big government. By contrast, the new ergonomics rule from the U.S. Labor Department's Occupational Safety and Health Administration (OSHA) represents a "1,000-plus page, top-down approach that just won't work for workers. What small business can assure compliance with a 1,000-page rule from Washington, D.C.? The trial lawyers and the unions who have been pushing for this for years will have a field day. It is a big, new hunting license for big government and trial lawyers to declare open season on law-abiding employers with safe workplaces and deep pockets. We need to build public support against this big-government assault on Americans.

Here are OSHA specifications for ordinary ladders: "The following general requirements apply to all ladders, including job-made ladders: A double-cleated ladder or two or more ladders must be provided when ladders are the only way to enter or exit a work area having 25 or more employees, or when a ladder serves simultaneous two-way traffic. Ladder rungs, cleats, and steps must be parallel, level, and uniformly spaced when the ladder is in position for use. Rungs, cleats, and steps of portable and fixed ladders (except as provided below) must not be spaced less than 10 inches (25 cm) apart, nor more than 14 inches (36 cm) apart, along the ladder's side rails. Rungs, cleats, and steps of step stools must not be less than 8 inches (20 cm) apart, nor more than 12 inches (31 cm) apart, between center lines of the rungs, cleats, and steps. Rungs, cleats, and steps at the base section of extension trestle ladders must not be less than 8 inches (20 cm) nor more than 18 inches (46 cm) apart, between center lines of the rungs, cleats, and steps. The rung spacing on the extension section must not be less than 6 inches (15 cm) nor more than 12 inches (31 cm). Ladders must not be tied or fastened together to create longer sections unless they are specifically designed for such use. A metal spreader or locking device must be provided on each stepladder to hold the front and back sections in an open position when the ladder is being used. When splicing side rails, the resulting side rail must be equivalent in strength to a one-piece side rail made of the same material. Two or more separate ladders used to reach an elevated work area must be offset with a platform or landing between the ladders, except when portable ladders are used to gain access to fixed ladders. Ladder components must be surfaced to prevent injury from punctures or lacerations, and prevent snagging of clothing. Wood ladders must not be coated with any opaque covering, except for identification or warning labels that may be placed only on one face of a side rail." There are tens of thousands of other products with similar specifications, and OSHA can fine anyone for not complying. Any questions?

1.   http://coffman.house.gov/index.php?option=com_content&task=view&id=455&Itemid=10

2.   http://news.investors.com/article/576009/201106211745/as-incandescent-bulb-ban-looms-opposition-grows.htm?p=full

3.   http://www.foxnews.com/politics/2009/09/16/obamas-osha-nominee-bad-business-critics-say/

10 GOVERNMENT WASTE

I would issue an order that there will be no funding of any programs or agencies other than the Defense Advanced Research Projects Agency (DARPA), the National Aeronautics and Space Administration (NASA), and the National Institute of Health (NIH). These three agencies have resulted in more innovation and technology for Americans than any other government entities. There will be no subsidies or funding for education, agriculture, infrastructure, or any other Federal Department that I eliminated (See Executive Branch). There will be no taxpayer bailouts of any company, financial institution, or governmental entity and no takeover of any company by the Federal Government. All funding will be managed by the individual states, where there is more accountability to the voters.

For the first time in United States history, a President of the United States fired the CEO of a major corporation, with the coerced resignation of GM president Rick Wagner. This is another example of President Obama's distaste for capitalism and the free market. He also abrogated the rights of GM bondholders (never before done in the history of the United States) in favor of the United Auto Workers. In the thirty-one months he has been in office, he has basically nationalized major insurance and banking companies and is now threatening other industries that did not accept taxpayer money, costing us tens of billions of dollars. Why doesn't the American public recognize that Obama is destroying the private sector institutions that made the United States the greatest economic and military engine in world history? The private businesses in our country are learning to their dismay that "if you take the king's shillings, you do the king's bidding". British Petroleum CEO Tony Hayward left his post and transferred to Russia for participation in a joint venture. This is another scalp for President Obama to hang on his wall of private company executives he has brought down, including GM's Rick Wagner and some bank CEO's. Since BP is not an American company, Obama had to do it surreptitiously. It was initiated at a meeting in the White House Roosevelt Room on June 16, 2010, with several BP executives, Obama, Biden, some cabinet members and staff. Sources in attendance said VP Joe Biden leaned forward and bluntly informed the BP officials they had no choice. If they didn't do the right thing and put $20 billion in an escrow account, it would be done to them.

The Federal Government admits that last year it wasted a total of $125 billion in "improper payments" alone. Now $125 billion is a large amount of money. It's only slightly less than the GDP of Hungary. It's enough to buy around 2,700 tons of gold. It's more than the combined Federal taxes paid by: Nevada, Delaware, Rhode Island, Mississippi, New Hampshire, New Mexico, Idaho, Hawaii, West Virginia, Maine, South Dakota, Alaska, Montana, North Dakota, Wyoming, and Vermont. Yes, combined. The people in those states paid the Federal Government a total of almost $116 billion in 2009 - 16 states worth of tax revenue gone. Upon presentation of these facts, liberals inevitably respond with some variation of: "We don't need to cut program X, we just need to cut the waste, it needs to be run better." There's no possible way you could be so naive and irresponsible as to promote bestowing more power to an organization with a monopoly on the use of force. The states could be called "The Gang of 16" (giving politicians the taste of their own medicine) or "The Forgotten States" or possibly some hilarious double entendre. Contact your State Representatives and strongly "suggest" they propose bills declaring solidarity with the other 15 states. Bring this up at town halls, get the word to your federal representatives. They should be holding press conferences on the steps of the capital with fellow congressman from those 16 states. When everyone starts realizing where all that money missing from their paychecks is going, any argument for bigger government will seem laughable.

Soaring government spending and trillion-dollar budget deficits have brought fiscal responsibility -- and reducing government waste -- back onto the national agenda. President Obama recently identified 0.004 of 1 percent of the federal budget as wasteful and proposed eliminating this $140 million from his $3.6 trillion fiscal year 2010 budget request. Aiming higher, the President recently proposed partially offsetting a costly new government health entitlement by reducing $622 billion in Medicare and Medicaid "waste and inefficiencies" over the next decade. Taxpayers may wonder why reducing such waste is now merely a bargaining chip for new spending rather than an end in itself. It is possible to reduce spending and balance the budget. In the 1980s and 1990s, Washington consistently spent $21,000 per household (adjusted for inflation). Simply returning to that level would balance the budget by 2012 without any tax hikes. Alternatively, merely returning to the 2008 (pre-recession) spending level of $25,000 per household (adjusted for inflation) would likely balance the budget by 2019 without any tax hikes.[1]

Most have heard the saying that no one takes care of a rental car like they take care of their own. Why not floor the gas pedal or track sand into the car -the reasoning goes -if you'll never see it again after this week? In many ways, this is a perfect analogy to government waste. No matter which party is in power, spending other people's money rarely compels one to be as prudent as if they were spending their own. Combine this with the typical politician's time horizon (the next election) and it's easy to see why so many government projects and initiatives have been swallowed by waste over the years. The six categories of wasteful and unnecessary spending are: programs that should be devolved to state and local governments; programs that could be better performed by the private sector; mis-targeted programs whose recipients should not be entitled to government benefits; outdated and unnecessary programs; duplicated programs; and inefficiency, mismanagement, and fraud.[2]

The federal government made at least $72 billion in improper payments in 2008.

Washington spends $92 billion on corporate welfare (excluding TARP) versus $71 billion on homeland security.

Washington spends $25 billion annually maintaining unused or vacant federal properties.

Government auditors spent the past five years examining all federal programs and found that 22 percent of them -- costing taxpayers a total of $123 billion annually -- fail to show any positive impact on the populations they serve.

The Congressional Budget Office published a "Budget Options" series identifying more than $100 billion in potential spending cuts.

Examples from multiple Government Accountability Office (GAO) reports of wasteful duplication include 342 economic development programs; 130 programs serving the disabled; 130 programs serving at-risk youth; 90 early childhood development programs; 75 programs funding international education, cultural, and training exchange activities; and 72 safe water programs.

Washington will spend $2.6 million training Chinese prostitutes to drink more responsibly on the job.

A GAO audit classified nearly half of all purchases on government credit cards as improper, fraudulent, or embezzled. Examples of taxpayer-funded purchases include gambling, mortgage payments, liquor, lingerie, iPods, Xboxes, jewelry, Internet dating services, and Hawaiian vacations. In one extraordinary example, the Postal Service spent $13,500 on one dinner at a Ruth's Chris Steakhouse, including "over 200 appetizers and over $3,000 of alcohol, including more than 40 bottles of wine costing more than $50 each and brand-name liquor such as Courvoisier, Belvedere and Johnny Walker Gold." The 81 guests consumed an average of $167 worth of food and drink apiece.

Federal agencies are delinquent on nearly 20 percent of employee travel charge cards, costing taxpayers hundreds of millions of dollars annually.

The Securities and Exchange Commission spent $3.9 million rearranging desks and offices at its Washington, D.C., headquarters.

The Pentagon recently spent $998,798 shipping two 19-cent washers from South Carolina to Texas and $293,451 sending an 89-cent washer from South Carolina to Florida.

Over half of all farm subsidies go to commercial farms, which report average household incomes of $200,000.

Health care fraud is estimated to cost taxpayers more than $60 billion annually.

A GAO audit found that 95 Pentagon weapons systems suffered from a combined $295 billion in cost overruns.

The refusal of many federal employees to fly coach costs taxpayers $146 million annually in flight upgrades.

Washington spent $126 million in 2009 to enhance the Kennedy family legacy in Massachusetts. Additionally, Senator John Kerry (D-MA) diverted $20 million from the 2010 defense budget to subsidize a new Edward M. Kennedy Institute.

Federal investigators have launched more than 20 criminal fraud investigations related to the TARP financial bailout.

Despite trillion-dollar deficits, last year's 10,160 earmarks included $200,000 for a tattoo removal program in Mission Hills, California; $190,000 for the Buffalo Bill Historical Center in Cody, Wyoming; and $75,000 for the Totally Teen Zone in Albany, Georgia.

The federal government owns more than 100,000 vacant homes.

The Federal Communications Commission spent $350,000 to sponsor NASCAR driver David Gilliland.

Members of Congress have spent hundreds of thousands of taxpayer dollars supplying their offices with popcorn machines, plasma televisions, DVD equipment, ionic air fresheners, camcorders, and signature machines - plus $24,730 leasing a Lexus, $1,434 on a digital camera, and $84,000 on personalized calendars.

More than $13 billion in Iraq aid has been classified as wasted or stolen. Another $7.8 billion cannot be accounted for.

Fraud related to Hurricane Katrina spending is estimated to top $2 billion. In addition, debit cards provided to hurricane victims were used to pay for Caribbean vacations, NFL tickets, Dom Perignon champagne, "Girls Gone Wild" videos, and at least one sex change operation.

Auditors discovered that 900,000 of the 2.5 million recipients of emergency Katrina assistance provided false names, addresses, or Social Security numbers or submitted multiple applications.

Congress recently gave Alaska Airlines $500,000 to paint a Chinook salmon on Boeing airplanes.

The Transportation Department will subsidize up to $2,000 per flight for direct flights between Washington, D.C., and the small hometown of Congressman Hal Rogers (R-KY) -- but only on Monday mornings and Friday evenings, when lawmakers, staff, and lobbyists usually fly. Rogers is a member of the Appropriations Committee, which writes the Transportation Department's budget.

Washington has spent $3 billion re-sanding beaches -- even as this new sand washes back into the ocean.

A Department of Agriculture report concedes that much of the $2.5 billion in "stimulus" funding for broadband Internet will be wasted.

The Defense Department wasted $100 million on unused flight tickets and never bothered to collect refunds even though the tickets were refundable.

Washington spends $60,000 per hour shooting Air Force One photo-ops in front of national landmarks.

Over one recent 18-month period, Air Force and Navy personnel used government-funded credit cards to charge at least $102,400 on admission to entertainment events, $48,250 on gambling, $69,300 on cruises, and $73,950 on exotic dance clubs and prostitutes.

Members of Congress are set to pay themselves $90 million to increase their franked mailings for the 2010 election year.

Congress has ignored efficiency recommendations from the Department of Health and Human Services that would save $9 billion annually.
Taxpayers are funding paintings of high-ranking government officials at a cost of up to $50,000 apiece.

The state of Washington sent $1 food stamp checks to 250,000 households in order to raise state caseload figures and trigger $43 million in additional federal funds.

Suburban families are receiving large farm subsidies for the grass in their backyards -- subsidies that many of these families never requested and do not want.

Congress appropriated $20 million for "commemoration of success" celebrations related to Iraq and Afghanistan.

Homeland Security employee purchases include 63-inch plasma TVs, iPods, and $230 for a beer brewing kit.

Two drafting errors in the 2005 Deficit Reduction Act resulted in a $2 billion taxpayer cost.

North Ridgeville, Ohio, received $800,000 in "stimulus" funds for a project that its mayor described as "a long way from the top priority."

The National Institutes of Health spends $1.3 million per month to rent a lab that it cannot use.

Congress recently spent $2.4 billion on 10 new jets that the Pentagon insists it does not need and will not use.

Lawmakers diverted $13 million from Hurricane Katrina relief spending to build a museum celebrating the Army Corps of Engineers -- the agency partially responsible for the failed levees that flooded New Orleans.

Medicare officials recently mailed $50 million in erroneous refunds to 230,000 Medicare recipients.

Audits showed $34 billion worth of Department of Homeland Security contracts contained significant waste, fraud, and abuse.

Washington recently spent $1.8 million to help build a private golf course in Atlanta, Georgia.

The Advanced Technology Program spends $150 million annually subsidizing private businesses; 40 percent of this funding goes to Fortune 500 companies.

Congressional investigators were able to receive $55,000 in federal student loan funding for a fictional college they created to test the Department of Education.

The Conservation Reserve program pays farmers $2 billion annually not to farm their land.

The Commerce Department has lost 1,137 computers since 2001, many containing Americans' personal data, and a cost of $800,000.

These are just a sampling of thousands of wasteful or redundant programs, and do not include bailouts of financial institutions, auto companies, and real estate firms at a taxpayer commitment of $11.0 trillion. These are detailed in my chapter on bailouts.

1. http://hoguenews.com/?p=4834
2. http://thesenewtimes.com/i-just-made-you-punch-your-computer-monitor/

11 BAILOUTS AND STIMULUS

I would issue an order that, effective immediately, all Federal Government bailouts and stimulus packages will be outlawed for states, counties, municipal governments, school districts, banks, insurance companies, auto companies, or any other private enterprises. There is a precedent for the bailout of a municipality (New York City -1975). The free market will determine winners and losers, not the government. Bankruptcies will be allowed to run their normal course.

On February 6, 2009, President Obama quietly issued Executive Order 13502 that encourages federal agencies to "consider requiring the use of labor agreements in connection with large- scale construction projects in order to promote economy and efficiency in Federal procurement". A project labor agreement requires contractors and sub-contractors to pay union wages and to recognize collective bargaining agreements. It is reasonable to say the "encouragement" from the president is likely to carry considerable weight with Federal agencies. The order constitutes "payback" for the unions who supported Obama's presidential campaign. Union construction workers constitute only 15 percent of that segment of the labor force. Therefore 85 percent of construction workers will not be eligible for any of the $864 billion stimulus money. Obama says the policy will help make labor costs more predictable and will prevent construction delays by preventing labor disputes. Critics, such as the Associated Builders and Contractors, a trade group representing non-union construction firms, say that by eliminating bids from their companies, the measure will increase costs for American taxpayers. Since Obama now owns a majority of two major automobile companies to protect unions, it makes sense that the stimulus money should be steered toward another voting block that can contribute more to Democrat politicians.

Unless the stimulus policies of the Obama administration and the Federal Reserve are changed, I believe the Dow Jones Industrial Average will drop below 8,000 before the end of President Obama's second term. Buckle up and hold on -- a new round of quantitative easing is here and things could start getting very ugly in the financial world over the coming months. The truth is that many economists fear that an out of control Federal Reserve is "crossing the Rubicon" by announcing another wave of quantitative easing. Have we now reached a point where the Federal Reserve is simply going to fire up the printing presses and shower massive wads of cash into the financial system whenever the U.S. economy is not growing fast enough? If so, what does the mean for inflation, the stability of the world financial system and the future of the U.S. dollar? The Fed says that the plan is to purchase $600 billion of U.S. Treasury securities by the middle of 2011. In addition, the Federal Reserve has announced that it will be "reinvesting" an additional $250 billion to $300 billion from the proceeds of its mortgage portfolio in U.S. Treasury securities over the same time period. So that is a total injection of about $900 billion. Perhaps the Fed thought that number would sound a little less ominous than $1 trillion. In any event, the Federal Reserve seems convinced that quantitative easing is going to work this time. So should we believe the Federal Reserve? The truth is that the Federal Reserve has tried this before. In November 2008, the Federal Reserve announced a $600 billion quantitative easing program. Four months later the Fed felt that even more cash was necessary, so they upped the total to $1.8 trillion. So did quantitative easing work then? No, not really. It may have helped stabilize the economy in the short-term, but unemployment is still staggeringly high. Monthly U.S. home sales continue to come in at close to record low levels. Businesses are borrowing less money. Individuals are borrowing less money. Stores are closing left and right.

There is a debate raging right now about whether Congress should create legislation giving states the option to file for bankruptcy, something along the lines of the existing law allowing for Chapter 9 municipal bankruptcy. To be sure, states are in big trouble: Total state debt is estimated at over $1 trillion, and that's in addition to unfunded liabilities (from pensions and other obligations), which are estimated at over $3 trillion. Given the federal government's $14 trillion in existing debt - which, according to a recent CBO report, will double in the next ten years - taxpayers cannot afford to bail out the states. Nor can we afford the precedent it would set. Federal bailouts should be off the table.[1] The bankruptcy idea is definitely appealing, but after reviewing arguments from both sides, I think that state bankruptcy could create more problems than it would solve. For instance, critics of the plan contend that bankruptcy will only make states' problems worse by jeopardizing their ability to continue to borrow and finance their debt.

States have and are already using other options to force concessions from powerful public-employee unions. For instance, E.J. McMahon writes in this Wall Street Journal article, "Yet state officials committed to cutting costs already have options for putting the squeeze on their unions. One is the threat of mass layoffs, which most governors can impose unilaterally. Governors and legislators also can prospectively freeze wages or even cut them through involuntary furloughs, as California and several other states did over the past two years."[2] Other options include reforming collective bargaining and state-workforce rules. McMahon suggests removing the protections that allow state workers to collectively bargain with government employers for wages and benefits, that would give lawmakers more leeway during negotiations and would open the door to outsourcing and privatization: At least 18 states already outlaw collective bargaining with some categories of government employees; Virginia and North Carolina prohibit it for all public workers. Two newly elected Republican governors, Scott Walker in Wisconsin and John Kasich in Ohio, have threatened to dismantle their state bargaining statutes if unions fail to make concessions.

With the flurry of recent government bailouts, we have to remember that they did not begin with the Bush or Obama administration Here is a chronological list of bailouts beginning in 1970:

Penn Central Railroad - $3.2 billion -In May, 1970, on the verge of bankruptcy, Penn appealed to the Fed that it provided crucial national defense transportation services. The Nixon administration and the Fed supported providing assistance, but Congress refused. Penn declared bankruptcy in June, and to counteract devastating ripple effects to the money market, the Fed told commercial banks it would provide the reserves needed to meet the credit requirements.

Lockheed - $1.4 billion -In August, 1971, Congress passed the Emergency Loan Guarantee Act, to provide funds for any major business in crisis. Lockheed was the first recipient, because failure would have meant significant job loss in California.

Franklin National Bank - $7.8 billion - In the first five months of 1974 the bank lost $63.6 million. The Federal Reserve stepped in with a loan of $1.75 billion.

New York City - $9.4 billion - During the 1970s, New York City became over-extended and entered a period of financial crisis. In 1975 President Ford signed the New York City Seasonal Financing Act, which released $2.3 billion in loans to the city.

Chrysler - $4.0 billion - In 1979 Chrysler suffered a loss of $1.1 billion. That year the corporation requested aid from the government. In 1980 the Chrysler Loan Guarantee Act was passed, which provided $1.5 billion in loans to rescue Chrysler from insolvency. In addition, the government's aid was to be matched by U.S. and foreign banks.

Continental Illinois National Bank and Trust Company - $9.5 billion -In 1984, then the nation's eighth largest bank, Continental Illinois had suffered significant losses after purchasing $1 billion in energy loans from the failed Penn Square Bank of Oklahoma. The FDIC and Federal Reserve devised a plan to rescue the bank that included replacing the bank's top executives

Savings & Loan - $293.9 billion -In 1989, after the widespread failure of savings and loan institutions, President George H. W. Bush signed and Congress enacted the Financial Institutions Reform Recovery and Enforcement Act in 1989

Airline Industry - $18.6 billion -In 2001, the terrorist attacks of September 11 crippled an already financially troubled industry. To bail out the airlines, President Bush signed into law the Air Transportation Safety and Stabilization Act, that compensated airlines for the mandatory grounding of aircraft after the attacks. The act released $5 billion in compensation and an additional $10 billion in loan guarantees or other federal credit instruments.

Bear Stearns -$30 billion -In 2008, JP Morgan Chase and the federal government bailed out Bear Stearns when the financial giant neared collapse. JP Morgan purchased Bear Stearns for $236 million; the Federal Reserve provided a $30 billion credit line to ensure the sale could move forward.

Fannie Mae / Freddie Mac - $400 billion - On Sep. 7, 2008, Fannie and Freddie were essentially nationalized: placed under the conservator ship of the Federal Housing Finance Agency. Under the terms of the rescue, the Treasury has invested billions to cover the companies' losses. Initially, Treasury Secretary Hank Paulson put a ceiling of $100 billion for investments in each company. In February, Tim Geithner raised it to $200 billion. The money was authorized by the Housing and Economic Recovery Act of 2008.

American International Group (A.I.G) - $180 billion -in 2008, on four separate occasions, the government has offered aid to AIG to keep it from collapsing, rising from an initial $85 billion credit line from the Federal Reserve to a combined $180 billion effort between the Treasury ($70 billion) and Fed ($110 billion). ($40 billion is included in TARP).

Auto Industry - $25 billion - In late September 2008, Congress approved a more than $630 billion spending bill, which included a measure for $25 billion in loans to the auto industry. These low-interest loans are intended to aid the industry in its push to build more fuel-efficient, environmentally friendly vehicles. The Detroit 3 -- General Motors, Ford and Chrysler -- will be the primary beneficiaries.

Troubled Asset Relief Program (TARP) - $700 billion - In October 2008, Congress passed the Emergency Economic Stabilization Act, which authorized the Treasury Department to spend $700 billion to combat the financial crisis. The Treasury has been doling out the money via an alphabet soup of different programs.

Citigroup - $280 billion –In 2008, they received a $25 billion investment through the TARP in October and another $20 billion in November. (That $45 billion is also included in the TARP total.) Additional aid has come in the form of government guarantees to limit losses from a $301 billion pool of toxic assets. In addition to the Treasury's $5 billion commitment, the FDIC has committed $10 billion and the Federal Reserve up to about $220 billion.

Bank of America - $142.2 billion -In 2009, they received $45 billion through the TARP, which includes $10 billion originally meant for Merrill Lynch. (That $45 billion is also included in the TARP total.) In addition, the government has made guarantees to limit losses from a $118 billion pool of troubled assets. In addition to the Treasury's $7.5 billion commitment, the FDIC has committed $2.5 billion and the Federal Reserve up to $87.2 billion.

Federal Reserve Rescue Efforts - $6.4 trillion -In 2009, the Fed committed to Commercial Paper Funding Facility $1.8 trillion, Foreign Exchange Dollar Swaps $29.1 billion, GSE debt purchases $200 billion, GSE mortgage-backed securities purchases $1.25 trillion, Money Market Investor Funding Facility $800 billion, Term Asset-backed Securities Loan Facility $1 trillion, Term Auction Facility $500 billion, Term Securities Lending Facility $250 billion, U.S. government Bond Facilities $300 billion.

FDIC Bank Takeovers - $46.4 billion -2008 takeovers $17.6 billion, 2009 takeovers $27.8 billion.

Other Financial Initiatives - $1.7 trillion -Credit Union Deposit Insurance Guarantee $80 billion, Money Market Guarantee $50 billion, NCUA bailout of U.S. Central and Wescorp Credit Unions $57 billion, U.S, Central Federal Credit Union Investment $1 billion, Temporary Liquidity Guarantee Program $1.5 trillion.

Other Housing Initiatives -FHA Housing Rescue 320 billion, Making Home Affordable Investment $20 billion.

All these are funded with taxpayer money. It traces every dollar, recipient, and program in the current financial crisis. The total is over $11 trillion, almost as large as the stated national debt. How many of these programs have never been exposed to scrutiny by the public?

1. http://www.nationalreview.com/corner/258356/should-states-be-able-file-bankruptcy-veronique-de-rugy
2. http://online.wsj.com/article/SB10001424052748704881304576094091992370356.html?KEYWORDS=state+bankruptcy

12 HOUSING

I would issue an order that the United States Government will stay out of anything to do with housing and let banks and other financial institutions in the free market determine prices, interest rates, and terms of payment. The government has spent $1.5 Trillion on housing programs and the problem is getting worse. Housing is the largest single purchase most persons make, and government interference has ruined many lives.

Liberal Democrats are constantly manipulating public sentiment in a steady effort to disestablish the free market as they push the nation down the road to disaster. They have built an enormous maze of government agencies and programs that grow from year to year and intervene in and interfere with the free market. Then, the central planners create economic perversions that are seriously detrimental to the public, blame the free market and insist on seizing additional authority to correct the failures created by their own direction. In 1977, Congress passed the Community Reinvestment Act (CRA) to address alleged discrimination by banks in making loans to poor people and minorities in inner-cities. They called it 'red-lining'. The act provided that banks have 'an affirmative obligation' to meet the credit needs of the communities in which they are chartered. In 1989 Congress amended the Home Mortgage Disclosure Act requiring banks to collect racial data on mortgage applications. University of Texas economics professor Stan Liebowitz has written, "In 1995 the Clinton administration's Treasury Department issued regulations tracking loans by neighborhoods, income groups and races to rate the performance of banks. The ratings were used by regulators to determine whether the government would approve bank mergers, acquisitions, and new branches."[1]

There are all kinds of finger pointing going around as to why our economy is the way it is. With four million homes in foreclosure it's no wonder our economy is where it is with so many people dependent on the real estate market and home building. They say Wall Street, banks, and speculators brought about the real estate home collapse, and this is true. However, the real culprits are in Congress and the Executive branch. In 1992, Andrew Cuomo was Secretary of the Department of Housing and Urban Development (HUD). HUD pressured two government-chartered corporations known as Freddie Mac and Fannie Mae to purchase large bundles of loans for conflicting purposes of diversifying the risk and making even more money available to banks for risky loans. Congress also passed the Federal Housing Enterprises Financial Safety and Soundness Act eventually mandating that these companies, Freddie Mac and Fannie Mae. Assume 45% of all loans from people of low and moderate incomes. Consequently, a second market was created for these loans by Fannie Mae and Freddie Mac.

In 1995 the Treasury Department established the Community Development Financial Institutions Fund that provided banks with tax dollars to encourage even more risky loans. This was still not enough. Top congressional Democrats including Representative Barney Frank, Senator Chris Dodd and Senator Charles Schumer, among others, repeatedly ignored warnings of pending disaster, insisting that they were overstated and opposed efforts to force Freddie Mac and Fannie Mae to comply with the usual business and oversight practices, like SEC reporting. Top executives of these corporations, most of whom had worked in Democrat administrations, resisted reform while they were actively "cooking the books" in order to reward themselves with tens of millions of dollars in bonuses. Barney Frank, who was head of the Banking and Finance Committee in the House, and Sen. Chris Dodd, who headed the Banking and Finance Committee in the Senate, are the ones who got us into this mess. Both of them decided that just about anyone who walks through the doors should own a home. They told the banks and mortgage companies to lower their standards on qualifying for a mortgage. That brought about interest only and adjustable rate mortgages with little or no money down, putting people in homes that they could not afford, along with speculators with buy today and sell tomorrow thinking. Dodd and Frank did this for one reason, and one reason only, to get votes.[1]

Top headlines a couple years ago were about the failures and buyouts of some of the largest financial institutions in the United States, like Lehman Brothers, Bear Stearns, Merrill Lynch, AIG and Washington Mutual. Freddie and Fannie have become wards of the state and have put the taxpayers on the hook for up to $1.5 Trillion dollars. Somehow you understand that all these problems go back to bad mortgages and that a combination of falling home prices and mortgage defaults have put these investment banks into deep trouble. So who is to blame? The Democrat politicians (and some Republicans) would like us to believe that the problem rests squarely on "greedy" mortgage brokers and lenders. Nothing could be further from the truth. The responsibility for this whole debacle can be laid at the feet of Congress and HUD for political meddling in the credit decisions of the mortgage lenders. A byproduct of this government intervention and social engineering was a financial instrument called the derivative which turned the sub-prime mortgage market into a ticking time-bomb that would magnify the housing bust by orders of magnitude. A derivative is, in essence, a contract where one party sells the risk associated with the mortgage to another party in exchange for payments to that company based on the value of the mortgage. In other words, it's a bet. It's a bet that the mortgage will last or will go under; you bet on one side or the other. In some cases investors who did not even make the loans would bet on whether the loans would be subject to default. Although imprecise, perhaps derivatives in this context can best be understood as a form of insurance. Now, derivatives allowed commercial and investment banks, individual companies and private investors to further spread and ultimately multiply the risk.

Twenty years ago the buzz-word in the media was "redlining", or mapping out districts in a city where loans from applicants would not be accepted. Newspapers across the country were filled with hard hitting investigative reports about evil and racist mortgage lenders refusing to make real estate loans to minority applicants living in lower income neighborhoods. These claims were absurd, because when credit histories, job stability, loan-to-value ratios and income levels were considered, there was no evidence of racial discrimination. However, political correctness won out. Washington made it clear that if the banks and other lending institutions didn't do something to bring more minorities into the world of home ownership there would be a heavy price to pay. The Community Reinvestment Act permitted community activist groups like ACORN (Association of Community Organizations for Reform Now) and NACA (Neighborhood Assistance Corporation of America) to browbeat the banks and force them to make $20 billion dollars in loans to unqualified borrowers. Bruce Marks, the CEO of NACA, said that they always took the junk-yard dog approach, "once we grab on we never let go." They drove Fleet Financial, The Associates, and First Union into virtual bankruptcy. Instead of the old rule of 20% down and a good credit history for a borrower, the rules were changed to no money down, no closing costs, no fees, no requirement for good credit, and a below-market interest rate.

NACA said, "Everyone gets the same incredible terms, including the below-market interest rate, regardless of their credit score or other factors. 'Minority mortgage applications were rejected more frequently than other applications but the overwhelming reason wasn't racial discrimination but simply that minorities tend to have weaker finances.

So what happened to these garbage loans? The hot potatoes were bundled up and sold to Freddie and Fannie. These agencies had the best of both worlds, because they were semi-private institutions with the tacit backing of the Federal Government. They also had their protectors in Congress, and contributed heavily to election campaigns of these Representatives and Senators (mostly Democrats). A review of Federal Election Commission records back to 1989 shows Barack Obama in his three complete years in the Senate is the second largest recipient of Freddie and Fannie campaign contributions - receiving $126,349 since being elected to the Senate in 2004. In his three years, he got more dollars/year than any other Senator in history. Since the government takeover, attention has focused on three Fannie Mae executives who have close ties to Obama: Franklin Raines, former Clinton administration budget director; James Johnson, former aide to Democratic Vice President Walter Mondale; and Jamie Gorelick, former Clinton administration deputy attorney general. Johnson earned $21 million in his last year as Fannie Mae CEO. Raines earned $90 million in his five years as Fannie Mae CEO. Gorelick earned an estimated $26 million as vice chair of Fannie Mae from 1998 to 2003. Raines and several top Fannie Mae executives were ordered to pay $31.4 million for manipulating Fannie Mae earnings to trigger their massive bonuses. Last year, the SEC imposed a $50 million fine on Freddie Mac and four executives for accounting fraud.

How do NACA and ACORN fit into this? The Community Reinvestment Act pumped up the volume of lending and bank deregulation set off a wave of mega-mergers. Regulatory approval of such mergers depended, in part, on positive CRA ratings. To avoid the possibility of denied or delayed applications, the lending institutions had an incentive to make formal agreements with community organizations (NACA and ACORN). *One of the lawyers for ACORN was Barrack Obama.* So these left-wing nonprofit urban terrorists were able to gain control over billions of dollars by threatening to intervene in the CRA review process of the banks. These billions were parceled out to individual low-income mortgage seekers. These applicants had to attend "workshops" that promote a left-wing activist political agenda and to participate they had to register to vote. So Obama and his fellow Democrats in control of Congress recognized that they had a symbiotic relationship with these groups, and needed each other as they washed money around in circles. Congressional Democrats forced banks to provide money for "CRA" purposes. The banks 'lend' the money through NACA and ACORN, who get fee-income that finance voter registration. These voters happen to vote Democrat. The loans are bundled neatly and sent to Fannie and Freddie so that Raines, Johnson, and Gorelick can show that they are lending to the disadvantaged, thereby inflating their salaries, bonuses, and stock-options rights. Fannie and Freddie executives then make significant donations to Obama, Frank, Dodd, and other Democrats to make sure they get re-elected. When Fannie and Freddie go belly up, it's no big deal. The taxpayers will pick up the tab.

The Federal Reserve Board's role in the housing boom and bust cannot be understated. The Pacific Research Institute's Robert Murphy explains that the Federal Reserve slashed interest rates while this was going on; slashed them repeatedly starting in January 2001 from 6.5% percent until they reached a low of 1% in June 2003. When the easy money policy became too inflationary for comfort, the Fed under Alan Greenspan and then new chairman Ben Bernanke, at the end, began a steady process of raising interest rates back up from 1% in June 2004 to 5.25% in June 2006. Therefore, when the Federal Reserve ended its role as steward of the monetary system and instead used interest rates to artificially and inappropriately manipulate the housing market, it interfered with the normal market conditions.[1]

The U.S. government may continue to play an outsized role in the nation's roughly $10 trillion home loan market under a proposal President Barack Obama is set to endorse. The plan, along with a sweeping set of new and old housing recommendations and ideas, will be unveiled in Phoenix, as Obama launches his second-term housing policy agenda in the same city where he made one of the biggest broken promises of his first term. Under Obama's plan, mortgages provided by private-sector lenders that are bundled into securities and sold to investors could obtain a taxpayer guarantee in return for a fee, according to the White House. The private sector would have to shoulder some of the initial losses if defaults were to rise, a condition usually triggered by falling home prices. After that, taxpayers would absorb the remainder of losses stemming from an extreme downturn in the nation's property market. The insurance fee collected by the government should be "actuarially-fair," the White House said, meaning it should equal the expected payout. Obama's endorsement of such a plan marks a turning point in the ongoing Washington debate over how to reform the nation's housing finance system. Five years after twin housing giants Fannie Mae and Freddie Mac were rescued by taxpayers, policymakers have struggled to advance a proposal that would ensure continued access to a bedrock of the U.S. housing market -- the fixed-rate 30-year mortgage -- but also would reduce the government's role in funding home loans.

Fannie Mae and Freddie Mac own or guarantee nearly half of all outstanding home loans. In the aftermath of the 2008 financial crisis, Fannie Mae, Freddie Mac and the rest of the U.S. government have backstopped more than 90 percent of new home loans. Taxpayers now own or guarantee roughly three of every five outstanding mortgages. Policy analysts reckoned there's little chance Obama's plan could make it into law before the 2014 election, despite what appears to be a growing bipartisan consensus on the future of U.S. housing finance.

1. http://www.amazon.com/Liberty-Tyranny-Conservative-Mark-Levin/dp/0743572203

13 ENERGY

I would issue an order that United States will drill and mine wherever coal, oil, natural gas, and liquefied gas are found. Since I will have eliminated the Environmental Protection Agency (EPA) and the Occupational Safety and Health Administration (OSHA), they will not present an obstacle to producing new energy sources. I will also issue an order that no source of energy will be subsidized by the Federal Government, including ethanol, oil, gas, wind, or solar. They will have to compete in a free market without taxpayer money. I would also issue a statement that global warming is a myth, not to be taken seriously, and that "cap and trade" is dead.

For a generation, extreme environmentalists have conditioned us to resist any progress in production of fossil fuels. This NIMBY (Not In My Back Yard) syndrome has now evolved into NIABY (Not In Anyone's Back Yard). The lies and distortions about drilling in the ANWR -Arctic National Wildlife Refuge - a barren wasteland, are an example. Pictures of pristine forests and bubbling streams were taken 1000 miles from the refuge. The profusion of protests and lawsuits over new energy sources resulted in power shortages and rolling blackouts in California. Energy giant American Electric Power (AEP) is closing five coal-fired power plants that will dramatically increase the cost of electricity in the Mid-Atlantic states because they cannot comply with the Obama administration carbon dioxide (CO2) emissions under the Clean Air Act. The radical environmentalists don't want nuclear plants, coal fired plants, or even windmills because they shred birds. I saw a large billboard in the mining area of Montana that suggested an appropriate fate for these people and their anti-energy supporters in Congress. It read: "Stop all drilling and mining. Let them all freeze to death in the dark."

Lisa Jackson, President Obama's EPA director, has just announced the agency's new auto regulations of gas mileage based on global warming. In addition, the agency asserts the right to regulate (CO_2) under the Clean Air Act. There is no need to limit greenhouse gas emissions because there is no "global warming". There is absolutely no scientific justification for this, and indeed, many observers believe the EPA lacks the legal authority regarding its stance on CO_2. Greenhouse gases are purported to be the primary cause of this fraud. The EPA, like a dozen other U.S. agencies, has been pushing the global warming fraud for decades. One more lie, even a whopper of a lie about CO_2, is of little concern to the EPA at this point. Beyond the issue of scientific fraud, there are the scientific facts that demonstrate that CO_2 plays a miniscule role, if any, as regards the Earth's climate. Carbon dioxide is less than one percent of the Earth's atmosphere (386 parts per million). The EPA will blame the generation of CO_2 on energy use, but 97% of the Earth's CO_2 is produced by Nature. Only about 3% of all the CO_2 in the atmosphere is produced by humans via industrial and transport activity. This estimate, in fact, comes from the United Nations Intergovernmental Panel on Climate Change.[1]

Despite the overwhelming evidence to the contrary, most Americans still believe that the EPA is dedicated to making our lives better. In the minds of America, the EPA ensures we have clean air and clean water. They punish people who dump dangerous waste and pollute our country. The truth is much uglier. The truth is that the EPA pushes a radical environmentalist agenda at the expense of American's quality of life. They have a dubious scientific basis for their actions, and they certainly have no constitutional authority. First, let's dismiss the notion that our environment would be dirty and unfit for human life without an EPA. We don't need the EPA to stop people that cause scientifically provable harm to other people or their property. People dumping industrial waste into rivers, or releasing poisonous gas into the air can be taken to court. The EPA is "needed" only when you want to have blanket prohibitions or regulations on actions that cannot be proven to harm anyone. For instance, Anthropogenic Global Warming couldn't be shown to exist to a fair court, and it certainly couldn't be shown to be harming specific individuals. Therefore, if you want to strangle industry based on unproven assertions, the EPA is needed. Strangling industry is exactly what President Obama is directing the EPA to do. You may remember that Obama has promised to make electric rates skyrocket and to bankrupt the coal industry.[2] Here are his words in an interview with the San Francisco Chronicle, "The only thing I've said with respect to coal, I haven't been some coal booster. What I have said is that for us to take coal off the table as an ideological matter as opposed to saying if technology allows us to use coal in a clean way, we should pursue it. So if somebody wants to build a coal-powered plant, they can. It's just that it will bankrupt them because they're going to be charged a huge sum for all that greenhouse gas that's being emitted."[3] It's amazing that this statement by Obama about bankrupting the coal industry has been kept under wraps until this time.

The Environmental Protection Agency will focus its national study of hydraulic fracturing on seven areas in five states, but will exclude the two Wyoming gas fields where agency researchers have already collected some of the most in-depth data on drilling's environmental impacts. The study, that was announced last March without specifics on research sites -will investigate alleged water contamination from drilling in five areas in Texas, Colorado, North Dakota and Pennsylvania. It also will encompass cradle-to-grave research projects in Pennsylvania and Louisiana, where the agency will track drilling's effects on water quality from before the drill bit hits the ground to after hydraulic fracturing has been performed. Fracturing is a process used to extract trapped oil and gas from thousands of feet below ground by injecting a mixture of water, sand and chemicals under enough force to shatter the rock and allow the oil and gas to flow out. Advancements in the technology have made large, deeply buried natural gas deposits in the Marcellus Shale, Bakken Formation, and elsewhere accessible for the first time. But the process is exempt from federal regulation and the EPA is trying to find another way to hinder U.S. energy production. [4]

The United States produces about 20%, or 1.1 billion tons, of the world's coal supply - second only to China. Coal generates about half of the electricity used in the United States. More than 2 million acres of mined land have been reclaimed over the past 25 years - that's an area larger than the state of Delaware. The United States has about a 245-year supply of coal, if it continues using coal at the same rate at which it uses coal today. Montana is the state with the most coal reserves (119 billion tons). But Wyoming is the top coal-producing state - it produced about 400 million tons in 2004. Texas is the top coal-consuming state. It uses about 100 million tons each year. The average coal miner is 50 years old and has 20 years of experience. Coal ash, a byproduct of coal combustion, is used as filler for tennis rackets, golf balls, and linoleum. U.S. coal deposits contain more energy than that of all the world's oil reserves. Each person in the United States uses 3.8 tons of coal each year.[5]

The U.S. Geological Service issued a report in April, 2008, on how much oil is in the western 2/3 of North Dakota, western South Dakota, and extreme Eastern Montana, known as the Bakken Formation. The

Bakken is the largest domestic oil discovery since Alaska's Prudhoe Bay, and has the potential to eliminate all America's dependence on foreign oil. The Energy Information Administration (EIA) estimates it at 503 billion barrels. Even if just 10% of the oil is recoverable, at $107 a barrel, it's a resource worth more than $5.3 Trillion. "This sizeable find is now the highest-producing onshore oil field found in the past 56 years." reports the Pittsburgh Post-Gazette. It's a formation known as the Williston basin, but it's more commonly known as the "Bakken", and it stretches from northern Montana, through North Dakota and into Canada. For years, U.S. oil exploration had been considered a dead end. Even "Big Oil" gave up searching for major oil years ago. However, a recent technological breakthrough has opened up Bakken's massive reserves, and we could have access of up to 500 billion barrels. Because this is light sweet oil, those billions of barrels will cost Americans just $16 a barrel. That's enough crude to fuel the American economy for 41 years. Lynn Helms, director of the state Department of Mineral Resources, said recent production results from 103 newly tapped wells in the Three Forks-Sanish formation show many that are "as good or better" than some in the Bakken. President Obama was wrong when he said, "the U.S. has just 2 percent of the world's oil reserves, yet uses 25 percent of them. Even if we drilled every drop of oil out of every one of those reserves, it still wouldn't be enough to meet our long-term needs. One way to meet this need is to partner with Canada, Mexico and Brazil. A second way is 'safe and responsible' off-shore drilling".[6]

Harold Hamm, the Oklahoma-based founder and CEO of Continental Resources, the 14th-largest oil company in America, is a man who thinks big. He came to Washington last month [Sept. 2011] to spread a needed message of economic optimism: With the right set of national energy policies, the United States could be "completely energy independent by the end of the decade. We can be the Saudi Arabia of oil and natural gas in the 21st century." "President Obama is riding the wrong horse on energy," he adds. We can't come anywhere near the scale of energy production to achieve energy independence by pouring tax dollars into "green energy" sources like wind and solar, he argues. It has to come from oil and gas. You'd expect an oilman to make the "drill, baby, drill" pitch. But since 2005 America truly has been in the midst of a revolution in oil and natural gas, which is the nation's fastest-growing manufacturing sector. No one is more responsible for that resurgence than Mr. Hamm. He was the original discoverer of the gigantic and prolific Bakken oil fields of Montana and North Dakota that have already helped move the U.S. into third place among world oil producers. How much oil does Bakken have? The official estimate of the U.S. Geological Survey a few years ago was between four and five billion barrels. Mr. Hamm disagrees: "No way. We estimate that the entire field, fully developed, in Bakken is 24 billion barrels." If he's right, that'll double America's proven oil reserves. "Bakken is almost twice as big as the oil reserve in Prudhoe Bay, Alaska," he continues. According to Department of Energy data, North Dakota is on pace to surpass California in oil production in the next few years. Mr. Hamm explains over lunch in Washington, D.C., that the more his company drills, the more oil it finds. Continental Resources has seen its "proved reserves" of oil and natural gas (mostly in North Dakota) skyrocket to 421 million barrels this summer from 118 million barrels in 2006. "We expect our reserves and production to triple over the next five years." And for those who think this oil find is only making Mr. Hamm rich, he notes that today in America "there are 10 million royalty owners across the country" who receive payments for the oil drilled on their land. "The wealth is being widely shared." One reason for the renaissance has been OPEC's erosion of market power. "For nearly 50 years in this country nobody looked for oil here and drilling was in steady decline. Every time the domestic industry picked itself up, the Saudis would open the taps and drown us with cheap oil," he recalls. "They had unlimited production capacity, and company after company would go bust." Today OPEC's market share is falling and no longer dictates the world price. This is huge, Mr. Hamm says. "Finally we have an opportunity to go out and explore for oil and drill without fear of price collapse." When OPEC was at its peak in the 1990s, the U.S. imported about two-thirds of its oil. Now we import less than half of it, and about 40% of what we do import comes from Mexico and Canada. That's why Mr. Hamm thinks North America can achieve oil independence. The other reason for America's abundant supply of oil and natural gas has been the development of new drilling techniques. "Horizontal drilling" allows rigs to reach two miles into the ground and then spread horizontally by thousands of feet. Mr. Hamm was one of the pioneers of this method in the 1990s, and it has done for the oil industry what hydraulic fracturing has done for natural gas drilling in places like the Marcellus Shale in the Northeast. Both innovations have unlocked decades worth of new sources of domestic fossil fuels that previously couldn't be extracted at affordable cost. Mr. Hamm's rags to riches success is the quintessential "only in America" story. He was the last of 13 kids, growing up in rural Oklahoma "the son of sharecroppers who never owned land." He didn't have money to go to college, so as a teenager he went to work in the oil fields and developed a passion. "I always wanted to find oil. It was always an irresistible calling." He became a wildcat driller and his success rate became legendary in the industry. "People started to say I have ESP," he remarks. "I was fortunate, I guess. Next year it will be 45 years in the business." Mr. Hamm ranks 33rd on the Forbes wealth list for America, but given the massive amount of oil that he owns, much still in the ground, and the dizzying growth of Continental's output and profits (up 34% last year alone), his wealth could rise above $20 billion and he could soon be rubbing elbows with the likes of Warren Buffett. His only beef these days is with Washington. Mr. Hamm was invited to the White House for a "giving summit" with wealthy Americans who have pledged to donate at least half their wealth to charity. (He's given tens of millions of dollars already to schools like Oklahoma State and for diabetes research.) "Bill Gates, Warren Buffett, they were all there," he recalls. When it was Mr. Hamm's turn to talk briefly with President Obama, "I told him of the revolution in the oil and gas industry and how we have the capacity to produce enough oil to enable America to replace OPEC. I wanted to make sure he knew about this." The president's reaction? "He turned to me and said, 'Oil and gas will be important for the next few years. But we need to go on to green and alternative energy. [Energy] Secretary [Steven] Chu has assured me that within five years, we can have a battery developed that will make a car with the equivalent of 130 miles per gallon.'" Mr. Hamm holds his head in his hands and says, "Even if you believed that, why would you want to stop oil and gas development? It was pretty disappointing." Washington keeps "sticking a regulatory boot at our necks and then turns around and asks: 'Why aren't you creating more jobs,'" he says.[7]

Keystone XL pipes lie in wait in North Dakota. According to Senator John Hoeven Keystone XL would take 500 trucks a day off the road in Western North Dakota.

A recent accident in North Dakota involving crude-by-rail transport prompted the U.S. Department of Transportation Pipeline and Hazardous Materials Safety Administration (PHMSA) to release an alert on January 2, 2014, which suggested that "the type of crude oil being transported from the Bakken region may be more flammable than traditional heavy crude oil." This alert has raised very important questions regarding the safety of crude oil transportation. "Before any oil goes into pipeline systems, it has to meet specific safety and regulatory standards. The oil that enters the pipeline at the Hardisty Terminal is tested upon injection for viscosity, temperature, water content, suspended solids and other characteristics to ensure it meets current regulatory requirements," said Vern Meier, TransCanada's vice president of pipeline safety and compliance. "Bakken oil is subject to the same type of product content disclosure requirements as any other crude oil that is transported in a pipeline and will have to meet all of the same content specifications for transportation that other crude oils are required to. The Keystone XL Pipeline is considered, under PHMSA's pipeline safety regulations, to be a hazardous liquid pipeline. The pipeline design, construction and operation will ensure it meets all of the required standards and regulations governing pipelines transporting a wide range of hydrocarbon-based hazardous liquid products, including crude oil, but also refined products such as gasoline and jet fuel," said Vern. "Safety is our number one priority at TransCanada, our construction standards are the highest in the industry and we have an industry-leading safety record to prove it." In 2012 alone, TransCanada invested $1 billion in our infrastructure safety and integrity program, which includes proactive inspection and maintenance programs to protect our pipelines and energy facilities, and we plan to have invested another $1 billion on safety and integrity in 2013. During our more than 60 years of operation, we have earned a reputation for delivering energy safely and efficiently and the Keystone and Keystone XL Pipelines will continue that commitment.

On April 25, 2011 Shell Oil Corporation announced it was dropping its efforts to drill for oil in the Arctic Sea off the northern coast of Alaska. This decision comes after 5 long years of jumping through the governmental hoops of massive regulations, careful, tedious exploration and the expense of investing over 4 billion dollars in the project. So just what caused Shell to accept the massive monetary losses and drop the project? Was it due to the fact that they couldn't find enough oil there to make a profit? Apparently that is not the case, as there are an estimated 27 billion barrels of oil just sitting there waiting for extraction. Could Shell's reason for dropping a 4 billion dollar project be that there is no demand for all of that oil in the U.S. today? With current gasoline prices over $4.00 a gallon across the nation that hardly seems like a valid reason to not extract that domestic oil in the Arctic Sea. Supply and demand are what drive gasoline prices, no matter who tells you anything different. So why is Shell being forced to accept 4 billion dollars in losses in pulling out its drilling operations in the Arctic Sea near Alaska? The answer to that question can be found in 3 simple little letters: EPA as in the infamous Environmental Protection Agency. Just do not try to get an exact answer from Obama appointee Lisa Jackson, the current EPA administrator, as she refuses to answer phone calls or E-mails to explain this ludicrous decision by her four radical Democrats on the board that denied an "air quality permit" for Shell to drill in the region. So much for accountability in our government once again from an Obama appointee. They have a pattern of making radical decisions, and then refusing to explain them to the very people who pay their salaries. I offer this article from Fox News as proof of just who is behind this ludicrous decision, and how they refuse to tell the people why they have made such a blatantly extreme decision.

The EPA's appeals board ruled that Shell had not taken into consideration emissions from an ice-breaking vessel when calculating overall greenhouse gas emissions from the project. Environmental groups were thrilled by the ruling. After 5 years and 4 billion dollars, the Democratic extremists on a panel for the EPA have denied the extraction of 27 billion barrels of our very own oil for the fact that ice-breaking vessels burn fuel, and therefore emit pollution. Does this mean that every ship traveling in our waters will be shut down also because they all burn fuel of one type or another. No, this only means that the evil capitalists at Shell Oil will be stopped from producing millions of dollars of oil for U.S. consumption because they did not include the emissions from the ice breaking ships in their total environmental impact figures for air quality control. If crab fishermen in Alaska get stuck in the ice this year, does this mean that the ice breaking ships will be told to let them sit there and freeze to death until Lisa Jackson's radical EPA board checks their emission statements too? There is no difference there. These people on this EPA board, including Lisa Jackson are extreme activists, hypocrites and liars, period. From the prior mentioned Fox News article we see who they really are: The EPA did not return repeated calls and e-mails. The Environmental Appeals Board has four members: Edward Reich, Charles Sheehan, Kathie Stein and Anna Wolgast. All are registered Democrats and Kathie Stein was an activist attorney for the Environmental Defense Fund. Members are appointed by the EPA administrator. Alaska's Republican senator thinks it's time to make some changes.

There you have it, an EPA board which includes an appointed political activist lawyer, all of them Democrats, has denied Shell Oil the rights to extract the oil in the Arctic Sea due solely to the emissions of the ice breaking ships. Will Lisa Jackson and this board write the refund check to Shell oil for the billions of dollars they are out of due to this environmental extremist board's decision? No, I'm not talking about a check drawn on the taxpayers account here, but instead a personal check drawn on the accounts of these five people who bear responsibility for this nonsense. Maybe that would make them think twice before trying a politically motivated stunt like this the next time they get asked to make a decision that will affect every single tax paying American citizen. The real motivation, the real prize, is the Trans-Alaska Pipeline System. The design throughput of the pipe is in excess of 2 million barrels of oil per day; recent throughput is around 600,000 barrels per day. At some limiting rate (I've heard 200,000 barrels per day), the cost to operate the line will exceed the value of operating it, and it will be shut down. Pipeline shut-down is the ultimate goal of the environmental movement. Not just ANWR, but any new development must be stopped so that TAPS dies an early and unnatural death. Since the U.S. House of Representatives recently voted to de-fund the domestic terrorists over at the EPA, only to be denied by the career politicians in the

U.S. Senate, I think we need to remember these Senate tyrants in 2012, and replace them with some people who will actually protect U.S. citizens from this kind of blatant abuse of power. [8]

Thanks to new drilling technologies that are unlocking substantial amounts of natural gas from shale rocks, the nation's estimated gas reserves have surged by 35 percent, according to a recent study. The report by the Potential Gas Committee, the authority on gas supplies, shows the United States holds far larger reserves than previously thought. The jump is the largest increase in the 44-year history of reports from the committee. The finding raises the possibility that natural gas could emerge as a critical transition fuel. With current usage, gas reserves give the U.S. an 86-year supply. Estimated natural gas reserves rose to 2,074 trillion cubic feet in 2008, from 1,532 trillion cubic feet in 2006, when the last report was issued. This includes the proven reserves compiled by the Energy Department of 237 trillion cubic feet, as well as the sum of the nation's probable, possible and speculative reserves. Much of that jump comes from estimated gas in shale rocks, which drilling companies have only recently learned how to tap. They have developed a technique called hydraulic fracturing, in which water is injected at high pressure into wells to shatter rocks deep underground, helping to release trapped gas. The method, perfected in recent years in places like Texas and Pennsylvania, has set off a boom in new drilling, but is coming under increasing regulatory and environmental scrutiny. Shale gas accounts for 616 trillion cubic feet of reserves, or a third of the total, according to the report. Higher drilling costs and the extensive use of water to fracture shale rocks have raised concerns about the long-run commercial potential of these supplies. Some environmental groups fear that hydraulic fracturing will pollute drinking water, and Congress is considering tighter regulation of the practice. Gas prices needed to be around $4 to $6 per thousand cubic feet to justify developing shale beds. They have fallen below that level at times in recent months. For advocates of the gas industry, the report vindicates the potential of natural gas in the economy. [9]

1. http://factsnotfantasy.blogspot.com/2010/04/destroying-america-with-epas-carbon.html

2. http://www.rationalpublicradio.com/the-epa-is-destroying-america-electricity-rates-to-jump-by-10-35.html

3. http://mediamatters.org/research/200811030006

4. http://www.propublica.org/article/epa-fracking-study-to-focus-on-five-states-but-not-wyoming

5. http://www.semissourian.com/blogs/lindsey/entry/34160/
6. http://thomasjeffersonclub.org/index.php?option=com_content&view=article&id=65:americas-unlimited-domestic-oil-reserves&catid=10:cap-a-trade&Itemid=16

7. http://online.wsj.com/article/SB10001424052970204226204576602524023932438.html?mod=rss_opinion_main

8. http://www.conservativedailynews.com/2011/04/epa-extreme-political-activism/

9. http://www.nytimes.com/2009/06/18/business/energy-environment/18gas.html?_r=2

14 FEDERAL RESERVE

I would issue an order that the Federal Reserve Corporation (Fed) and the Securities and Exchange Commission (SEC), will be abolished immediately. We have taken the creation of money out of the hands of Congress, who are accountable to the people, and given it to an independent Corporation of bankers that is not answerable to anyone, in a misguided attempt to take politics out of the currency supply.

Few Americans realize why the Founding Fathers wrote into Article I of the U.S. Constitution: "Congress shall have the Power to Coin Money and Regulate the Value Thereof". They did this in prayerful hope it would prevent "love of money" from destroying the Republic they had formed. We shall see how subversion of Article I has brought on the "evil" that God warned about in the Bible. How true Solomon's words are: "The rich rule over the poor, and the borrower is servant to the lender" (Proverbs 22:7). God warned in the Bible that one of the curses that would come upon His people for disobeying His Laws was: "The stranger that is within you shall get up above you very high; and you shall come down very low. He shall lend to you, and you shall not lend to him; he shall be the head, and you shall be the tail" [Deut. 28: 44-45].

Not since 1833 have there been calls to abolish a United States bank. At the time, it was President Andrew Jackson who succeeded in abolishing The Second Bank of the United States. Today Rep. Ron Paul (R -TX) is calling for an end to the Federal Reserve. Paul calls for an audit, then an end to the Fed. He thinks the Fed permitted exorbitant risk-taking by companies ranging from Bank of America (NYSE: BAC) to Citigroup (NYSE: C) and from Morgan Stanley (NYSE: MS) to AIG (NYSE: AID). He believes abolishing the Fed would spur people to save more and become more prudent with their finances because free market forces, instead of a central bank, would set interest rates, limiting the amount of credit in the economy. He is in favor of returning to the Gold Standard and believes an end to the Fed will put an end to the dollar's long-trending depreciation. He also calls for more regulation on the government and not the markets.

He believes the Fed caused the current financial crisis. A monetary policy of easy credit and artificially low interest rates was the main source of the financial bubble, and the correction is always trying to fix what the Federal Reserve has done. The only way you can address the business cycle and prevent wild swings in the business cycle is by addressing the Federal Reserve and how they cause nothing but mischief. He said, "I believe in free markets. We don't have free markets and haven't had them. So it's convenient for people to blame the free market for the problems, but that's a fallacy. In a free market, capital would come from savings. People put their money in a savings account or something of real value, and that determines the interest rates. When people don't save, and we as a nation have not saved for many decades, there is this illusion that there is still so-called capital, or money made for investments. In reality, that capital came from a computer at the Federal Reserve. Therefore it sent the wrong information to businesses and savers, claiming that there was a lot of savings out there. Based on that, people over invested and built too many houses. It's the Federal Reserve that sends out the incorrect information".

There would be less credit, but it would still be steady growth. You would never have periods of economic tumult if you had economic growth of 4% or 5%, so you would never have the temptation to turn it off. There would be enough credit, but there wouldn't be an excess amount. It would be determined by the marketplace rather than by the artificialness of the Federal Reserve. I don't know of any risk in abolishing the Fed. The biggest challenge is that people might not understand it. If there are problems, they might blame the problems on getting rid of the Fed, while the problem would really be coming from the fact that it had existed. The first year would be tough. The problems would be due to the fact that the Fed would cause so much harm in the correction phase, which is always necessary. Reaction from the global economy to eliminating the Fed depends what you replace it with. If you allow the market to replace it with commodity money and make sure various countries believe in free trade, tariffs should go down, and free trade should reign. You should be able to have much freer travel, so it would be a real move towards globalization and global trade. If only one country does it, there's more of a challenge, and only the person who goes onto the Gold Standard would benefit. Abolishing the Fed will thwart the dollar's long-trending depreciation.

Governments want to spend more than they have and go to war when they shouldn't, and the only way they can finance it is through the printing press. The period of time when the world accepted a notion of an international Gold Standard was a time of tremendous economic growth. Paul has introduced HR 1207, the Federal Reserve Transparency Act, in which the Comptroller General audits the Fed and then gives a detailed report to Congress. He said the bill very popular. Every Republican in the House has signed on, and 111 Democrats have signed on. He has over 290 supporters, which in theory means that it could pass under suspension because he already has two-thirds in Congress as co-signers of the bill. It depends on the opposition, but there's a very good chance it will get passed. The opposition argues that auditing the Fed would open up the central bank to the political process and subject the bank to making monetary policy decisions based on lobbyists, politicians, and special interest groups, rather than the necessary economics. The Fed wants to use the political influence that they already have because it's been in secret. If you have a political influence of a company like Goldman Sachs (NYSE: GS) that can manipulate the benefits toward them and away from Lehman Brothers, that's political, too. It's been known for decades that the chairman of the Federal Reserve Board always accommodates a president and tries to have the right part of a cycle come up for election time. But, the audit bill has nothing to do with managing monetary policy.

In terms of reforming the financial regulatory structure, he says the SEC has been a total failure. Now people have this moral hazard of saying "It's OK, the SEC has looked at their books." That encourages people to make mistakes. People should be much more cautious. What we need is more regulation of the government - the Federal Reserve and Treasury - not to interfere in the markets. We should let bankruptcy laws work. The most important way to regulate markets is to never prop up the bad investments. Regulation should be defined as enforcing contracts, no fraud, and making sure the government doesn't interfere for the benefit of special interests. Let state laws take care of fraud cases. Insurance and ratings would all be market-oriented.[1]

Economists use the term "create" when speaking of the process by which money comes into existence. Now, creation means making something that did not exist before. Lumbermen make boards from trees, workers build houses from lumber, and factories manufacture automobiles from metal, glass and other materials. But in all these they did not "create", they only changed existing materials into a more usable and, therefore, more valuable form. This is not so with money. Here alone, man actually "creates" something out of nothing. A piece of paper of little value is printed so that it is worth a piece of lumber. With different figures, it can buy the automobile or even the house. Its value has been "created" in the true meaning of the word.[2]

Money is very cheap to make, and whomever does the "creating" of money in a nation can make a tremendous profit! That profit is part of our story, but first let us consider another unique characteristic of the thing - money, the love of which is the "root of all evil." An adequate supply of money is indispensable to civilized society. Money is the blood of civilized society, the means of all commercial trade except simple barter. It is the measure and instrument by which one product is sold and another purchased. Remove money or even reduce the supply below that necessary to carry on current levels of trade, and the results are catastrophic.

Since 1913, all our money has been created and issued by an illegal method that will eventually destroy the United States if it is not changed. Prior to 1913, America was a prosperous, powerful, and growing nation, at peace with its neighbors and the envy of the world. But, in December of 1913, Congress, with many members away for the Christmas holidays, passed what has since been known as the Federal Reserve Act. It simply authorized the Federal Reserve Corporation, with a Board of Directors to run the money system. This simple but terrible law completely removed from Congress the right to "create" money or to have any control over its "creation" and gave that function to the Federal Reserve Corporation. This was done with appropriate fanfare and propaganda that this would "remove money from politics". They didn't say "and therefore from the people's control". The people were not told then, and most still do not know today, that the Federal Reserve Corporation is a private corporation controlled by private bankers and therefore is operated for the financial gain of the bankers over the people, rather than for the good of the people.

In 1930 America did not lack industrial capacity, fertile farmland, skilled and willing workers or industrious farm families. It had an extensive and highly efficient transportation system in railroads, road networks, inland and ocean waterways. Communications between regions were the best in the world, utilizing telephone, teletype, radio, and a well-operated government mail system. No war had ravaged the cities or the countryside, no pestilence weakened the population, nor had famine stalked the land. The United States of America in 1930 lacked only one thing: an adequate supply of money. In the early 1930's, bankers, the only source of new money and credit, deliberately refused loans to industries, stores and farms. Payments on existing loans were required however, and money rapidly disappeared from circulation. Goods were available to be purchased, jobs waiting to be done, but the lack of money brought the nation to a standstill. By this simple ploy, America was intentionally put in a "depression" and the greedy bankers took possession of hundreds of thousands of farms, homes, and business properties. The people were told, "times are hard," and "money is short". Not understanding the system, they were cruelly robbed of their earnings, their savings, and their property.

World War II ended the "depression". The same bankers who in the early 1930's had refused loans for peacetime houses, food and clothing, suddenly had unlimited billions to lend for Army barracks, K-rations and uniforms! A nation that in 1934 couldn't produce food for sale, suddenly could produce bombs to send free to Germany and Japan! With the sudden increase in money, people were hired, farmers sold their produce, factories went to two shifts, mines re-opened, and "The Great Depression" was over! Some politicians were blamed for it and others took credit for ending it. The truth is the lack of money (caused by the bankers) brought on the depression, and adequate money ended it. The people were never told that simple truth, and in this article we will endeavor to show how these same bankers who control our money and credit today have used their control to plunder America and place us in bondage.

When some few Patriotic people or organizations who know the truth begin to expose the Fed or try to stop any of their mad schemes, they are ridiculed and smeared as "conspiracy theorist," "right-wing extremists," "super-patriots," "ultra-rightists," "bigots," "racists," even "fascists" and "anti-Semites." Some, who are especially vocal in their exposure of this treason against our people, are harassed by government agencies such as the EPA, OSHA, or the IRS, causing them financial loss, embarrassment, or other hardships. By these methods, most Americans have been prevented from learning the truth. Therefore, to prevent violence or armed resistance in their plunder of America, they plan to eventually disarm all citizens. They have to eliminate most guns, except those in the hands of government police and army. Fortunately, groups of patriots in every state (and now a growing number of citizens of other countries) know the truth and are helping to fight the bankers' plans to dump the Constitution into the UN garbage pail. When the bankers prick the credit/debt bubble they will foreclose on America. Then they will own it all.

Buckle up and hold on -- a new round of quantitative easing is here and things could start getting very ugly in the financial world over the coming months. The truth is that many economists fear that an out of control Federal Reserve is "crossing the Rubicon" by announcing another wave of quantitative easing. Have we now reached a point where the Federal

Reserve is simply going to fire up the printing presses and shower massive wads of cash into the financial system whenever the U.S. economy is not growing fast enough? If so, what does the mean for inflation, the stability of the world financial system and the future of the U.S. dollar? The Fed says that the plan is to purchase $600 billion of U.S. Treasury securities by the middle of 2011. In addition, the Federal Reserve has announced that it will be "reinvesting" an additional $250 billion to $300 billion from the proceeds of its mortgage portfolio in U.S. Treasury securities over the same time period. So that is a total injection of about $900 billion. Perhaps the Fed thought that number would sound a little less ominous than $1 trillion. In any event, the Federal Reserve seems convinced that quantitative easing is going to work this time. So should we believe the Federal Reserve? The truth is that the Federal Reserve has tried this before. In November 2008, the Federal Reserve announced a $600 billion quantitative easing program. Four months later the Fed felt that even more cash was necessary, so they upped the total to $1.8 trillion. So did quantitative easing work then? No, not really. It may have helped stabilize the economy in the short-term, but unemployment is still staggeringly high. Monthly U.S. home sales continue to come in at close to record low levels. Businesses are borrowing less money. Individuals are borrowing less money. Stores are closing left and right. The Fed is desperate to crank the debt spiral that our economic system is now based upon back up again. The Fed thinks that somehow if it can just pump enough nearly free liquidity into the banking system, the banks will turn around and lend it out at a markup and that this will get the debt spiral cranking again. The sad truth is that the Federal Reserve is not trying to build an economic recovery on solid financial principles. Rather, what the Federal Reserve envisions is an "economic recovery" based on new debt creation. So will $900 billion be enough to get the debt spiral cranked up again? No. If 1.8 trillion dollars didn't work before, why does the Federal Reserve think that 900 billion dollars is going to work now? This new round of quantitative easing will create more inflation and will cause speculative asset bubbles, but it is not going to fix what is wrong with the economy. The damage is just too vast. Anyone who believes a meager one or two trillion dollars in pump-priming can overcome $15-$20 trillion in overpriced assets and $10 trillion in uncollectible debt may well be disappointed. In fact, economists over at Goldman Sachs estimate that it would take a staggering $4 trillion in quantitative easing to get the economy rolling again. Of course that may eventually be what happens. The Fed may be starting at $900 billion just to get the door open. With these kinds of bureaucrats, once you give them an inch they usually end up taking a mile. So why should we be concerned about quantitative easing?

1. http://www.fool.com/investing/international/2009/09/25/should-we-abolish-the-federal-reserve.aspx

2. http://www.buildfreedom.com/tl/rape3.shtml

15 GOLD STANDARD

I would issue an order that would return the United States to the Gold Standard as quickly as practicable. This will help keep the federal government from out-of-control spending policies and stop the Federal Reserve from printing more money. This would be academic, as I would eliminate the Federal Reserve.

The growing disillusionment with politically controlled monetary policies has produced an increasing number of advocates for a return to the Gold Standard - including at times President Reagan. In years past, a desire to return to a monetary system based on gold was perceived as nostalgia for an era when times were simpler, problems less complex and the world not threatened with nuclear annihilation. But after a decade of destabilizing inflation and economic stagnation, the restoration of a Gold Standard has become an issue that is clearly rising on the economic policy agenda. A commission to study the issue, with strong support from President Reagan, was in place. The increasingly numerous proponents of a Gold Standard persuasively argue that budget deficits and large federal borrowings would be difficult to finance under such a standard. If we don't go on the Gold Standard, it is predicted that gold will reach $20,000 an ounce by 2016.

Heavy claims against paper dollars cause few technical problems, for the Treasury can legally borrow as many dollars as Congress authorizes. But with unlimited dollar conversion into gold, the ability to issue dollar claims would be severely limited. Obviously if you cannot finance federal deficits, you cannot create them. Either taxes would then have to be raised or expenditures lowered. The restrictions of gold convertibility would therefore profoundly alter the politics of fiscal policy that have prevailed for half a century. Disturbed by alternatives, even some of those who conclude a return to gold is infeasible remain deeply disturbed by the current situation. For example, William Fellner of the American Enterprise Institute in a forthcoming publication remarks, "I find it difficult not to be greatly distressed by the very large damage done to the economies of the industrialized world by the monetary management that has followed the era of (gold) convertibility... It has placed the Western economies in acute danger."

Yet even those of us who are attracted to the prospect of gold convertibility are confronted with a seemingly impossible obstacle: the latest claims to gold represented by the huge world overhang of fiat currency, many dollars.

The immediate problem of restoring a gold standard is fixing a gold price that is consistent with market forces. Obviously if the offering price by the Treasury is too low, or subsequently proves to be too low, heavy demand at the offering price could quickly deplete the total U.S. government stock of gold, as well as any gold borrowed to thwart the assault. At that point, with no additional gold available, the U.S. would be off the gold standard and likely to remain off for decades.

Alternatively, if the gold price is initially set too high, or subsequently becomes too high, the Treasury would be inundated with gold offerings. The payments the gold drawn on the Treasury's account at the Federal Reserve would add substantially to commercial bank reserves and probably act, at least temporarily, to expand the money supply with all the inflationary implications thereof.

Monetary offsets to neutralize or "earmark" gold are, of course, possible in the short run. But as the West Germany authorities soon learned from their past endeavors to support the dollar, there are limits to monetary countermeasures.

The only seeming solution is for the U.S. to create a fiscal and monetary environment which in effect makes the dollar as good as gold, i.e., stabilizes the general price level and by inference the dollar price of gold bullion itself. Then a modest reserve of bullion could reduce the narrow gold price fluctuations effectively to zero, allowing any changes in gold supply and demand to be absorbed in fluctuations in the Treasury's inventory.

What the above suggests is that a necessary condition of returning to a gold standard is the financial environment which the gold standard itself is presumed to create. But, if we restored financial stability, what purpose is then served by return to a gold standard?

Certainly a gold-based monetary system will necessarily prevent fiscal imprudence, as 20th Century history clearly demonstrates. Nonetheless, once achieved, the discipline of the gold standard would surely reinforce anti-inflation policies, and make it far more difficult to resume financial profligacy. The redemption of dollars for gold in response to excess federal government-induced credit creation would be a strong political signal. Even after inflation is brought under control the extraordinary political sensitivity to inflation will remain.

Concrete actions to install a gold standard are premature. Nonetheless, there are certain preparatory policy actions that could test the eventual feasibility of returning to a gold standard, that would have positive short-term anti-inflation benefits and little cost if they fail.

The major roadblock to restoring the gold standard is the problem of re-entry. With the vast quantity of dollars worldwide laying claims to the U.S. Treasury's 264 million ounces of gold, an overnight transition to gold convertibility would create a major discontinuity for the U.S. financial system. But there is no need for the whole block of current dollar obligations to become an immediate claim.

Convertibility can be instituted gradually by, in effect, creating a dual currency with a limited issue of dollars convertible into gold. Initially they could be deferred claims to gold, for example, five-year Treasury Notes with interest and principal payable in grams or ounces of gold.

With the passage of time and several issues of these notes we would have a series of "new monies" in terms of gold and eventually, demand claims on gold. The degree of success of restoring long-term fiscal confidence will show up clearly in the yield spreads between gold and fiat dollar obligations of the same maturities. Full convertibility would require that the yield spread for all maturities virtually disappear. If they do not, convertibility will be very difficult, probably impossible, to implement.

A second advantage of gold notes is that they are likely to reduce current budget deficits. Treasury gold notes in today's markets could be sold at interest rates at approximately 2% or less. In fact from today's markets one can construct the equivalent of a 22-month gold note yielding 1%, by arbitraging regular Treasury note yields for June 1983 maturities (17%) and the forward delivery premiums of gold (16% annual rate) inferred from June 1983 futures contracts. Presumably five-year note issues would reflect a similar relationship.

The exchange risk of the Treasury gold notes, of course, is the same as that associated with our foreign currency Treasury note series. The U.S. Treasury has, over the years, sold significant quantities of both German mark - and Swiss franc denominated issues, and both made and lost money in terms of dollars as exchange rates have fluctuated. And indeed there is a risk of exchange rate loss with gold notes.

However, unless the price of gold doubles over a five-year period (16% compounded annually), interest payments on the gold notes in terms of dollars will be less than conventional financing requires. The run-up to $875 per ounce in early 1980 was surely an aberration, reflecting certain circumstances in the Middle East which are unlikely to be repeated in the near future. Hence, anything close to doubling of gold prices in the next five years appears improbable. On the other hand, if gold prices remain stable or rise moderately, the savings could be large: Each $10 billion in equivalent gold notes outstanding would, under stable gold prices, save $1.5 billion per year in interest outlays.

A possible further side benefit of the existence of gold notes is that they could set a standard in terms of prices and interest rates that could put additional political pressure on the administration and Congress to move expeditiously toward non-inflationary policies. Gold notes could be a case of reversing Gresham's Law. Good money would drive out bad.

Those who advocate a return to a gold standard should be aware that returning our monetary system to gold convertibility is no mere technical, financial restructuring. It is a basic change in our economic processes. However, considering where the policies of the last 50 years have eventually led us, perhaps there are lessons to be learned from our more distant gold standard past.[1]

"The United States will likely go back on the gold standard within five years in order to correct fiscal and monetary imbalances." says former GOP presidential candidate and Forbes Magazine Publisher Steve Forbes. The gold standard, under which the dollar is pegged to gold instead of other currencies as it is today was abandoned by President Richard Nixon in 1971. "What seems astonishing today could become conventional wisdom in a short period of time." says Forbes. A return to the gold standard would stabilize the dollar by discouraging hefty fiscal spending as well as preventing the Federal Reserve from printing excess money. "People know that something is wrong with the dollar." he says, adding "You cannot trash your money without repercussions." The dollar would not only be stronger today if the gold standard were in place, it would be less volatile. Currency volatility has helped open the doors for speculators to invest in commodities as a hedge against swinging currency values, which has helped stoke inflationary concerns.

Under a gold standard, it is "much harder" for governments to borrow excessively like they are doing today. The housing bubble, partly the product of loose monetary policy, would never have been so severe under a gold standard. "When it comes to exchange rates and monetary policy, people often don't grasp what is at stake for the economy", he said. By restoring the gold standard, the country would move away from "less responsible policies" and toward a stronger dollar and a stronger America. "If the dollar was as good as gold, other countries would want to buy it." Talk of returning the country to the gold standard has risen in recent months. Sean Fieler and Jeffrey Bell, respectively the chairman and policy director of the American Principles Project, say resurrecting the gold standard can tame the Federal Reserve's money printing campaign.

"Members of Congress seeking to restrict the Fed's power need to consider what oppositional force is truly capable of hemming it in," the two write in a recent The Wall Street Journal editorial. "One answer is a revived gold standard, which would once again obligate the Fed to redeem dollars for gold at a fixed rate." With the dollar weakening and with the Fed in no hurry to change its policies, gold has been soaring. Precious metals often do when paper currencies soften. Gold recently hit a record $1,577.57 an ounce, which is six times higher than the precious metal's low in August 1999, according to Bloomberg. Gold's rally did take a breather recently, falling 1.6 percent after the Wall Street Journal reported that Soros Fund Management sold precious-metal assets. Still, others say the metal has a ways to go before truly peaking. "I'm bullish on gold despite its current levels." says Hal Lehr, Deutsche Bank's managing director for cross-commodity trading, according to Bloomberg. "It could reach $2,000 an ounce in the next eight months."[2]

1. Alan Greenspan, "Can the US Return to a Gold Standard?" *The Wall Street Journal*, Sept. 1, 1981. Online version here: http://www.gold-eagle.com/greenspan011098.html

2. http://www.moneynews.com/StreetTalk/Steve-Forbes-Gold-Standard/2011/05/11/id/395949

16 WALL STREET

I would issue an order that there will be a separation of business operations in the financial world. Banks will be limited to traditional functions of the banking industry, brokerage houses will be limited to traditional roles in stocks and bonds, and insurance companies will be limited to traditional roles for selling insurance. One of the major problems with Wall Street had been a blurring of roles for these industries. The financial crisis was the result of a fundamental failure from Wall Street to Washington. Wall Street took irresponsible risks that they didn't fully understand, and Washington did not have the authority to properly monitor or constrain risk-taking at the largest firms. When the crisis hit, they did not have the tools to break apart or wind down a failing financial firm without putting the American taxpayer and the entire financial system at risk. Also, hedge funds, derivatives, and speculators will be outlawed. Compensation for all company officers will be voted on at annual stockholder meetings, not by Corporate Board of Directors. This will make compensation packages responsive to the shareholders and what they feel is the performance of the management team. In addition, Congress will be directly responsible for corporate negligence or fraud (Bernard Madoff), and not delegated to some third party or agency. Since I eliminated the Securities and Exchange Commission (SEC) and Federal Reserve (Fed), Congress will be accountable to the voters for the control and health of these industries. Finally, I would issue an order repealing the Sarbanes-Oxley Act and the Dodd/Frank bill that have been obstacles to the fundamental operation of banks.

There has been a move under way by some economists and liberals in Congress to cap CEO salaries at $500,000. This shows that Marxism/Communism and class envy/class warfare are alive and well. Karl

Marx said, "From each according to his abilities, to each according to his needs." Limiting CEO salaries to $500,000 for top managers who are responsible for the livelihood of thousands of people is ridiculous. Steve Jobs, Apple, Inc., had an annual salary of $1, but made $616 million in 2010. Why should only executives of corporations be subject to the cap? There is no reason movie directors, movie stars, and athletes should be immune. Why not limit the compensation for Steven Speilberg ($332 million), Angelina Jolie ($20 million per movie), or Alex Rodriquez ($28 million)? In a free capitalist society, the marketplace and stockholders determine the compensation package. CEO's are paid what the board of directors and stockholders decide is the value of their contribution to the organization. There is a quote attributed to Babe Ruth, when asked by a reporter why he was demanding $80,000 a year when President Herbert Hoover was only paid $75,000. Ruth replied, "I had a better year than Hoover."

"The point is, ladies and gentleman, that greed, for lack of a better word, is good. Greed is right, greed works. Greed clarifies, cuts through, and captures the essence of the evolutionary spirit. Greed, in all of its forms; greed for life, for money, for love, for knowledge has marked the upward surge of mankind." - Gordon Gekko -In the movie Wall Street (1987).

As Gordon Gekko said, "Greed is good." However, hedge fund managers have taken greed to a new level, and hedge funds need to be outlawed. As major markets and economies careened downward last year, 25 top managers reaped a total of $11.6 billion in pay by trading above the pain in the markets, according to an annual ranking of top hedge fund earners by Institutional Investor's Alpha magazine James H. Simons, a former math professor who has made billions year after year for the hedge fund Renaissance Technologies, earned $2.5 billion running computer-driven trading strategies. John A. Paulson, who rode to riches by betting against the housing market, came in second with reported gains of $2 billion, and George Soros, also a perennial name on the rich list of secretive moneymakers, pulled in $1.1 billion. Their earnings were not unscathed by the extensive shakeout in the markets. In a year when losses were recorded at two of every three hedge funds, pay for many of these managers was down by several million, and the overall pool of earnings was about half the $22.5 billion the top 25 earned in 2007. The managers' compensation, which was breathtaking in the best of times, is eye-popping after a year when hedge funds lost 18 percent on average, and investors withdrew money en masse.

Government scrutiny over Wall Street pay is also mounting. Hedge funds are facing proposals for new taxes on their gains, and Treasury Secretary Timothy F. Geithner said he would seek greater power to regulate hedge funds. To make the cut this year, a hedge fund hotshot needed to earn $75 million, down sharply from the $360 million cutoff for 2007's top 25. Still, amid the financial shakeout, the combined pay of the top 25 hedge fund managers beat every year before 2006. "The golden age for hedge funds is gone, but it's still three times more lucrative than working at a mutual fund, and most other places on Wall Street," said Robert Sloan, managing partner of S3 Partners, a hedge fund risk management firm. "But this shouldn't pop up on the greed meter. They made money. That's what they're supposed to do." In an interview, Paulson, whose lofty 2008 earnings were down from the $3.7 billion that Alpha estimated he earned in 2007 - said his pay was high in large part because he is the biggest investor in his fund. In fact, he said he receives no bonus. The pensions, endowments and other institutions that invest in his fund do not mind the hefty cut of profits he and his team take, he said. "In a year when all their other investments lost money, we're like an oasis," Paulson said. "We have investors who were invested with Bernard Madoff, and they can't thank me enough," he added.[1]

There have been several attempts in Congress to reform Wall Street. The laws enacted have met with some success, but the Wall Street gurus have managed to outsmart the politicians. Here are the major Congressional Acts:

The Glass-Steagall Act of 1933 - This placed a "wall of separation" between banks and brokerages, which was largely repealed by the Financial Services Modernization Act of 1999. Though some commentators regard the restoration of the 1933 bill as crucial, even calling it "the most vital element of Wall Street reform", House Democratic leaders refused to allow an amendment by Rep. Maurice Hinchey (D-NY) to restore Glass-Steagall as part of the 2009 Frank bill. Hinchey introduced his proposal as a separate bill, the Glass-Steagall Restoration Act of 2009. Nonetheless, the "Volcker rule" proposed by the Obama administration has been described as a "new Glass-Steagall Act for the 21st century", as it establishes stringent rules against banks using their own money to make risky investments.

Sarbanes-Oxley Act of 2002 -This Act, by Sen. Paul S. Sarbanes (D-MO) and Rep. Michael G. Oxley (R OH), was signed into law by George W. Bush in July 2002. The bill was enacted as a reaction to a number of major corporate and accounting scandals, including those affecting Enron and WorldCom.

The "Volcker Rule" - This was proposed by President Obama based on advice from Paul Volcker, and a draft of the proposed legislation was prepared by the U.S. Treasury Department. It limited any one bank from holding more than 10% of FDIC-insured deposits, and prohibited any bank with a division holding such deposits from using its own capital to make speculative investments. The Volcker rule faced heavy resistance in the Senate and was introduced as part of the subsequent Dodd bill only in a limited form.

Financial Stability Oversight Council - Chaired by the United States Secretary of the Treasury, a new multi-authority oversight body called the Financial Stability Oversight Council of regulators will be established. The council will consist of nine members including regulators from the Federal Reserve System, U.S. Securities and Exchange Commission, Federal Housing Finance Agency, and many other agencies. The main purpose of the council is to identify risk in the Financial system. Also, the council will look at the interconnectivity of the highly leveraged financial firms and can ask companies to divest holdings if their structure poses a great threat to the Financial system. The council will have a solid control on the operations of the leveraged firms and also help in increasing the transparency.

House Bill H.R. 4173, the Wall Street Reform and Consumer Protection Act of 2009, and Senate Bill S.3217, (the Dodd bill) that included a $50 billion liquidation fund that drew criticism as a continuing bailout, was removed by pressure from Republicans and the Obama administration. Both passed. Differences between the bills were to be worked out in United States congressional conference committee, including whether the new consumer protection agency would be independent (Senate) or part of the Federal Reserve, whether to require banks to issue credit derivatives in separately capitalized affiliates (Senate); how exactly the Federal Deposit Insurance Corporation (FDIC) will wind down or bail out large institutions that fail; the circumstances under which large institutions could be broken up; a 15 to 1 leverage limit in the House bill; the terms of a Fed audit (continuous as in the House bill or one-time as in the Senate bill). Both bills include the Volcker rule that prohibits proprietary trading by bank holding companies, but both have a caveat that would allow regulators to overrule the rule. Both bills propose to regulate credit rating agencies, but the Senate's bill is much stronger.

The wizards of Wall Street have figured out that it's a lot easier to make a buck off basic needs -commodities - than corporate paper, and they are fueling another commodities bubble that is pushing millions of people around the globe into poverty and despair. Not content with destroying America's housing market, they are now forcing us to pay higher prices for gas and groceries. It's a Wall Street tax. The mainstream business press would have us believe higher prices are being driven by the specter of

Parson Malthus, who argued more than 200 years ago that food production could not keep pace with population growth. Wall Street analysts describe a "super cycle" in commodities being driven by growth in emerging market economies like Brazil, India, and China. While true to a certain extent, the facts are that the current upward trend in prices and increased volatility is mainly fueled by speculative investment activity from Wall Street. There's nothing like a good bubble for Wall Street profits, and there's nothing like profiting on the things people need. From 2000 to 2008, financial flows into commodities increased from $10 billion to $270 billion - an increase of over 2,500 percent! And these same forces that pushed oil and food prices up in 2008 are driving the current commodity bubble.

Since the mid-2000s, Wall Street banks have been investing in companies that transport and store commodities, "These days, the Wall Street banks are more like those grain traders than you might think." *Business Week* reported last July. "They have equipped themselves to take delivery of raw materials when they choose to…Goldman owns a global network of aluminum warehouses. Morgan Stanley (MS) chartered more tankers than Chevron (CVX) last year." In other words, Wall Street banks are now commodity traders. But it takes two to tango, and Wall Street needed chumps who would blindly increase demand for futures contracts. Enter the Exchange Traded Fund (ETF), an investment product that is a hybrid of mutual funds and stocks. A mutual fund buys assets and sells "shares" to investors that can be bought/sold at the end of each day. An ETF buys a fixed bundle of assets, and sells shares that can be traded during the day like a stock. The first commodity ETFs were created around 2001-2002 to invest in gold and silver.

The current oil price spike is being blamed on turmoil in the Middle East and North Africa (affectionately known as MENA) that is supposedly disrupting the supply of oil, causing gas prices to exceed $4/gallon. However, oil storage facilities in Cushing, Oklahoma, one of the largest in the US, are at capacity - it's awash in oil. Why? Because markets make it profitable to buy and store oil, which is exactly what the big players, including Wall Street banks, are doing. Supply is not the problem. It's the huge flow of speculative money betting on oil, and other commodities, causing increased prices and greater volatility. The Fed's QE2 bond-buying program has added fuel to the fire by raising inflationary expectations, causing investors to put even more money into ETF commodity investments, thus creating a self-fulfilling prophecy. Wall Street banks have taken control of the futures markets, and the regulators have let them. They make more money when markets are rigged to function more like casinos than providing the true economic function of price hedging. Speculative investment flows are the major influence on commodity prices now, and the more money that flows in, the higher prices go, and the more profits Wall Street makes.

Futures markets, like the Chicago Mercantile Exchange (CME), were created to allow farmers and merchants to protect themselves against price movements. A futures contract is an obligation by the seller to deliver (or take delivery if one is a buyer) a given quantity of wheat (5,000 bushels, for example) at some point in the future (say, six months) at a price determined today (say $2/bushel). Rather than worry about what prices will be at harvest time, farmers can lock in a price today by selling futures contracts at the time they plant their crops. Note, in this example, the total value of the contract is $10,000 ($2 times 5,000 bushels), but the farmer is only required to put up about five percent of the value as collateral ($500 in this case), known as margin. With margins so low, futures markets naturally attracted speculators. Speculators have always been welcome participants in futures markets because they provide liquidity - they make it easier to buy and sell contracts. However, since commodity markets are significantly smaller in size than other asset markets, they are easier to manipulate. Because of this, speculators were limited in the number of contracts they could hold, known as position limits. This was done to ensure that fundamentals - the underlying supply and demand from producers and consumers - determined commodity prices, not speculative activity. Note also, that true speculators make bets on price movements up or down. This is a hugely significant innovation. If the hedge fund directly used the futures market to bet on commodities, it would have position limits, but in using OTC swaps from Goldman, there are no position limits on either firm. The hedge fund is no longer restricted in the number of bets it makes, which means speculative investment flows will have a greater impact on prices.[2]

A pending lawsuit against the Dodd-Frank Wall Street Reform and Consumer Protection Act exemplifies several aspects of the complaints legal scholars have against the president's treatment of the Constitution. The State National Bank of Big Spring, Texas launched a lawsuit against Dodd-Frank, joined by the Competitive Enterprise Institute and the 60 Plus Association. The lawsuit argues that three parts of the bill - the Consumer Financial Protection Bureau (CFPB), the Orderly Liquidation Authority, and the Financial Stability Oversight Counsel (FSOC) - all violate the Constitution, according to Adam White, a lawyer at Boyden Gray & Associates who is working on the lawsuit. Three states - Oklahoma, South Carolina, and Michigan - joined the lawsuit in September, arguing that the Orderly Liquidation Authority is unconstitutional. The CFPB and the FSOC, said White, both violate the separation of powers. "Dodd-Frank authorizes the CFPB to define and prosecute unfair, deceptive, or abusive practices," White said, and this ability to define constitutes legislation, which is forbidden under the separation of powers. "Title X of the Dodd-Frank Act delegates effectively unbounded power to the CFPB, and couples that power with provisions insulating the CFPB against meaningful checks by the Legislative, Executive, and Judicial Branches," reads the lawsuit. White said that the CFPB does not receive its money through congressional appropriations, but rather from the Federal Reserve, insulating it from congressional oversight. He also emphasized that CFPB director, Richard Cordray, has a high level of job security, as the president cannot fire him at will as he can with Cabinet appointees. The lawsuit says that the FSOC "has sweeping and unprecedented discretion to choose which non-bank financial companies to designate as 'systemically important,'" that is, too big to fail. Yet this discretion is "not limited by any meaningful statutory directives," giving the FSOC "virtually boundless discretion in making consequential designations," says the lawsuit. The president initially justified the appointment on pragmatic grounds. "When Congress refuses to act, and as a result hurts our economy and puts people at risk, I have an obligation as president to do what I can without them," Obama said when announcing Cordray's appointment.

1. http://www.nytimes.com/2009/03/25/business/25hedge.html

2. http://artvoice.com/issues/v10n17/news_feature

17 LAWYERS

I would issue an order that no lawyers will be permitted to run for any national elective office. In the present U.S. Congress, there are 132 lawyers in the House (32%) and 60 lawyers in the Senate (60%). That is why we have legislation that no one understands, with parsing of words to confuse the citizenry. With 307,000,000 people, we can find enough capable non-lawyer candidates to run for federal offices. I would also issue an order that attorneys will not be allowed to advertise on television, radio, internet, or newspapers. No class action lawsuits would be permitted, and lawyers would not be involved in any medical malpractice, product liability, or accident suits. There would be panels of doctors and/or qualified "experts" in each city and jurisdiction who would determine malpractice or damage awards, with national caps of $500,000 for pain and suffering. Who do you trust most, a panel of doctors or a panel of trial lawyers? I would also institute a loser pay system as they have in all of Europe and most other nations. Finally, I will issue an order that the maximum contingency fee that a lawyer may charge a client is 10% of the monies awarded the client when winning a suit. This will prevent most frivolous lawsuits. These are true tort reforms that will save Americans hundreds of billions of dollars each year.

On October 24, 2004, I wrote a letter to the editor of The Roanoke Times, my local newspaper, about John Edwards, the poster boy for trial lawyers. They wouldn't publish it because it was too close to the election, and they have a liberal bias. In retrospect, my words have been completely vindicated. Didn't he turn out to be a prince of a fellow? Here is the letter: "The presidential election on November 2 is a referendum on a struggle between doctors and trial lawyers. If President Bush is re-elected, the doctors win. He has made medical liability reform a priority in his next administration. If Senator Kerry is elected, the trial lawyers win. He has selected as his vice presidential nominee Senator John Edwards, one of the most successful personal injury lawyers in North Carolina history. Trial lawyers are our one of our highest paid professions. Mr. Edwards won 31 medical malpractice suits against doctors and hospitals with awards over $1 million, including one $23 million settlement in 1995. Linking complications during childbirth to cerebral palsy became his specialty. Dr. Craig VanDerVeer, a Charlotte neurosurgeon said, "John Edwards crushed obstetrics, gynecology, and neurosurgery in North Carolina. As a result, thousands of patients lost their healthcare." Trial lawyers have driven some of the largest companies in the United States into bankruptcy, including Dow Chemical and Johns-Manville, costing tens of thousands of jobs. In Luke 11:46, Jesus said, "Woe to you lawyers also; for you load men with burdens hard to bear, and you yourselves do not touch the burdens with one of your fingers." His words are still true today.

In a handbook for trial lawyers, people who actually believe in our Nation's Founding Values are identified as being not desirable for juries because they are biased towards personal responsibility. We've all heard of race bias, gender bias, class bias, sexual orientation bias, et cetera. But maybe only a psychotherapist turned trial lawyer could come up with something called "personal responsibility bias." Apparently this affliction is especially pronounced among strange people with "traditional family values" and "strong religious beliefs". There are many men and women who have chosen to be a lawyer and devoted their professional lives to equity and justice. There are a greater number of the lawyer fraternity however, who have different motives and have not been so noble. In fact, as a general culture and class, lawyers are destroying America, turning this nation and American justice into a financial and political self-serving game.

Plea bargaining, bonding and judicial politics offer a revolving door justice system for criminals. There are two standards of justice for criminals: the rich walk, and the poor go to bankruptcy court or prison. Over 100,000 formal complaints are filed annually against lawyers and lawyer judges with only 2% formally prosecuted. Over 80% of low to middle income Americans cannot afford to pay the lawyer ransom for justice in America. Lawyer monopoly of the legal services profession now constitutes the most blatant illegal monopoly in America. Lawyers are robbing their clients through over billing and outright theft, conspiracy and fraud. Lawyer-judges have created class discrimination against non-lawyer pro se litigants nationwide. How lawyers and lawyer-judges have become a closed member country club with the masses picking up the tab. The American jury is being manipulated by the lawyers to get the verdict they want. America has become a giant law factory of self-interest laws hurting law-abiding citizens.

Lawyers criminalize Americans, attempting to assist citizens with generic legal procedures.[1]

The "case law" jungle created by the lawyer culture leads away from the Constitutional law. Extortion is going after the deep pockets. Lawyers are destroying America! Put aside for the time being the lawyer contributions on the national character issue, the ethical and moral issues, the spiritual issues of the nation, put aside the issues caused by the largest criminal culture on earth. Let's just take the economic ground in this issue. Case histories reveal that lawyers will go after what they perceive to be the "deep pockets" even when there is not a shred of evidence that the deep pocket party should be in the lawsuit. Often the best way to correct a problem on anything is to go back to the drawing board, see if we have strayed from the pilot model and make adjustments. The drawing board in this case is thirteen tiny early American colonies from whence sprang the greatest governing document in the world - the U. S. Constitution! You may not know this but lawyers were absolutely forbidden in those colonies for many years - in fact Virginia held them off for over 100 years. Disputes were settled by the CHURCH. We now have a grim picture of a great nation in an unconstitutional takeover by a dominant lawyer culture. With lawyers making up 36% of the federal Congress, lawyers holding the office of American President 57% of the time and 100% lawyers in the judicial branch, the three-branch of government concept has been breached! This constitutional nightmare now has lawyers making the laws, lawyers judging us in the laws, lawyers defending us in the laws, lawyers prosecuting us in the laws, lawyers interpreting the laws and lawyers administering the laws. Under this tyrannical monopoly of justice our freedoms, rights and privileges are under assault!

Trial lawyers' misleading Internet solicitations pose risk to public health. A new report from the Center for Medicine in the Public Interest shows that Internet searches for medical information predominantly lead to trial lawyer-run Web sites designed to gin up lawsuits. The often inaccurate and misleading information offered on these sites, says the report, frightens some patients away from beneficial drugs and treatment and thus endangers public health. Since President Obama was inaugurated, there has been a proliferation of television commercials by law firms. Trial lawyers were major contributors to his campaign, and after January 20 they immediately started to troll for perceived victims of the medical industry or product manufacturers. As an example, there are constant daily TV appeals to contact an attorney if suffering from Mesothelioma because of exposure to asbestos decades earlier. President Obama says he wants healthcare reform legislation to reduce medical costs. He was booed by doctors in a speech to the American Medical Association in Chicago on June 15, 2010, when saying he would not support caps on medical malpractice. Tort reform limiting outrageous jury awards is a legislative priority for the AMA. There are many categories listed on the internet as reasons for suing doctors, hospitals, or manufacturers, encouraging people to fill out a form if they have been injured by faulty medications, malfunctioning medical devices, or medical negligence. Doctors perform many unnecessary tests as protection against frivolous lawsuits, greatly increasing healthcare costs. It has been said, "Give a man a fish and he will eat for a day. Teach a man to sue and he will eat for a lifetime."

America differs from all other Western democracies (indeed, from virtually all nations of any sort) in its refusal to recognize the principle that the losing side in litigation should contribute toward "making whole" its prevailing opponent. It's long past time this country joined the world in adopting that principle; unfortunately, any steps toward doing so must contend with deeply entrenched resistance from the organized American Bar Association, which likes the system the way it is. As other countries recognize, the arguments in support of the indemnity principle are overwhelming. They include basic fairness, compensation of the victimized opponent, deterrence of tactical or poorly founded claims and legal maneuvers, and the provision of incentives for accepting reasonable settlements. Sad to say, the American Bar, though loud in proclaiming that every other industry and profession should be made to pay for its mistakes, changes its mind in this one area, demanding an across-the-board charitable immunity for its own lucrative industry of suing people. In the United Kingdom, as throughout Europe, the general loser-pays principle enjoys strong support among social democrats and conservatives alike. In a 1999 debate in Britain's House of Lords (January 21), in response to an objection that applying loser-pays in cases before employment tribunals might discourage workers from bringing claims against their employers, Lord Irvine, who serves as Lord Chancellor in the Labor government of Prime Minister Tony Blair, responds that "It can be argued that one should discourage weak cases. Very often applicants bring weak cases before employment tribunals inspired by animus against their employers arising out of their dismissal. If the effect of [a costs] rule were to deter weak claims and prevent employers being vexed by them there is a highly respectable argument in favor of that change."

Just as liability insurance covers the risks of being a defendant in litigation, so nations with loser-pays have developed markets for what is called legal expenses insurance, which helps manage the financial risks of becoming a plaintiff including the chance of becoming liable for costs in the event of a courtroom loss. (This chance is, in fact, quite remote since abroad, as in the United States, well over 90 percent of cases settle out of court before a final legal resolution. The primary influence of loser-pays is in the "shadow" it casts on the size and timing of this settlement.) Legal expenses insurance is typically available at quite a modest cost, often as an added rider to homeowners' or automobile policies. Its cost is modest in part because it can benefit from a self-financing fund. If the insurer correctly analyzes which cases brought in by its policyholder plaintiffs are worthy of being pressed, it will benefit from fee shifts paid by the defendants against whom it finances suits. A series of country-by-country reports from the European Commission indicate that legal expenses insurance is "almost universal in Denmark," "very common in Norway," and "widely available in the Netherlands," while "Germany has the largest LEI market of any EU country". [2]

1. http://100777.com/node/123

2. http://overlawyered.com/topics/lpays.html

18 LOBBYISTS

I would issue an order that no lobbyist firm will be allowed to have an office in Washington, D.C. or surrounding Maryland and Virginia areas. K-Street will be vacant. The 34,750 lobbyists in Washington will have to work from state capitals or Congressional districts in a state. They will be barred from visiting Congressional or Senate offices in Washington. Also, I will issue an order that any individual who was ever employed by the federal government or a state government in any capacity (even as a janitor) will have a lifetime ban on being a lobbyist.

To the great growth industries of America such as healthcare and home building add one more: influence peddling. The number of registered lobbyists in Washington has more than doubled since 2000 to more than 34,750 while the amount that lobbyists charge their new clients has increased by as much as 100 percent. Only a few other businesses have enjoyed greater prosperity in an otherwise fitful economy. The lobbying boom has been caused by three factors, experts say: rapid growth in government, Republican control of both the White House and Congress, and wide acceptance among corporations that they need to hire professional lobbyists to secure their share of federal benefits. "There's unlimited business out there for us", said Robert L. Livingston, a Republican former chairman of the House Appropriations Committee and now president of a thriving six-year-old lobbying firm. "Companies need lobbying help." Lobbying firms can't hire people fast enough. Starting salaries have risen to about $300,000 a year for the best-connected aides eager to "move downtown" from Capitol Hill or the Bush administration. Once considered a distasteful post-government vocation, big-bucks lobbying is luring nearly half of all lawmakers who return to the private sector when they leave Congress, according to a forthcoming study by

Public Citizen's Congress Watch. Political historians don't see these as positive developments for democracy. "We've got a problem here", said Allan Cigler, a political scientist at the University of Kansas. "The growth of lobbying makes even worse than it is already the balance between those with resources and those without resources."[1]

Why did the number of Washington, D.C. lobbyists double since 2000? In 2005, 43% of members who had left the U.S. Congress are now registered to become lobbyists. The lobbying of politicians for special favors has been going on since the beginning of the Union. The term "lobbyist" was originally coined by the British. It came about many years ago in England and the term at the time referred to those individuals who approached the members of Parliament for political favors by intercepting them in the "lobby" of the House of Commons. The term "lobbyist" for the United States started from a much different situation. During the presidency of Ulysses S. Grant (1869-1877), President Grant's wife Julie would not allow the President to smoke his cigars inside the White House. For that reason, many times the President could be found in the lobby of the nearby Willard Hotel by those looking for political favors. So American "favor seekers" became known as "Washington, D.C. Lobbyists". Over the years, local lobbyists earned questionable reputations as individuals who did not demonstrate a high level of personal integrity. At that time the term "lobbyist" was a casual name, not an official designation as it is today. For many years, previous members of Congress would shy away from becoming a "D.C. lobbyist" as prior Congressmen who had chosen that profession were considered "tainted ex-politicians".

There was an explosion of lobbyists in the 1980's. Since the mid-1930's, the Democrats controlled both the Congress and White House most years. Even when Republican Presidents Dwight Eisenhower and Richard Nixon were in office, he Congress was mostly under Democrat leadership, and they were major supporters of small business and anti- big business. Then in 1980, when Ronald Reagan and a Republican Congress both came to power, the world of the "Washington, D.C. lobbyist" began to change. As Republicans had always been such staunch supporters of big business, it became apparent to large U.S. corporations that they needed some local Washington, D.C. help for obtaining a chance at a bigger piece of the gigantic "government business pie". They also recognized that through their "hired lobbyist guns in D.C.", they could exert or "buy" congressional influence for future legislation that would support the goals of their big businesses. Due to this change in the controlling political party, during the 1980's the number of actual "paid lobbyists" increased many fold. In addition, during that period the salaries for those in the "government lobbying trade" began to increase exponentially. This is because, for what those individuals in D.C. were able to "bring to the party" for big business, it was many times in the millions to billions of dollars of new U.S. government business. As it turned out, even though they were located all over Washington, D.C., many of the large lobbying firms ended up with their headquarters on K-Street. Today K-Street is known as "The Street of Washington Lobbyists".[2]

In order to obtain a better level of "public transparency" about their lobbying activities, Congress eventually passed the Lobbying Disclosure Act of 1995. This act is still in force and it requires that all lobbyists must register if they are to have any contact with any government representative. They are also required to file reports detailing their lobbying activities every 6 months. Since George W. Bush was elected in 2000 and the Congress turned Republican in the mid-1990's, the number of registered lobbyists doubled to 34,750 registered Washington lobbyists. Even with the addition of the "lobbying act", over time, the activities of these lobbying efforts continued to get out of hand. In fact, previous House Representative and Majority Whip, Tom DeLay(R-TX), asked some "K-Street" lobbyists to help in drafting some of the language for bills that DeLay would be presenting on the floor of the House. In January 2006, under pressure from fellow Republicans, DeLay was indicted and announced he would not seek to return to his position in the House. In the months before and after that decision, two of DeLay's former House aids were convicted in the Jack Abramoff lobbying scandal.[3]

Upon taking office as the U.S. President, Barack Obama sent a clear message in a March 20, 2009 presidential directive specifying that lobbyists cannot be present at any meetings to discuss the new economic stimulus projects. The directive also said that federal officials cannot consider the opinions of lobbyists unless those opinions are put in writing and that any such written opinions must be posted online. However, in response to the President, there was also a recent high-profile editorial written by a Mr. Daryl Owen, owner of the Washington D.C. lobbyist firm Daryl Owen Associates. Mr. Owens wrote the following in the early part of his article: "Does anyone else detect a few inconsistencies? President Obama, a constitutional scholar and former head of the Harvard Law Review, has issued an edict barring behavior that appears to be protected by the Bill of Rights. Beyond that, the order, by its own terms, exempts lobbyists who handle tax matters. Are they less evil than the rest of us? And why should, say, General Electric chief executive Jeffrey Immelt be permitted to visit the Energy Department to talk about some federal grant in support of a "smart grid" project, while the head of his Washington [lobbying] office has to wait in the car?" Now Mr. Owen is not new to dealing within the US government in Washington, D.C. Before founding his lobbying firm, this writer was a lawyer and he served as staff director of the Senate Energy and Natural Resources Committee from 1986 to 1990. Mr. Owen is proud of that work in the Senate, and he feels it has seriously made him better at what he does today as a D.C. lobbyist. I think Mr. Owen needs to understand that now is not the time for his Washington, D.C. industry to present themselves in such a high-profile position.

Drug companies have spent more than any other segment of the medical industry to make sure that they come out winners in the effort to overhaul the nation's healthcare system. It's understandable the drug makers would want a roll-call accounting of who their friends and enemies are, considering the size of the investment they are making on Capitol Hill. In the first six months, drug and biotech companies and their trade associations spent more than $110 million - that's about $609,000 a day - to influence lawmakers, according to figures compiled by the nonpartisan watchdog group Center for Responsive Politics. The drug industry's legion of registered lobbyists numbers 1,228 or 2.3 for every member of Congress, and its campaign contributions to current members of the House Energy and Commerce Committee have totaled $2.6 million over the past three years. The return on that investment has been considerable, both in the House and in the Senate. "We've done very well," says lobbyist Jim Greenwood, a former Republican Congressman from Pennsylvania who was a member of the Energy and Commerce Committee and now heads the Biotechnology Industry Organization (BIO). "We carried a majority of the Democrats and a majority of the Republicans in each of the committees, and by very clear margins." Whether the broader public is benefiting from the industry's success is less clear. How Greenwood's group has scored decisive early victories on an obscure but crucial healthcare provision is a case study in how interest groups are shaping the contours of healthcare reform - and why that's not necessarily good news for consumers.[4]

1. http://www.washingtonpost.com/wp-dyn/content/article/2005/06/21/AR2005062101632.html

2. http://amchron.soundenterprises.net/articles/view/97416

3. http://commonsense-gater.blogspot.com/2009/04/washington-lobbyists-why-did-their.html

4. http://www.time.com/time/magazine/article/0,9171,1931729,00.html

19 PUBLIC SECTOR UNIONS

I would issue an order that all public sector unions, including teachers unions, will be abolished. I will also issue an order all states will be "right to work" states. Only secret ballots will be allowed in private sector union elections and "card check" (the use of cards so union officials will know how the member voted) will not be permitted. Since the National Labor Relations Board (NLRB) and the Department of Labor will have been eliminated - see Executive Branch - there will be no interference in where companies want to locate, such as the controversy about Boeing Corp. locating in South Carolina and the NLRB trying to interfere.

President Franklin D. Roosevelt, the patron saint of the American labor movement, was a man of strong character. One has to look no further than the heroic way he coped with his crippling polio. This dreadful disease undoubtedly made him the consummate realist. For example, although he had the lock on labor's vote, he expressed caution about public sector unions. In a little known letter he wrote to the president of the National Federation of Federal Employees in 1937, Roosevelt reasoned, "Meticulous attention should be paid to special relationships and obligations of public servants to the public itself and to the government. All government employees should realize that the process of collective bargaining, as usually understood, cannot be transplanted into the public service. It has its distinct and insurmountable limitations. The very nature and purposes of Government make it impossible for officials to bind the employer. The employer is the whole people, who speak by means of laws enacted by their representatives. Particularly, I want to emphasize my conviction that militant tactics have no place in the functions of any organization of government employees. Upon employees in the federal service rests the obligation to serve the whole people. This obligation is paramount. A strike of public employees manifests nothing less than an intent to prevent or obstruct Government. Such action, looking toward the paralysis of Government, is unthinkable and intolerable."[1]

"It is impossible to bargain collectively with the government." That wasn't Newt Gingrich, or Ron Paul, or Ronald Reagan talking. That was George Meany, the former president of the A.F.L.-C.I.O in 1955. Government unions are unremarkable today, but the labor movement once thought the idea absurd. Public sector unions insist on laws that serve their interests - at the expense of the common good. The founders of the labor movement viewed unions as a vehicle to get workers more of the profits they help create. However, Government workers don't generate profits. They merely negotiate for more tax money. When government unions strike, they strike against taxpayers. Government collective bargaining means voters do not have the final say on public policy. Instead their elected representatives must negotiate spending and policy decisions with unions. That is not exactly democratic -a fact that unions once recognized. George Meany was not alone. Up through the 1950s, unions widely agreed that collective bargaining had no place in government. But starting with Wisconsin in 1959, states began to allow collective bargaining in government. The influx of dues and members quickly changed the union movement's tune, and collective bargaining in government is now widespread. As a result, unions can now insist on laws that serve their interests -at the expense of the common good. Union contracts make it next to impossible to reward excellent teachers or fire failing ones. Union contracts give government employees gold-plated benefits -at the cost of higher taxes and less spending on other priorities.[2]

On August 5, 1981, President Ronald Reagan did one of the most important things in his Presidency. He fired more than 11,000 air traffic controllers who ignored his order to return to work. The sweeping mass firing of federal employees slowed commercial air travel, but it did not cripple the system as the strikers had forecast. Two days earlier, nearly 13,000 controllers walked out after talks with the Federal Aviation Administration collapsed. As a result, some 7,000 flights across the country were canceled on that day at the peak of the summer travel season. Robert Poli, president of the Professional Air Traffic Controllers Organization, sought an across-the-board annual wage increase of $10,000 for the controllers, whose pay ranged from $20,462 to $49,229 per year. He also sought a reduction of their five-day, 40-hour workweek to a four-day, 32-hour workweek. The FAA made a $40 million counteroffer, far short of the $770 million package that the union sought. Reagan branded the strike illegal. He threatened to fire any controller who failed to return to work within 48 hours. Federal judges levied fines of $1 million per day against the union. In 1955, Congress made such strikes punishable by fines or a one-year jail term - a law the Supreme Court upheld in 1971. To the chagrin of the strikers, the FAA's contingency plans worked. Some 3,000 supervisors joined 2,000 non-striking controllers and 900 military controllers in manning airport towers. Before long, about 80 percent of flights were operating normally. Air freight remained virtually unaffected. In carrying out his threat, Reagan also imposed a lifetime ban on rehiring the strikers. In October 1981, the Federal Labor Relations Authority decertified PATCO.

One of the most pressing issues in America today is public sector unions crippling state budgets. To make matters worse, in this time of economic upheaval, public sector unions are demanding more benefits, such as higher pensions and better health coverage, at the expense of overburdened taxpayers. Government employees do not innovate or create wealth, so how can many politicians justify such lavish benefits to public sector unions that the private sector can only dream of? Politicians simply cannot make a rational statement about public sector unions and their bloated benefits. However, politicians are experts at rationalization and will tell you that government employees are hard-working, decent Americans, while completely avoiding the question on public sector unions and their benefits. President Obama, in an interview with Charles Benson from an NBC affiliate in Milwaukee, had this to say, "Some of what I've heard coming out of Wisconsin, where you're just making it harder for public employees to collectively bargain, generally seems like more of an assault on unions. I think it's very important for us to understand that public employees, they're our neighbors, they're our friends." Government employees are our neighbors, and some may be our friends, but is anyone actually arguing for picking up your neighbor's health insurance premiums and pension contributions, while they contribute a less percentage of what you are required to pay? If you're shaking your head, then you are probably living in the wrong neighborhood like many Americans. So, how bad is the situation? Dennis Cauchon of USA TODAY said that according to the Bureau of Labor Statistics, average federal salary for 2008 was $67,691, while average private sector salary was only $60,046, which is a $7,645 difference. Federal employees are typically paid more than private sector employees. While the average federal salary has typically been increasing year to year the benefits granted to them remains incredibly high. Government health care plans, pension and other federal benefits, amounts to roughly $40,785 per worker a year, while private sector benefits are at a meager $9,882 per worker a year. Individual state benefits vary, but the majority of states give roughly the same amount of benefits that federal employees receive.

You may be wondering how public service unions can get away with this. It is no surprise that public service unions receive a large amount of benefits in exchange for votes and political contributions. For example, Wisconsin currently allows union dues to be collected through payroll taxes. These unions strong arm you to resign if you do not join their union. Speaking of strong arming, ever wonder why we have secret ballot elections? We do this so that organizations such as the Republican Party, Democrat Party or other political groups do not single you out and coerce you into voting for a particular candidate or referendum. Public service unions seem to despise this concept, which is not a surprise given that the structure of these unions typically has a top to bottom command structure in which the union bosses make most of the decisions. These practices are tolerated by the politicians because it helps guarantee them votes and contributions come election time. Worst of all, taxpayers are generally not represented in the negotiations with public sector unions. Taxpayers ultimately foot the bill for the generous benefits given to unions, so where are our interests represented during these negotiations. The sad fact is that we rarely have a say with regards to unions and our tax dollars. Who can we turn to if not the politicians, we elect to represent our interests as taxpayers? Luckily, there is always a light at the end of the tunnel.[3]

We can get public sector unions back to where they do not drive the state and even federal deficit spiraling out of control. Wisconsin's Governor Walker is a rare example of an elected official acting on behalf of taxpayers and those who elected him to public office to do his job and solve the problem at its root. The Democrats and unions tried to remove him from office with a recall petition that failed. Will Governor Walker's charge inspire others to take action against out of control government spending?[3] The alternative to Walker's budget was kicking 200,000 children off Medicaid. His plan reasserts voter control over government policy. Voters' elected representatives should decide how the government spends their taxes. More states should heed the A.F.L.-C.I.O. Executive Council's 1959 advice: "In terms of accepted collective bargaining procedures, government workers have no right beyond the authority to petition Congress - a right available to every citizen." It took long enough, but the State Senate finally came through for Governor Walker. They voted on a bill that the slick fourteen Democrats thought they could prevent by hiding out in Illinois. Democrats at their finest; don't like the other party, just flee your state and prevent a vote indefinitely. What person, who clearly sees that unions are destroying America, can be happy about it? We need strong leadership, whether it is Governors or State or Federal Representatives that fight back against these abuses of power. The idea behind Walker's budget is fair treatment. For too long the public sector unions have bilked the taxpayers, robbing them blind; $150,000 corrections officer salaries $150,000 for bus drivers; Viagra for teachers. That's right, under collective bargaining, not only did a porn-watching teacher get his job back, but Viagra is offered up to the teachers as part of their health care plan. Anyone wonders why test scores are so low?

Those who mock Governor Walker do not speak for the American people. They speak for the few who would like to get something for nothing. Unions were a good thing when fat cat business owners were putting the thumb on the little people. The problem with public sector unions is that the fat cat bosses with their supposed thumbs on the little people are the taxpayers. The taxpayers pay the salaries of the teachers, bus drivers and the corrections officers. The taxpayers also do the hiring, as it were, when we vote in our Representatives. The Governor and other representatives waited patiently and made requests for the cowardly Democrats that fled in the first place to come back and be part of the process. Should the Wisconsin people, or the American people for that matter, be held hostage by Representatives who don't want to do their job? By voting despite the absenteeism of their fellow Senators, Wisconsin took a stand. Those 18 Senators who voted yes and the one Senator who voted no spoke up and said that they would not allow fourteen other Senators to highjack our Republic. At one point in time this was a Constitutional Republic, where Representatives were elected and voting took place to decide various measures.[4]

1. http://www2.hernandotoday.com/news/hernando-news/2010/oct/17/ha-fdrs-warning-public-employee-unions-a-no-no-ar-291004/

2. http://www.nytimes.com/roomfordebate/2011/02/18/the-first-blow-against-public-employees/fdr-warned-us-about-public-sector-unions

3. http://newsflavor.com/opinions/public-sector-unions-destroying-america/

4. http://newsflavor.com/world/usa-canada/governor-walker-union-thugs-and-justice-for-wisconsin/

20 HEALTHCARE

I would issue an order to immediately repeal the Affordable Care Act (HR3200) and privatize the healthcare system for everyone, primarily based on a proposal by John Mackey, former CEO of Whole Foods, with modifications. Some Republican healthcare proposals are the much demonized plan by Representative Paul Ryan (R - WI), a bicameral coalition of the House and Senate titled "Patients Choice Act of 2009", a plan by Senator Jim DeMint (R -SC) "Healthcare Freedom Plan", and a plan led by Representative Tom Price (R -GA). Some of the provisions included in one or more of these bills include investing in preventive medicine, an overhaul of Medicaid, reduction of abuse and fraud in the Medicare program, supplemental health insurance for low-income families, tax credits for health insurance, and a ban on federal funds being used for abortions. My order would create high-deductible health insurance plans, equalize unfair laws between employer and individually-owned insurance, allow insurance companies to compete across state lines, remove mandates regarding what insurance companies must cover, enact stringent tort reform, make all healthcare costs transparent, and privatize Medicare and Medicaid. Programs for preventable maintenance of dental and vision care will be provided in all policies, as these should not be excluded from healthcare. High-deductible catastrophic health insurance will be encouraged for all individuals to remove the fear of losing all assets because of major illness or accident. Implementation of the FairTax is not considered in any of the proposed reforms, but this is necessary to eliminate any issues of trying to configure plans based on tax deductions or credits. There will be no need for deductions because income taxes and Federal Insurance Contributions Act (FICA) taxes will no longer exist, and free market forces and competition will determine costs.

The Democrat's 2,300-page 211,000-word monstrosity healthcare bill (HR 3200) has created 53 new boards, bureaucracies, commissions, and programs that will control every aspect of our healthcare system, and destroy the best healthcare system in the world.

Here is the list:

Health Benefits Advisory Committee, Health Choices Administration, Qualified Health Benefits Plan Ombudsman, Program of Administrative Simplification, Retiree Reserve Trust Fund, Health Insurance Exchange, Mechanism for Insurance Risk Pooling, Special Inspector General for the Health Insurance Exchange, Health Insurance Exchange Trust Fund, State-based Health Insurance Exchanges, Public Health Insurance Option, Ombudsman for Public Health Insurance Option, Telehealth Advisory Committee, Demonstration Program Providing Reimbursement for Culturally and Linguistically Appropriate Services, Demonstration Program for Shared Decision Making Using Patient Decision Aids, Accountable Care Organization Pilot Program, Independent Patient-centered Medical Home Pilot Program Under Medicare, Community-based Medical Home Pilot Program Under Medicare, Center for Comparative Effectiveness Research, Comparative Effectiveness Research Commission, Patient Ombudsman for Comparative Effectiveness Research, Quality Assurance and Performance Improvement Program for Nursing Facilities, Special Focus Facility Program for Nursing Facilities, National Independent Monitor Pilot Program for Skilled Nursing Facilities, Demonstration Program for Approved Teaching Health Centers with Respect to Medicare GME, Pilot Program to Develop Anti-fraud Compliance Systems for Medicare Providers, Medical Home Pilot Program Under Medicaid, Comparative Effectiveness Research Trust Funds, Identifiable Office or Program within CMS to Provide for Improved Coordination Between Medicare and Medicaid in the Case of Dual Eligibles, Public Health Investment Fund, Scholarships for Service in Health Professional Needs Areas, Loan Repayment Program for Service in Health Professional Needs Areas, Program for Training Medical Residents in Community-based Settings, Grant Programs for Training in Dentistry, Public Health Workforce Corps, Public Health Workforce Scholarship Program, Public Health Workforce Loan Forgiveness Program, Grant Program for Innovations In Interdisciplinary Care, Advisory Committee on Health Workforce Evaluation and Assessment, Prevention and Wellness Trust, Clinical Prevention Stakeholders Board, Community Prevention Stakeholders Board, Grant Program for Community Prevention and Wellness Research, Grant Program for Community Prevention and Wellness Services, Grant Program for Public Health Infrastructure, Center for Quality Improvement, Assistant Secretary for Health Information, Grant Program to Support the Operation of School-based Health Clinics, National Medical Device Registry, and Grants for Labor-management Programs for Nursing Training. Remember, HR 3200 has yet to be enacted, and yet these programs are already funded. Democrats are hoping all these bureaucracies will be so entrenched that the bill cannot be repealed. These entities to date have created 11,000 pages of new regulations that total 11,588,500 words.

In addition to the unimaginable bureaucracy noted above, Obama has planned for hundreds of thousands of additional federal employees to implement the program. If the employment numbers seem better than one might have expected during the next few months, it will have nothing to do with private companies hiring people to provide goods and services people actually want. It will instead relate to the army being hired to help individuals and families apply for ObamaCare subsidies starting on October 1, 2013. If California's situation is typical of what will be happening nationwide, the total number of "enrollment counselors," also known as "navigators," hired for this supposedly short-term task will be huge. In California alone, about 21,000 counselors will be hired from among an estimated 3,600 community organizations ranging from Native American tribes and chambers of commerce to labor unions and faith-based organizations that will be authorized to help people buy insurance. Project that to the entire country, and we're talking about 175,000 counselors. That would be Number 29 on Fortune's 500 list of largest private-sector employers in 2011. The state insurance commissioner and anti-fraud groups say the exchange is falling short in ensuring that the people hired as counselors are adequately screened and monitored. Consumers could fall prey to bogus health care products, identity theft and other abuses, and will have a hard time seeking justice if unscrupulous counselors get their Social Security number, bank accounts, health records or other private information. What kind of controls are in place to prevent phantom sign-ups, or to detect them if they're submitted?

During 2012, the corrupt media was able to keep the focus of the presidential election exactly where Obama wanted it, off his failed record. The media would never expose the White House's own hypocrisy on the issue -- including its own Solicitor General making the tax case for Obama Care before the Supreme Court. Something the media won't be able to spin is that though ObamaCare is a job killer in the private sector, it's a boon for federal employees who enjoy the kind of health and pension benefits you and I can only dream about, specifically IRS agents. How many, exactly? Numbers range from 2,700 to 16,500: The IRS says it is well on its way to gearing up for the new law but has offered little information about its long-term budget and staffing needs, generating complaints from Republican lawmakers and concern from government watchdogs. The IRS spent $881 million on the law from 2010 through 2013, hiring more than 2,700 new workers and upgrading its computer systems. But the IRS has not made public information about its spending plans in the following years, when the bulk of the health care law takes effect. The growing IRS targeting scandal will prevent the IRS' scheduled implementation of Obamacare from being sufficiently funded, even though the agency will have sweeping new powers to enforce President Obama's health care law, according to experts. "The IRS has 47 separate powers under Obamacare. That's a problem for the IRS because it is mired in scandal. Congress understandably is not moved to do more funding for IRS enforcement of Obamacare. Obamacare needs to be defunded.

President Obama's health care law will push 7 million people out of their job-based insurance coverage — nearly twice the previous estimate, according to the latest estimates from the Congressional Budget Office released Tuesday. CBO said that this year's tax cuts have changed the incentives for businesses and made it less attractive to pay for insurance, meaning fewer will decide to do so. Instead, they'll choose to pay a penalty to the government, totaling $13 billion in higher fees over the next decade. But the non-partisan agency also expects fewer people to have to pay individual penalties to the IRS than it earlier projects, because of a better method for calculating incomes that found more people will be exempt. Overall, the new health provisions are expected to cost the government $1.165 trillion over the next decade — the same as last year's projection. During the health care debate Mr. Obama had said individuals would be able to keep their plans.

Governor Sarah Palin was severely criticized for using the term "death panels" regarding the implementation of Obamacare. It has come to pass even before the law was begun. HHS Secretary Kathleen Sebelius became a one-woman death panel when she refused to allow 10-year old Sarah Murnaghan to be moved to the adult transplant list. A federal judge intervened and ordered Sebelius to make an exception, and the little girl is alive. Her mother said Sebelius was choosing to let children die.

"The problem with socialism is that eventually you run out of other people's money."
- Margaret Thatcher

With a projected $1.8 trillion deficit for 2012, several trillions more in deficits projected over the next decade, and with both Medicare and Social

Security entitlement spending about to ratchet up several notches over the next 15 years as baby boomers become eligible for both, we are rapidly running out of other people's money. These deficits are simply not sustainable. They are either going to result in unprecedented new taxes and inflation, or they will bankrupt us. While we clearly need healthcare reform, the last thing our country needs is a massive new healthcare entitlement that will create hundreds of billions of dollars of new unfunded deficits and move us much closer to a government takeover of our healthcare system. Instead, we should be trying to achieve reforms by moving in the opposite direction - toward less government control and more individual empowerment.

Here are reforms that would greatly lower the cost of healthcare for everyone:

Remove the legal obstacles that slow the creation of high-deductible health insurance plans and health savings accounts (HSAs). The combination of high-deductible health insurance and HSAs is one solution that could solve many of our healthcare problems. For example, high-deductible health insurance plans and use of additional healthcare dollars through deposits into employees' Personal Wellness Accounts to spend as they choose on their own health and wellness will create incentives to spend their health dollars Money not spent in one year rolls over to the next and grows over time. Individuals could therefore spend their own healthcare dollars until the annual deductible is covered (about $2,500) and the insurance plan kicks in. This creates incentives to spend the first $2,500 more carefully. Costs would be much lower than typical health insurance, while providing a very high degree of worker satisfaction.

Repeal all state laws that prevent insurance companies from competing across state lines. We should all have the legal right to purchase health insurance from any insurance company in any state, and we should be able use that insurance wherever we live. Health insurance should be portable. There is a barrage of television ads from automobile insurance companies touting their advantage over competitors because there is a free market to compete in any state, but a dearth of such ads for healthcare because of individual state regulations about coverage. Government mandates regarding what insurance companies must cover must be repealed. These mandates have increased the cost of health insurance by billions of dollars. What is insured and what is not insured should be determined by individual customer preferences and not through special-interest lobbying.

Enact tort reform to end the ruinous lawsuits that force doctors to pay insurance costs of hundreds of thousands of dollars per year. These costs are passed back to us through much higher prices for healthcare. I would also issue an order that attorneys will not be allowed to advertise on television, radio, internet, or newspapers. No class action lawsuits will be permitted, and lawyers will not be involved in any medical malpractice, product liability, or accident suits. There will be panels of doctors and/or qualified "experts" in each city and jurisdiction who will determine malpractice or damage awards, with national caps of $500,000 for pain and suffering. Who do you trust most, a panel of doctors or a panel of trial lawyers? I would also institute a loser pay system as they have in all of Europe and most other nations. Finally, I would issue an order that the maximum contingency fee that a lawyer may charge a client is 10% of the monies awarded the client when winning a suit. This will prevent most frivolous lawsuits. These are true tort reforms that will save Americans hundreds of billions of dollars each year.

Make costs transparent so that consumers understand what healthcare treatments cost. How many people know the total cost of their last doctor's visit and how that total breaks down? What other goods or services do we buy without knowing how much they will cost us? Virtually everything we buy has a published price except for healthcare. We would not buy a car from a dealer and wait a week for a statement to see how much we paid, hoping someone else will pay the bill and expressing outrage about the price. Healthcare should also have pre-determined published prices, with each doctor and dentist office having a price for the visit and a large billboard with the price for each procedure. Hospitals should provide the same information. It is understood that healthcare is different than any other service, because many times the visit is an emergency and dealing with life and death does not lend itself to asking how much it will cost.

Many promoters of healthcare reform believe that people have an intrinsic ethical right to healthcare - to equal access to doctors, medicines and hospitals. While all of us empathize with those who are sick, how can we say that all people have more of an intrinsic right to healthcare than they have to food or shelter? Healthcare is a service that we all need, but just like food and shelter it is best provided through voluntary and mutually beneficial market exchanges. A careful reading of both the Declaration of Independence and the Constitution will not reveal any intrinsic right to healthcare, food or shelter. That's because there isn't any. This "right" has never existed in America. Even in countries like Canada and the United Kingdom, there is no intrinsic right to healthcare. Rather, citizens in these countries are told by government bureaucrats what healthcare treatments they are eligible to receive and when they can receive them. All countries with socialized medicine ration healthcare by forcing their citizens to wait in lines to receive scarce treatments. Although Canada has a population smaller than California, 830,000 Canadians are currently waiting to be admitted to a hospital or to get treatment, according to a recent report in Investor's Business Daily. In England, the waiting list is 1.8 million. Employees of a company should be able to vote on what benefits they most want. Subsidiaries of Canadian and British companies usually express their benefit preferences very clearly - they want supplemental healthcare dollars that they can control and spend themselves without permission from their governments. Why would they want such additional healthcare benefit dollars if they already have an "intrinsic right to healthcare"? The answer is clear - no such right truly exists in either Canada or the U.K. or any other country. Rather than increase government spending and control, we need to address the root causes of poor health. This begins with the realization that every American adult is responsible for his or her own health.

Unfortunately, many of our healthcare problems are self-inflicted: Two-thirds of Americans are now overweight and one-third are obese. Most of the diseases that kill us and account for about 70% of all healthcare spending—heart disease, cancer, stroke, diabetes and obesity - are mostly preventable through proper diet, exercise, not smoking, minimal alcohol consumption and other healthy lifestyle choices. Recent scientific and medical evidence shows that a diet consisting of foods that are plant-based, nutrient dense and low-fat will help prevent and often reverse most degenerative diseases that kill us and are expensive to treat. We should be able to live largely disease-free lives until we are well into our 90s and even past 100 years of age.

Healthcare reform is very important. Whatever reforms are enacted it is essential that they be financially responsible, and that we have the freedom to choose doctors and the healthcare services that best suit our own unique set of lifestyle choices. We are all responsible for our own lives and our own health. We should take that responsibility very seriously and use our freedom to make wise lifestyle choices that will protect our health. Doing so will enrich our lives and will help create a vibrant and sustainable American society. [1]

1. http://online.wsj.com/article/SB100014240529702042514045743421700 72865070.html

21 SOCIAL SECURITY

I would issue an order to immediately privatize Social Security for everyone, with the government collecting the contributions but then directly forwarding them to private financial institutions. The government could ensure a level of security in the investment of the funds with Wall Street. I would also immediately increase the retirement age to 70 years, because of longer life expectancy.

In the 19th Century, German Chancellor Otto von Bismarck had a big idea - that a worker with a pension depends on the state and is a more docile worker. He invented a pay-as-you-go social security system with a moral flaw that destroys the link between effort and reward. It makes benefits the product of political pressure rather than what you contribute by your work. This dependency on political demagogues has spilled over into other areas besides retirement. People say "Offer me more, and I'll vote for you." That corruption of both workers and politicians has fed a culture of irresponsibility.

In the 1920's, legendary con man Charles Ponzi devised a scheme that still carries his name and is now illegal in all 50 states. It works much the same way as von Bismarck's system, and it is the way the U.S. Social Security works today. Ponzi convinced "investors" to put money in his coupons, promising big profits, but there were no profits, just a pyramid scam. Ponzi took money from the second round of investors and put it in the pockets of the first. Eventually he ran out of takers and money, was convicted of fraud and sent to prison. Like Ponzi's scheme, Social Security makes no investments. Its "investors" are taxpayers, who, like the folks Ponzi bilked, won't get paid unless there are enough new taxpayers to cover them. When the Baby Boomers begin retiring at the rate of 10,000 a day, there won't be enough young taxpayers to tap, and just like Ponzi's scheme, Social Security will collapse.

Is there a better way than Social Security to provide financial retirement security for U.S. workers? Yes! Personal retirement accounts are the answer. Here are examples:

The nation of Chile had a social security system that predated the U.S., having started in 1926. In the late 1970's the benefit payments were greater than taxes collected and there were no funded reserves. The anticipated decline in the support/benefit ratio meant the problems were only going to get worse. In 1981, midway through the dictatorship of General Augusto Pinochet, the system faced bankruptcy if the government didn't provide more subsidies. Pinochet hired a group of U.S. trained economists, who recommended personal accounts for the system, creating something like a mandatory 401(K) plan. Ten percent of a worker's wages is automatically deducted and sent to one of several independently managed mutual fund companies selected by the worker. Chile allowed each worker to choose whether to stay in the state run pay-as-you-go system or put the whole payroll tax into an individual retirement account. Some 93% of workers chose the new system. They trusted the private sector and preferred market risk to political risk. Chile's citizens proudly carry what looks like a standard bank passbook from the pre-computer age. They call it a "Libretta", a deliverer of liberty. Ownership has changed the way workers see life. They are no longer at the mercy of politicians or union bosses. The typical Chilean worker's main asset is not a small house, but the Libretta, with most worth over $100,000 that can be passed on to their heirs.

The United States also has an example of a personal retirement plan that works. The Social Security Act of 1935 permitted municipal governments to opt out of the system -a loophole that Congress closed in 1983. In 1981, employees of Galveston County, Texas, chose by a vote of 78 percent to 22 percent to leave Social Security for a personal account alternative. Brazoria and Matagorda counties soon followed, swelling the group to 5,000 participants. Employees now pay 6.13 percent of income and the counties contribute 7.65 percent -for a total of 13.78 percent. Of that 13.78 percent, 9.737 percent goes to the employee's individual retirement account that pays a 6.5 percent average interest rate, compounded daily. The cost of the program, known as the Alternative Plan, is virtually the same as Social Security, but the benefits are far greater. A person retiring at age 65 with 40 years of deposits and an annual wage of $20,000 will retire with $383,000 in a personal account and $2,740 a month vs. $775 per month from Social

Security. A person with a wage of $50,000 for 40 years will retire with $956,303 in the account and $6,843 a month from the private plan vs. $1,302 a month from Social Security. The personal accounts are estates that can be left to their heirs. Social Security leaves nothing. Life insurance for the personal plan is three times the worker's annual pay (with a minimum of $50,000 and a maximum of $150,000). Social Security pays a one-time death benefit of $255 to a surviving spouse.

According to a recent Gallop poll, a lack of retirement funds is America's most pressing financial concern. The survey found Americans aged 30-49 are the most apprehensive about retirement. Americans who have yet to retire are already relying heavily on their personal retirement accounts such as 401Ks and IRAs. Every reform plan, from privatization to raising the retirement age is met with vicious opposition and insidious demagoguery about impoverishing seniors. With high unemployment and polls showing a precipitous drop in support for Obama among young voters, Congressman Pete Sessions is proposing the SAFE ACT (HR 2109), that would allow younger workers to control all their retirement savings.

Here are some of the key details of the proposal: Every American would be able to opt out of the current system and direct the full 6.2% of payroll taxes to a personal retirement account beginning January 1, 2012. After 15 years of the bill's enactment, employers would contribute their share of payroll taxes to the employee's SAFE account. Self-employed individuals would be able to divert the full amount of their payroll taxes to a SAFE account. The SAFE accounts would be tax free and any cash contributions would be tax deductible. Also, all post-retirement distributions from the account would be tax free. Upon the death of the account beneficiary, irrespective of age, the inheritors of the estate will assume full ownership of the account. While this is admirable, with the Fair Tax and complete privatization for everyone, this proposal becomes moot.

Because they were afraid voters would see through the Social Security scam, since 1983, members of Congress participate in Social Security. Senators and Representatives also participate in the Civil Service Retirement System or the Federal Employees Retirement System that went into effect in 1987. Like all federal government employees, current members of Congress contribute portions of their salaries to these programs as well as Social Security.

However, Congressional pensions accrue at a higher rate than average - 70 percent higher, according to Representative Asa Hutchinson of Arkansas. Congress also has a special retirement plan that they voted for themselves many years ago. It works like this: When they retire, they continue to draw their full pay until they die, increased by cost-of-living adjustments. For instance, calculating an average life span for each, former Senator Bill Bradley and his wife may be expected to draw $7,900,000, with Mrs. Bradley drawing $275,000 during the last year of her life. They paid nothing into this. It comes from our tax money. The Democrats in Congress, together with their willing sycophants in the AARP leadership, are trying to scare American senior citizens into believing personal accounts are a risky scheme that will take away their Social Security. If Social Security is so wonderful, we should take the Golden Fleece retirement plan away from Congress and put them in the system with the rest of us. Members of Congress who want to retain the existing pay-as-you-go system should share the fate of their mentor Charles Ponzi. They should be convicted of fraud and sent to prison. The government is spending our retirement, but for some reason we don't take it seriously. If Social Security were a private entity, its CEO and directors would be in jail long ago.

The Social Security "surplus" that was expected to vanish by 2017 may disappear sooner due to the current economic crisis. With unemployment rising, the payroll tax revenue that finances Social Security benefits for 51 million retirees and other recipients is falling, according to a report from the Congressional Budget Office. As a result, the trust fund's annual surplus is forecast to be gone nearly a decade early - and deprive the government of billions of dollars it had been counting on to balance the nation's books. The Treasury Department has for decades borrowed money from the Social Security trust fund to finance government operations. If it is no longer able to do so, it could be forced to borrow an additional $700 Billion over the next decade from China, Japan, and other investors.

Instead of temporarily patching the system by increasing taxes, decreasing benefits, or increasing the retirement age, we must look for a permanent fix. The best solution is to completely privatize Social Security. The government could mandate a minimum level of contribution to private retirement plans instead of running the Social Security scam. The government could even collect the contributions, but they should be immediately forwarded to a private financial institution rather than being spent by the Federal Government. Some people are hesitant to privatize Social Security, but that is illogical. The most corrupt, most poorly-run private system has a better chance of working over the long term than our current government-run system. We cannot wait to do something, because the longer we mark time, the higher the probability that the system will collapse and we will lose all the money we have contributed over our lifetime.[1]

1. http://www.redstate.com/dhorowitz3/2011/06/16/time-to-opt-out-of-the-social-security-ponzi-scheme/

22 WELFARE

I would issue an order that direct welfare to individuals will be stopped immediately because it is unconstitutional. The Preamble to the Constitution reads, "We the People of the United States, in Order to form a more perfect Union, establish Justice, insure domestic Tranquility, provide for the common defense, promote the general Welfare, and secure the Blessings of Liberty to ourselves and our Posterity, do ordain and establish this Constitution for the United States of America." Promote the general Welfare does not mean to fund. I would issue an order to provide block grants to the individual states for an interim period of time and let them "promote the general welfare". I would also issue an order to have mandatory drug testing for able-bodied welfare recipients once a year.

You cannot legislate the poor into prosperity by legislating the wealthy out of prosperity. What one person receives without working for, another person must work for without receiving. The government cannot give to anybody anything that the government does not first take from somebody else. You cannot multiply wealth by dividing it. When half of the people get the idea that they do not have to work because the other half is going to take care of them, and when the other half gets the idea that it does no good to work, because somebody else is going to get what they work for, that is the beginning of the end of any nation.

In the 1990's, there was a serious attempt at welfare reform. The Personal Responsibility and Work Opportunity Reconciliation Act (PRWORA), was signed by President Clinton on August 22, 1996, a bill aimed at substantially reconstructing the welfare system. Introduced by Rep. E. Clay Shaw, Jr., the act gave state governments more autonomy over welfare delivery, while also reducing the federal government's responsibilities. It instituted the Temporary Assistance to Needy Families program, which placed time limits on welfare assistance and replaced the longstanding Aid to Families with Dependent Children program. Other changes to the welfare system included stricter conditions for food stamps eligibility, reductions in immigrant welfare assistance, and recipient work requirements. President Clinton stated that the act "gives us a chance we haven't had before to break the cycle of dependency that has existed for millions and millions of our fellow citizens, exiling them from the world of work. It gives structure, meaning and dignity to most of our lives." Under the Obama administration, it has been so diluted and changed by regulation that it is ineffective.[1]

Is welfare unconstitutional? No less than framers Madison and Jefferson, plus at least five presidents and dozens of prominent statesmen throughout American history thought so.

"Our peculiar security is in the possession of a written Constitution. Let us not make it a blank paper by construction." - President Thomas Jefferson (1803)

How do we interpret the Constitution? Though many erroneously view the Constitution as an intentionally vague and loosely interpreted document, by simply looking at the document one soon learns that there are many very distinct methods with which to interpret, define, and study the Constitution. The Constitution is a very defined and extremely straightforward text with many definitions inherent in the common logic behind it. The "necessary and proper" clause of Article I, Section 8, enumerated power of Congress #18, mandate that the aforementioned 17 enumerated powers are further defined and expanded upon through implications though limited on the whole by a "necessary and proper" relationship. McCulloch v. Maryland defined this as Congress may enact legislation within the powers (1) specifically enumerated by Article I, Section 8 and (2) that which reasonably "necessary and proper" in "carrying into execution" these powers and those elsewhere listed to Congress in the constitution (certain amendments). In other words, Congress is strictly defined to very specifically enumerated powers and that which draws a reasonable relationship to these specific powers as a "means" of carrying into play their execution. Much of what Congress does today is neither enumerated nor reasonably implied through clause 18 (the use of public monies for charity on the national level - what we know today as social welfare handouts).[2]

Federal welfare spending has grown by 32 percent over the past four years, fattened by President Obama's stimulus spending and swelled by a growing number of Americans whose recession-depleted incomes now qualify them for public assistance, according to numbers released Thursday. Federal spending on more than 80 low-income assistance programs reached $746 billion in 2011, and state spending on those programs brought the total to $1.03 trillion, according to figures from the Congressional Research Service and the Senate Budget Committee. That makes welfare the single biggest chunk of federal spending — topping Social Security and basic defense spending. Sen. Jeff Sessions, the ranking Republican on the Budget Committee who requested the Congressional Research Service report, said the numbers underscore a fundamental shift in welfare, which he said has moved from being a Band-Aid and toward a more permanent crutch. "No longer should we measure compassion by how much money the government spends but by how many people we help to rise out of poverty," the Alabama conservative said. "Welfare assistance should be seen as temporary whenever possible, and the goal must be to help more of our fellow citizens attain gainful employment and financial independence." Welfare spending as measured by obligations stood at $563 billion in fiscal year 2008, but reached $746 billion in fiscal year 2011, a jump of 32 percent.

The numbers tell a complex story of American taxpayers' generosity in supporting a varied social safety net, including food stamps, support for low-income AIDS patients, child care payments and direct cash going from taxpayers to the poor. By far, the biggest item on the list is Medicaid, the federal-state health care program for the poor, which at $296 billion in federal spending made up 40 percent of all low-income assistance in 2011. That total was up $82 billion from 2008. Beyond that, the next big program is food stamps at $75 billion in 2011, or 10 percent of welfare spending. It's nearly twice the size it was in 2008 and accounts for a staggering 20 percent of the total welfare spending increase over those four years. Several programs to funnel cash to the poor also ranked high. Led by the earned income tax credit, supplemental security income and the additional child tax credit, direct cash aid accounts for about a fifth of all welfare. States contributed another $283 billion to low-income assistance — chiefly through Medicaid.

The conservative Heritage Foundation said roughly 100 million Americans get benefits from at least one low-income assistance program each month, with the average benefit coming to around $9,000. The think tank estimates that if welfare spending were transferred as straight cash instead, it would be five times more than needed to lift every American family above the poverty line — though many of the programs help those above the poverty line. Mr. Sessions' Budget Committee staff said that at current projections, the 10 biggest welfare programs will cost $8.3 trillion over the next decade. The Congressional Research Service looked at obligations for each program as its measure of spending. It included every program that had eligibility requirements that seemed designed chiefly to benefit those with lower or limited incomes. The report looked at programs that had obligations of at least $100 million in a fiscal year, which meant some small-dollar welfare assistance wasn't included.

What is the intent of the Constitution and the role of government in the welfare of its people? Who should take care of the poor and unfortunate? It has always been the assumption that government has a responsibility to provide for the needy. The government shouldn't act as a charitable institution. It's not the role of the government to hand out money because it's not the government's money to give. It's the taxpayer's money and the money should be used to support the citizens' basic rights. The original authors of the Constitution and other major documents that formed our nation were quoted as saying that forcing taxpayers to give the government money, and then handing that money over to other citizens for free is hurtful to the country. There is a famous quote, and it applies perfectly to this argument against social welfare: "Give a man a fish and he will eat for a day. Teach him how to fish and he will eat for a lifetime." It's true. How can you learn how to do something for yourself if someone is just providing for you for free? Better yet, why would someone bother to work for something when they know they can get it for free? Welfare should not come from the federal government. Thank a Democrat politician, who needs to buy votes, for the "gimme", uneducated, permanently government dependent underclass. The New Deal coming out of the depression has long since passed its usefulness like so many laws and programs from decades ago.

Tax Day is a dreaded deadline for millions, but for nearly half of U.S. households it's simply somebody else's problem. About 47 percent paid no federal income taxes at all for 2009. Either their incomes were too low, or they qualified for enough credits, deductions and exemptions to eliminate their liability. That's according to projections by the Tax Policy Center, a Washington research organization. Most people still are required to file returns by the April 15 deadline. The penalty for skipping it is limited to the amount of taxes owed, but it's still almost always better to file. That's the only way to get a refund of all the income taxes withheld by employers. In recent years, credits for low- and middle-income families have grown so much that a family of four making as much as $50,000 owed no federal income tax for 2009, as long as there are two children younger than 17, according to a separate analysis by the consulting firm Deloitte Tax.

The result is a tax system that exempts almost half the country from paying for programs that benefit everyone, including national defense, public safety, infrastructure and education. It is a system in which the top 10 percent of earners - households making an average of $366,400 in 2006 - paid about 73 percent of the income taxes collected by the federal government. The bottom 40 percent, on average, make a profit from the federal income tax, meaning they get more money in tax credits than they would otherwise owe in taxes. For those people, the government sends them a payment. In 2007, about 38 percent of households paid no federal income tax, a figure that jumped to 49 percent in 2008, according to estimates by the Tax Policy Center. In 2008, President George W. Bush signed a law providing most families with rebate checks of $300 to $1,200. In 2010, President Obama signed the economic recovery law that expanded some tax credits and created others. Most targeted low- and middle-income families. Obama's Making Work Pay credit provides as much as $800 to couples and $400 to individuals. The expanded child tax credit provides $1,000 for each child under 17. The Earned Income Tax Credit provides up to $5,657 to low-income families with at least three children. "We have 50 percent of people who are getting something for nothing." said Curtis Dubay, senior tax policy analyst at the Heritage Foundation. The number of households that don't pay federal income taxes increased substantially in 2008, when the poor economy reduced incomes and Congress cut taxes in an attempt to help recovery.[3]

What's the most misused verse of the Bible? The field of candidates is as crowded as the field of GOP presidential aspirants is this year (2012), but a leading contender is Matthew 25:40, "As you did to one of the least of these my brothers, you did to me." Many people use that verse to vindicate everything from giving an alcoholic a dollar to adding to the US budget billions more for what passes as welfare - even though such spending does not help the poor to fare well. In the 1960's, the Protestant debates concerning welfare essentially pitted theological liberals against Evangelicals. In one corner stood the liberal National Council of Churches, which in a great reversal from church positions of the 19th century, favoured fighting poverty through forced redistribution by government. Liberal use of the Matthew 25 quotation (and many others) raises severe questions of biblical interpretation. The Old Testament emphasizes not alms but opportunities to glean, and not subsidies for sitting but exhortations to be industrious. If we use Matthew 25 to baptize the welfare state, even though its result has been two generations that never learned about the importance of work, what do we do with dozens of verses from Proverbs? Some examples: "Lazy hands make a man poor... Diligent hands will rule, but laziness ends in slave labor. The sluggard's craving will be the death of him, because his hands refuse to work." The apostle provided to the Thessalonians and us not a suggestion but a rule: "In the name of the Lord Jesus Christ, we command you, brothers, to keep away from every brother who is idle. We gave you this rule: 'If a man will not work, he shall not eat.'" Jesus could have turned stones into bread to feed all the hungry people in Israel, but instead He fed only those who came to hear Him, and He didn't feed them that quickly either: In Matthew 15, Jesus fed 4,000 men, along with women and children, only after they were with Him, gaining spiritual nourishment, for three days.

If Matthew 25:40 exhorts us to be compassionate, as it does, we need to understand what biblical compassion means. "Helping widows, orphans, the sick, and others who temporarily cannot help themselves is fine, but anything more than that is an anti-Biblical trap into which some evangelicals are falling." We should not spiritualise away real material needs, but we should also not deny Christ by giving needy people only physical sustenance. We should challenge able-bodied, able-minded people to leave poverty, instead of enabling them to remain in poverty. If given work instead of handouts, what a better life they would have. I Timothy 5 states the church is to take care of widows. Even Christianity Today no longer blows clear trumpet sounds, which is one reason why World magazine (with its doctrine of Biblical "objectivity") and Christianity Today are now vying for the circulation leadership among evangelicals. Here is how Jesus' words, in light of his own teaching and the whole counsel of God, could be modernized for application to welfare statists: "I despaired and you gave me stew, when what I truly needed was my birthright. I was an alcoholic and you gave me money that I used to buy another bottle, while you walked away applauding yourself. I lived for immediate gratification and needed the discipline of work and family, but you gave me shelter without responsibility so that I did not have to look back or ahead. Now depart from me into the eternal fire." Those who profess Christ need to be careful to avoid the same pit.[4]

1. http://www.answers.com/topic/personal-responsibility-and-work-opportunity-reconciliation-act-1996

2. http://gopcapitalist.tripod.com/constitution.html

3. http://www.cleverdude.com/content/is-welfare-unconstitutional-and-bad-for-society/

4. http://www.torenewamerica.com/the-bibles-most-misused-verse

23 CHRISTIANITY AND SOCIALISM

I would issue an order stating that the United States is a Capitalist free enterprise country and that the tenants of Capitalism are not in conflict with Christianity.

A group of self-described "progressive" Christian evangelicals calling themselves "Red Letter Christians," and led by the left-oriented Sojourners magazine and left-oriented religious pundits like Jim Wallis and Tony Campolo, has recently emerged in the body politic. These self-proclaimed "progressives" have been making a lot of noise recently complaining about the ties that other Christian evangelicals have long held with the conservative movement in the United States, including the conservative movement in the Republican Party.

One policy under attack by these "progressives" is the conservative effort to "cut programs to the poor". They say that such a policy goes against Jesus Christ's commands in chapter 24 of the book of Matthew to feed those who are hungry. These "Red Letter Christians" are making a lot of noise, but they are just a bunch of clanging cymbals, and the love that they claim to spout has no truth in it whatsoever. What these misguided religious zealots conveniently fail to note is that nowhere in the New Testament or the other books of the Bible do Jesus Christ, His apostles, God the Father, the Holy Spirit, Moses or the Hebrew prophets command the government to take money from its citizens and transfer it to poor people. In fact, the Bible says just the opposite.

God presents us with three general ways in the Bible to take care of the poor and needy:
1) through the family,

2) through the church, and

3) through individual charity.

The applicable passages for these three ways are Deuteronomy 14:28, 29, Numbers 18:24, Matthew 6:1-4 and 1 Timothy 5:3-16.

Now, the first two ways are pretty clear. People's first obligation is to the needy, poor, widowed and orphaned in their own families. Only after they do this do they have any obligation to help the needy, poor, widowed and orphaned through their local church organization. God established the pattern for this kind of church giving in Numbers 18:24 and Deuteronomy 14:28, 29. As David Chilton points out in his great book Productive Christians in an Age of Guilt Manipulators the bulk of Christian giving to the local church should be geared toward financing professional theologians, experts in biblical law and church discipline, teachers of God's word and leaders skilled in worship. It was only every third year that all the giving was set aside to help the needy, poor, widowed and orphaned. Even then, the money was not given just to anyone who showed up. Those able to work but don't do not qualify for help. Also, those who have families to take care of them don't qualify, nor do widows under age 60 qualify, according to the Apostle Paul in 1 Timothy 5:3-16.

Jesus Christ, who is God in the flesh, talks about the third way in Matthew 6. He tells His listeners that they should give individual charity. He also says they should give such charity secretly: "Do not let your left hand know what your right hand is doing." In other words, Jesus is not a socialist. Nor is he a liberal. In fact, in none of the Bible passages just cited, nor in any others I know of, does Jesus, God or even Moses cite the government as the means by which the poor, needy, widowed and orphaned are housed, clothed and fed. Thus, a simple, straightforward reading of the Bible, God's Word, including the "Red Letter" words of Jesus Christ, the Son of God, clearly shows that the American welfare state is anti-Christian and unbiblical. Any Christian who advocates such a government welfare system (including clergymen or women) should be harshly rebuked. Furthermore, any members of any political party, including Republicans, Democrats, Reform Party members, Libertarians or whatever, who advocate such a socialist system yet claim to be Christian should be reprimanded by their fellow brothers and sisters in Christ and by all church leaders.

If any such party members refuse to repent and change their ways, then their names should be posted at their church and throughout the whole land so that all Christians in the United States can know not to vote for these people or place them in positions of authority and leadership. Of course, all Christians should encourage families to take care of their own. And they should also encourage their churches to give at least one-third of their gross income to help the poor, needy, widowed and orphaned. On that note, it is interesting to recall that the 10th Commandment in Exodus 20:17 actually protects private property by commanding people not to covet their neighbor's house or belongings. That commands applies to the average citizen as well as the elected official, the judge and all other government officials. Furthermore, the Bible condemns laziness and praises hard work. Proverbs 10:4 says, "Lazy hands make a man poor, but diligent hands bring wealth." Proverbs 14:23 says, "All hard work brings a profit, but mere talk leads only to poverty."

Finally, it is interesting to note that, in Mark 7:20-23, not only does Jesus Christ declare that all sex outside of heterosexual marriage, including homosexuality, pre-marital sex and adultery, is evil, he also declares that both greed and envy are evil. Thus, Jesus Christ condemns both the greed of the rich man as well as the greed of the poor man, and the envy of the poor man as well as the envy of the rich man.

Thus, God condemns the politics of envy of the left, and he extols the virtues of hard work and capitalism, not just the value of charity! Liberals and socialists like the "Red Letter Christians," Secretary of State Hillary Clinton, and former Vice President Al Gore are violating the commands of Jesus Christ, who is God in the Flesh. They are also violating the commands that God gives all of us in the Hebrew Scriptures as well. If they truly want to follow the words of Jesus in the New Testament, they should stop their opposition to the real Christian movement in America and join it. One of the first things they should do immediately is help cut government programs for the poor. Christians must stop the ungodly, immoral rape of American citizens with the totalitarian, socialist welfare state! They must establish a proper and godly system of family, church and private charity. Not just Christians, but all true Americans should follow God's clear guidance in this matter. God will reward us mightily for our obedience in these matters.[1]

1. http://www.wnd.com/2006/10/38336/

24 CHRISTIANITY AND PACIFISM

I would issue an order stating that the primary duty of the Federal Government is to protect us from enemies, foreign and domestic. The Preamble to the Constitution reads: "We the People of the United States, in Order to form a more perfect Union, establish Justice, insure domestic Tranquility, provide for the common defense, promote the general Welfare, and secure the Blessings of Liberty to ourselves and our Posterity, do ordain and establish this Constitution for the United States of America." "Provide for" the common defense means to fund, as opposed to "Promote" the general Welfare that means to lobby support, not fund. Some mainstream Protestant churches mistakenly think Jesus was a pacifist. President Ronald Reagan had it right when he said, "Freedom is never more than one generation away from extinction. We didn't pass it on to our children. Democracy is worth dying for because it is the most deeply honorable form of government ever devised by man. Of the four wars in my lifetime, none came about because the U.S. was too strong".

The Savior clearly said He would fight! The prophecies concerning Christ said He would fight, and wage war! Specific prophecies said He would cheerfully carry out the death penalty for evil, wicked men. Yet, Jesus Christ is usually portrayed as a "peacenik," an anti-war, non-violent, pacifistic person who would invariably turn the other cheek, overlook every affront, appease and placate every aggressor. Isaiah prophesied of Christ, "...the spirit of the LORD shall rest upon him, the spirit of wisdom and understanding, the spirit of counsel and might, the spirit of knowledge and of the fear of the LORD. And shall make him of quick understanding in the fear of the LORD: and he shall not judge after the sight of his eyes, neither reprove after the hearing of his ears: But with righteousness shall he judge the poor, and reprove with equity for the meek of the earth: and he shall smite the earth with the rod of his mouth, and with the breath of his lips shall he slay the wicked. And righteousness shall be the girdle of his loins, and faithfulness the girdle of his reins." (Isaiah 11:2-5). This is hardly the mental image of Christ that has been planted in the minds of millions of nominal Christians. "Slay the wicked?" The average nominal Christian who possesses a mental image of Jesus would never believe such a thing.

Christ's disciples flocked to Him not because they believed they would become gray-haired old patriarchs who would die and molder in their graves for twenty or so centuries awaiting His second coming. Instead, they believed He would become the King of Israel, that He would usurp the corrupt throne of the Herods, that He would expel the occupying Roman forces, and that He would reestablish the greater Solomonic Kingdom of Israel, which at one time extended from modern Iraq to the seven streams of the Nile in Egypt. These young men were would-be revolutionaries, expecting a complete regime change in Israel. They were not vying for positions in the clergy, nor did they covet a religious office. At the famous "Last Supper," they argued vehemently over which one of them would be at a Cabinet-level position, like viceroys or chiefs of staff: "And there was also a strife among them, which of them should be accounted the greatest" (Luke 22:24). This was not merely a laid-back, casual discussion. It was strife. Voices were raised. Anger was present. Jesus rebuked them, saying "The kings of the Gentiles exercise lordship over them, and they that exercise authority upon them are called benefactors. But ye shall not be so: but he that is greatest among you, let him be as the younger; and he that is chief, as he that doth serve" (Luke 22:25,26).

Yet, moments later, He reassured them, "And I appoint unto you a kingdom, as my Father hath appointed unto me; That ye may eat and drink at my table in my kingdom, and sit on thrones judging the twelve tribes of Israel" (Luke 22:29,30). They could hardly interpret this in terms of two thousand hazy years in the future! To them, it meant "here and now!" Sitting on thrones? Judging, ruling, handing down decisions? This was hardly a "religious" calling; hardly a description of somber religious rites, echoing chants, or administering communion. The proof of this is easily discerned. At the feeding of the four and the five thousand, when the miraculous cornucopia basket gave forth its inexhaustible supply of bread and fish, the crowd assayed to take Him, hoist Him on their shoulders, and march on Jerusalem. Jesus went into a boat and crossed Galilee to avoid the crowd (John 6:14,15).

When Jesus twice cleansed the temple, He did so in what anyone would characterize as a violent act! He did not strike or injure any person, but He did throw over tables, crates and pens, and, using a hand-made cord, drove animals outside. Money changers were scrambling around on the floor, where their coins had been thrown; doves were flying wildly around inside; sheep, goats and cattle were adding their voices to the cacophony. What could anyone think who had been there? That this was the moment. This was it! He was exerting His authority, taking over. The Temple was the very center of religious and social life among the Jews; it was, in a real sense, the religious capital. He was taking charge of the temple. Or so they thought.

At the triumphal march into Jerusalem in those final days before His arrest and mock trial, Christ rode on a white colt, while the enthusiastic crowd played the game of using their garments to place on the rocky trail up from Kidron, insuring not a hoof touched the ground. Others were picking them up as the donkey passed, running to the head of the line, to place them on the path again. Many were waving palm fronds in the air, and the crowd took up a chant, "Hosanna! Hosanna! Glory to God in the Highest, Jerusalem, behold your king!" They did not say, "behold your vicar, or your right reverend, or your priest!" No, they used a "political" term, "King!" This was in every sense a huge, exciting political rally - a crowd of thousands, fully expecting that at the terminus of their march would come the culmination of their hopes and dreams; Christ mounting the throne of Israel!

Continually, the disciples were frustrated when it seemed He was determined to delay; to dash their hopes. Finally, at the moment of His arrest in the garden, Peter tried to precipitate the revolution! Just as they were arresting Jesus, He whipped out his sword, and tried to kill the person nearest him, Malcom, the servant of the High Priest. Malcom dodged, and Peter succeeded only in slicing off his ear. Christ bent over, picked up the ear, stuck it back on Malcom's head, and, as he uttered a quick prayer, Malcom's ear was healed - perfectly whole as before. Christ then rebuked Peter for striking with his sword. Peter was outraged! He faded back into the darkness in shame, dismay, anger and disbelief. He felt betrayed! Only a few hours later, Peter cursed and swore three times, disclaiming any knowledge of Jesus, just as prophesied. He bitterly believed his hopes and dreams had been dashed into pieces. Not only Peter was disappointed. All of the disciples "forsook Him and fled." They didn't stand around with their hands steeled, with a beatific expression of holy martyrdom on their faces, but they ran and hid. To them, the revolution was a complete failure!

It was not until these most unwilling witnesses were finally convinced, against their will, by Christ's many miraculous appearances to them, that they believed - truly believed at last - that He really was the Son of God, that He had been murdered, buried, and had risen again. Finally, just before He was taken up, the anxious group asked the most important question which had perplexed them from the beginning. Time and time again they had supposed He would establish His government, overthrow the Herodian line, and expel the Romans. Time and time again their hopes were dashed when He did not continue the events in motion that would have completed the revolution. Now, they asked, "Lord, wilt thou at this time restore again the kingdom to Israel?" (Acts 1:6). Ponder that question carefully. Think about what they did not ask.

The language is clear. They did not ask, "Would He give them religious rites and orders? Would He tell them which one should be the chief apostle? Would He tell them what kind of liturgy to follow?" No, they asked in plain language if He now, finally, at long last, would "restore again the kingdom to Israel!"

Their hopes and dreams were born in an occupied country; the hopes of a downtrodden, exploited people under a brutal dictatorship, and the fear of the dreaded Sanhedrin, whose agents could carry out death sentences. They wanted a new government, a righteous, fair, equitable government. They knew He was the most qualified man they had ever known. Had not He continually talked about His coming Kingdom? But now, Christ told them it was not for them to know "the times and the seasons," and they watched open mouthed as He ascended from them.

Christ was not, and is not now, a pacifist. When being grilled by Pilate, He said, "My kingdom is not of this world: if my kingdom were of this world, then would my servants fight, that I should not be delivered to the Jews: but now is my kingdom not from hence." (John 18:36). It was only because His time was not yet that He desisted from fighting. The question is not whether Jesus Christ would fight, but in whose cause? He ultimately intends to fight the war to end all wars, not become embroiled in half measures of corrupt human politics.[1]

1. http://www.garnertedarmstrong.org/GTA_Wordfroms/gtanews81.htm

25 IMMIGRATION

I would issue an order that Section I of Article 2 of the U.S. Constitution shall have the term natural born citizen defined about children of illegal aliens born in the United States: "No person born in the United States where both parents are illegal aliens shall be considered a citizen." I would issue an order that illegal aliens could get ten-year renewable work permits, but they would never be eligible for citizenship unless they had an honorable discharge after serving a term of active duty in a branch of the United States military. There would be no monetary penalties for illegal entry, but they would not be eligible for welfare or any federal government subsidies. I would also issue an order that a double-barrier fence be completed along the entire 1,954-mile border between Mexico and the United States as initiated in House Resolution 6061(H.R. 6061) "Secure Fence Act of 2006". Finally, I would issue an order that the E-Verify provision of the Illegal Immigration Reform and Immigrant Responsibility Act of 1996 be made mandatory for all employers and that any employer not complying with this Act will be subject to a fine and/or jail term.

From Section 1 of Article 2 of the United States Constitution: "No person, except a natural born Citizen, or a Citizen of the United States, at the time of the Adoption of this Constitution shall be eligible to the office of President, neither shall any Person be eligible to that Office who shall not have attained to the Age of thirty five years and been fourteen years a Resident within the United States. The Constitution does not provide a definition of natural born citizen. Neither does the Immigration and Naturalization Act, nor has the U.S. Supreme Court defined the term. Consequently, there has been much debate over its meaning. What is certain, is a person who has become a citizen through naturalization is not considered to be a natural born citizen and therefore not eligible to be

President of the United States. The question of citizenship to children born in the U.S to illegal aliens has not been addressed. Fathom the odd hypocrisy that our government wants every citizen to prove they are insured, but they don't have to prove they are citizens.

In his speech in El Paso on immigration reform on May 10, 2011, President Obama declared that the fence along the border with Mexico is "now basically complete." Still, he predicted that many Republican opponents won't be satisfied. "We have gone above and beyond what was requested by the very Republicans who said they supported broader reform as long as we got serious about enforcement", Obama said. "They wanted more agents on the border. Well, we now have more boots on the ground on the southwest border than at any time in our history. The Border Patrol has 20,000 agents - more than twice as many as there were in 2004, a build up that began under President Bush and that we have continued. All the stuff they asked for, we've done. But even though we've answered these concerns, I've got to say I suspect there are still going to be some who are trying to move the goal posts on us one more time. They'll want a higher fence.", Obama said. "Maybe they'll need a moat. Maybe they want alligators in the moat. They'll never be satisfied. And I understand that. That's politics."

Fencing along the U.S.-Mexico border has long been a thorny political issue, so with Obama declaring mission accomplished, we decided to check it out. Richard Stana, director of homeland security issues for the Government Accountability Office, informed the Senate Homeland Security Committee in March that there are only 129 miles of the 1,954-mile-long U.S.-Mexico border where the Border Patrol can prevent or stop an illegal entry from taking place at the border itself. There are another 744 miles where it can stop an illegal entry at "distances of up to 100 miles or more away from the immediate border." That leaves at least 1,081 miles of border where Homeland Security has anything but "operational control." In written testimony presented to the committee on May 4, 2010, Stana said Homeland Security had built 646 miles of border fence (of 652 miles it intended to build) as of April 2010. This generally was not the "2 layers of reinforced fencing" described in the Secure Border Act. Three hundred forty-seven miles was what the GAO described as "pedestrian" fencing, and 299 miles was "vehicle" fencing. "Pedestrian fencing is designed to prevent people on foot from crossing the border and vehicle fencing consists of physical barriers meant to stop the entry of vehicles.", Stana testified. Stana told the committee that Homeland Security had increased the total length of border fence to 649 miles -- an increase of 3 miles in a year. In the first half of the decade, an average of 850,000 people a year entered the United

States without authorization, according to a recently released report. As the economy plunged into recession between 2007 and 2009, that number fell to 300,000 a year.

House Resolution 6061(H.R. 6061) "Secure Fence Act of 2006", was introduced on September 13, 2006. It passed through the U.S. House of Representatives on September 14, 2006 with a vote of 283–138. On September 29, 2006, by a vote of 80–19 the U.S. Senate confirmed H.R. 6061 authorizing, and partially funding the "possible" construction of 700 miles (1,125 km) of physical fence/barriers along the border. The very broad support implies that many assurances have been made by the Administration, to the Democrats, Mexico, and the pro "Comprehensive immigration reform" minority within the GOP, that Homeland Security will proceed very cautiously.

The proverb "Good fences make good neighbors" has been around for a couple centuries, in different forms. One place it can be found is in Poor Richard's Almanac, by Benjamin Franklin. His version is "Love your neighbor, but don't pull down your hedge." It's interesting that the specific wording of the proverb, "Good fences make good neighbors" is fairly modern. It comes from Robert Frost's poem "Mending Wall" in 1914. The Great Wall of China was started during the Qin Dynasty (221-206 B.C.) and enlarged to 4,000 miles during the Ming Dynasty (1368-1644 A.D.). The largest construction project ever completed, it is a feature visible from Earth orbit. Made with human labor from masonry, rocks, and packed earth, the wall has a thickness of from 15 to 30 feet and a height up to 25 feet. Many walls have been built throughout man's history to hinder foreign invaders, including the walled cities described in the Bible. An exception was the Berlin Wall, used to keep East Germans from leaving. A recent controversial wall and fence being built by Israel has been largely successful in deterring suicide bombers. The 1,954- mile border between the United States and Mexico traverses a variety of terrains, including urban areas and deserts. Barriers have been built in metropolitan centers, the locations of the greatest number of illegal crossings. U.S. Congressman Duncan Hunter has proposed the construction of a reinforced fence along the entire United States -Mexican border. In 1962, Vice President Lyndon Johnson received the following message from a Native American Chief on a reservation. "Be careful with your immigration laws. We were careless with ours."[1]

There is a tool available to preserve jobs for legal workers: E-Verify. But the program is voluntary. Congress has the opportunity to expand E-Verify, including making it mandatory, with more job opportunities made available to unemployed Americans. Created under the Illegal Immigration Reform and Immigrant Responsibility Act of 1996, E-Verify is a Web-based system that allows employers to electronically verify the work eligibility of newly hired employees. The Social Security numbers and alien identification numbers of new hires are checked against Social Security Administration and Department of Homeland Security records to weed out fraudulent numbers and help ensure that new hires are legally authorized to work in the United States. The program quickly confirms 99.5% of work-eligible employees. Even though E-Verify is not mandatory, many employers willingly use the program. More than 250,000 American employers currently use it, and an average of 1,400 new businesses sign up each week. Over 16 million queries run through the system in fiscal year 2010. There have been over 3 million cases run through the system in fiscal year 2011 (as of December 11, 2010). E-Verify is mandatory for some employers, such as those employers with federal contracts or subcontracts that contain the Federal Acquisition Regulation (FAR) E-Verify clause and employers in certain states. It is a voluntary program for most employers, with limited exceptions. Companies can access E-Verify online and compare an employee's Form I-9 information with over 455 million records in the Social Security Administration database, and more than 80 million records in Department of Homeland Security immigration databases. Part of the reason for E-Verify's success is that participating employers are happy with the results. Outside evaluations have found that the vast majority of employers using E-Verify believe it to be an effective and reliable tool for checking the legal status of their employees. In fact, after being subjected to several Immigration and Customs Enforcement I-9 audits, Chipotle now uses E-Verify at all of its restaurants nationwide to help ensure that it hires legal workers.

E-Verify has proved to be much more reliable than the current paper-based, error-prone I-9 system. Under the I-9 system, the employer only has to attest that an identification document "reasonably appears on its face to be genuine." The problem is that fake documents are produced by the millions and can be obtained cheaply. This has undermined the I-9 system. In addition, when the National Federation for Independent Business polled its members, 76% said it would be a minimal or no burden if "there was one telephone number and/or a single Internet website where you could check a new employee's eligibility to work, something like a merchant's capacity to check the validity of a credit card." This describes E-Verify, and E-Verify recently received an exceptionally high overall customer satisfaction score - 82 out of 100 on the American Customer Satisfaction Index scale. The government's overall satisfaction score is only 69. With this sort of track record, it is no surprise that 82% of likely voters, responding to a recent Rasmussen poll, thought businesses should be required to use E-Verify. Last year, the U.S. Bureau of Citizenship and Immigration Services implemented a photo-matching tool as part of E-Verify. This allows an employer to view a picture of the employee -from a green card, an employment authorization document or a passport -to determine that the employee is in fact the person to whom the Social Security number or alien identification number was issued.[2]

1. http://www.politifact.com/truth-o-meter/statements/2011/may/16/barack-obama/obama-says-border-fence-now-basically-complete/

2. http://coloradoindependent.com/90936/house-immigration-subcommittee-will-discuss-mandatory-e-verify-bill

26 EDUCATION

I would issue an order that all teacher unions will be abolished. As noted in other chapters of this book, the Executive Branch and the Federal Department of Education will also be gone, removing a plethora of regulations and unfunded mandates. Also, I would institute a universal system of vouchers, where the money is given to the parents, not to school boards or politicians at the local, county, state, or national level. Parents of home-schooled children will be given the same funds as if they were sending their children to public or private schools. I would also issue an order that tenure will be eliminated for all school systems, including Universities. I would issue an order that all student loans for colleges or universities will be privatized, so the federal government will be out of the loan business. Finally, I will mandate sensible dress codes and/or uniforms for all students K through 12 to help erase economic differences and promote school safety.

Led by the American Federation of Teachers and the National Education Association, teacher unions contributed about $5.4 million to federal candidates, parties and committees during the 2008 election cycle. As is true with unions in general, most of the money coming from this category goes to Democrats. Teacher unions contribute 95 percent of their funds to Democrats -- a rate that's above average among labor unions across the board. The AFT contributed $2.8 million during the 2008 cycle, with 99 percent going to Democrats. For its part, the NEA contributed $2.5 million, with 91 percent going to Democrats. Teacher unions' primary goals include decreasing class sizes, defeating proposals to offer public school students vouchers for private schools and improving student/teacher interaction. The unions also focus on issues of pay, tenure and the availability of classroom resources. During 2008, teacher unions spent about $2.7 million on federal lobbying. This is down from a record $10.2 million in 2007. The NEA leads these groups in lobbying spending, doling out $1.5 million in 2008. The AFT also invests significantly on lobbying, spending about $960,000 in 2008.

Not since the late Albert Shanker has a teacher union official been so candid about the true priorities of the National Education Association. Shanker, president of the American Federation of Teachers famously said: "When school children start paying union dues, that's when I'll start representing the interests of school children." Now NEA general counsel Bob Chanin, speaking to the teacher union convention, goes even further. "Despite what some among us would like to believe, it is not because of our creative ideas; it is not because of the merit of our positions; it is not because we care about children; and it is not because we have a vision of a great public school for every child. The NEA and its affiliates are effective advocates because we have power. And we have power because there are more than 3.2 million people who are willing to pay us hundreds of millions of dollars in dues each year because they believe that we are the unions that can most effectively represent them; the union that can protect their rights and advance their interests as education employees."[1]

The education documentary "Waiting for Superman" makes one thing crystal clear, that the main problem with our public school education system is the teacher unions. It is self-evident that throwing more and more money into the Department of Education over the years has not solved the issues in relation to our educational system. Our educational system is broken.

For decades the unions have been creating generations of children who will be dependent on the government because of the teachers having no clear incentive to teach well. This is because the Democrats are in the teacher union's pockets, and they believe in Big Government and want to create an atmosphere where multitudes of adults are dependent on the government they put on a pedestal. One of the main problems with the teacher unions is that the teachers have a total lack of accountability. It doesn't matter to the unions if there are teachers who are incompetent and not meeting certain standards because as the head of the NTA stated they are "against proposals that divide people". There are no incentives for being a good teacher. One would think that all teachers are duty bound to teach their kids properly. But both the lackadaisical attitude and this "I-am-owed-something" attitude has spread so rampantly among all Democrat-controlled sectors of employment.

Democrats are a study in contradictions. They want a woman to have a choice in having or aborting a baby, but if she decides to have the child, that's where the choice should end. First, they and the teachers unions want the youngster put in government-funded day care so he or she can be indoctrinated with liberal philosophy. Then, at five or six years old, they want the child to enroll in the only true monopoly in our country - the public school system. They know that if given a choice, with vouchers, parents will abandon the failing public schools in droves. This would force school systems to examine their bloated bureaucracies and realize that more money isn't the answer. On November 9, 1998, the United States Supreme Court voted to let stand the decision to allow $5,000 vouchers for about five thousand students of poor families in Milwaukee, Wisconsin. Hopefully, this will open the floodgates for choice.

An analysis of the Milwaukee publicly-run voucher program shows the parents of "choice" kids are virtually unanimous in their opinion of the program. They love it. Parents are not only far more satisfied with their freely chosen private schools than they were with their former public schools, but they participate more actively in their children's education now that they've made the move. A re-analysis of the raw data by statisticians and educational researchers from Harvard and the University of Houston found that choice students do indeed benefit academically from the program, showing significant gains in both reading and mathematics by their fourth year of participation. Privately funded and operated voucher programs are perhaps the most effective way to help low-income families become active consumers in the educational marketplace, helping them to gain control over their children's education and encouraging them to become more involved. More than two dozen private voucher programs exist in cities across the United States, and Terry Moe, professor of political science at Stanford University, has collected some of the most interesting and compelling studies of these programs in Private Vouchers. The attitudes and motivations of participating parents are explored, as are the academic effects of programs from Texas to Wisconsin. It is truly an important source of empirical evidence for anyone interested in the impact of competition and choice on the ability of schools to serve the needs of families.[2]

A group called Students First has a mission to build a national movement that will defend the interests of children in public education and pursue reform so America will have the best education system in the world. They have put together some statistics that are quite alarming. The literacy rates among fourth grade students In the U.S. are sobering. In a recent report by the Annie E. Casey Foundation, one out of three students scored below "basic" on the 2009 National Assessment of Education Progress (NAEP) Reading Test. Among these low performing students, 49% come from low income families. Even more alarming is the fact that more than 67% of all U.S. fourth graders scored "below proficient", meaning they are not reading at grade level. Reading proficiency among middle and high school students isn't much better. On the test, about 26% of eighth graders and 27% of twelfth graders scored below the "basic" level and only 32% of eighth graders and 38% of twelfth graders are at or above grade level. It is going to be hard for our students to compete in the global market for jobs such as engineers, scientists, physicians, and creative entrepreneurs when according to an assessment by the Organization for Economic Cooperation and Development found that 15-year-olds in the U.S. placed 25th out of 30 countries in math performance and 21st in science. Test scores have not improved in decades. In April 2009, Education Week reported that average math and reading scores for 17-year-olds in the NAEP tests have remained stagnant since the 1970s. And, according to The Journal, fourth and eighth grade reading scores "have barely budged" since 1992, despite policy and investment focused on improving student achievement. This problem cannot be postponed because of union demands. Our public education priority is supposed to be about the students, not about the adults. If the teachers are not held accountable, the United States will no longer be a global leader in innovation or understand the meaning of hard work and responsibility.

Several states now have laws advancing through the legislatures that would change tenure for schoolteachers. Ohio Senate Bill 5 has many controversial provisions including the elimination of tenure. Proponents say this will prevent teachers who can't make the grade from keeping their jobs year after year. As passed by the state Senate, the bill would eliminate certain collective bargaining abilities for public employees, as well as the right to strike. It would also remove tenure for teachers who have not already earned it or would not earn it under their current contracts. Instead, they would be limited to a maximum five-year contract. Under a recent law passed during former Gov. Ted Strickland's administration, teachers must work in a district for 7 years before becoming eligible for tenure. Senate Bill 5 is being touted as a way to help address a looming $8 Billion deficit in the upcoming biennial budget. The law was enacted on March 11, 2011.

Wisconsin's new governor's attempts to overhaul its public employee collective bargaining rights received much attention early in 2011. In 2011, citing a large budget deficit, Governor Scott Walker proposed a new budget bill that would eliminate most collective bargaining rights for public employees and require workers to pay half of their pension costs and at least 12% of state health insurance premiums. The state's Democratic state senators left Wisconsin hoping to prevent a quorum and passage of the bill. Despite numerous protests and the absence of the state's Democratic senators, Wisconsin Act 10 was passed, and Governor Walker signed it on March 11, 2011. The law takes away all collective bargaining rights for state employees except for wages. Any raises beyond the rate of inflation would require voter referendum and approval. The law requires public employees to pay more for pensions and health insurance and prohibits state and municipal governments from collecting union dues. The Dane County District Attorney filed suit for violations of Wisconsin's open meeting laws and the Dane County, WI Circuit Court issued a permanent injunction against the Act, ruling that the joint Assembly-Senate conference committee violated the open meeting laws when it considered and passed Wisconsin Act 10. The Wisconsin Supreme Court held oral argument on June 6, 2011 on whether it should accept jurisdiction over an appeal. On June 14, 2011, the Wisconsin Supreme Court in a 4-3 decision vacated the lower court's injunction, stating the lower court "usurped the legislative power that the Wisconsin Constitution grants exclusively to the legislature" by enjoining publication of the law and further held that in enacting Wisconsin Act 10, the legislature did not violate the open meetings provisions of Wisconsin's Constitution. This was a major blow to unions nationwide.[3]

In recent years, schools across the country have experienced violence, gang activity, and thefts of clothing and accessories. Many school boards, mindful of their responsibility to provide safe school environments for students, have implemented policies specifying dress codes or the wearing of uniforms. As many as 25 percent of the nation's public elementary, middle, and junior high schools were expected to implement dress-related policies during the 1997-98 school year, according to the *California School News* (March 31, 1997). Ten states allow school districts to mandate school uniforms. One of the chief benefits of school uniforms is that they make schools safer. Uniforms are said to reduce gang influence, minimize violence by reducing some sources of conflict, and help to identify trespassers. Parents benefit because they are no longer pressured to buy the latest fashions, and they spend less on their children's clothing. Uniforms help erase cultural and economic differences among students, set a tone for serious study, facilitate school pride, and improve attendance. Uniforms also enhance students' self-concepts, classroom behavior, and academic performance.[4]

The Obama Administration has declared war on home schooling. In Germany home schooling is banned. The Romeike family from Germany were granted political asylum in Tennessee. US Attorney General Eric

Holder has appealed the judge's ruling. The case reveals how the US government regards individual rights and liberties. In their argument the US Department of Justice disregards the rights of an individual and considers only collective rights of members of a group. The implications are immense: The Home School Legal Defense Association sets out threats to individual liberty that are far wider than the home schooling issue. Michael Farris, J.D., LL.M., HSLDA Founder and Chairman said, "I immersed myself for about eight days in writing a brief for the Romeike family, who fled to the United States for political asylum. The U.S. law of asylum allows a refugee to stay in the United States permanently if he can show that he is being persecuted for one of several specific reasons. Among these are persecution for religious reasons and persecution of a "particular social group." The Romeikes' case went before the United States Court of Appeals for the Sixth Circuit, and they were allowed to stay. The case for the government was officially in the name of the Attorney General of the United States, and the case was called Romeike v. Holder. It is a statement of the position of our government at a very high level. . The central problem here is that the U.S. government does not understand that religious freedom is an individual right. One need not be a part of any church or other religious group to be able to make a religious freedom claim, one should be able to follow the dictates of God Himself. Does anyone think that our government would say to Orthodox Jewish parents, we can force your children to eat pork products for 22-26 hours per week because the rest of the time you can feed them kosher food? This argument necessarily means that the United States government believes that it would not violate your rights if our own government banned home schooling entirely. After all, you could teach your children your own values after they have had 22-26 hours of public school indoctrination aimed at counteracting religious and philosophical views the government doesn't like. Freedom for the mind and spirit is as important as freedom for the body and spirit.

Student-loan borrowers now owe the federal government more than $1-trillion for the first time, the Consumer Financial Protection Bureau announced on Wednesday. The swelling federal student-loan debt now sits at $1.2-trillion, the bureau estimated. The country passed the milestone with a fitting backdrop: the debate in Congress over student-loan interest rates. Rates for new borrowers of federally subsidized loans doubled, to 6.8 percent, on July 1, with Democrats and Republicans sparring, before and since, over the best way to set future rates. Total student debt, including private loans, passed $1-trillion in 2011 and has grown by one-fifth since then, the bureau reported. Most student loans come from federal sources. Politicians and policy makers are likely to use the figure to renew concerns about rising debt levels. The bureau reported in May that student-loan borrowing would have a significant economic impact, as it hurts young Americans' ability to save up to buy a house or car or to start a business.

1. http://www.markhillman.com/2009/07/10/nea-lawyer-its-all-about-power-money-job-protection/

2. http://catholicgossip.blogspot.com/2011/02/teachers-unions-destroying-education-in.html

3. http://www.studentsfirst.org/

4. http://character-education.info/Articles/Case_for_Uniforms.htm

27 DRUGS

I would issue an order that all drugs would be legalized, including cocaine and heroin, and be dispensed though pharmacies with a doctor's prescription. They would be taxed as any other commodity under the FairTax. There would also be a prohibition on advertising drugs in any media, including the Internet. I would also issue an order that all employees would be drug tested at the time of employment and once a year. Also, misuse of drugs would be treated the same as misuse of alcohol, with the same penalties. The "war on drugs" would be over, foreign drug cartels would disappear, and we could finally realize that we cannot legislate morality.

What if we legalized all drugs? How does a $50 billion boost to the US economy sound? Not bad? Well, what about all the new addicts we could see pop up on the streets? It's all possible. Every year, about 2 million people in the U.S. are arrested for drug offenses, including using or selling marijuana, heroin, cocaine or methamphetamines. About a third of the country's prisoners are held on drug charges or for crimes attributed to drug abuse. What if we legalized all street drugs? Youngsters would decide to try drugs "just once", and some would get hooked. Some lives would be ruined. But more lives would be saved. Gang murders would fall sharply. Thousands of people now in jail would be free to find work and feed their families. We'd save billions on the war on drugs, and a new drug industry would create jobs and loads of taxable revenue.

This may sound like madness. The gut feeling among many people is that it would be disastrous. Yet some economists, including American Nobel laureate Milton Friedman, have supported the idea of legalizing drugs. Friedman believed America's war on drugs was at the root of police corruption and caused thousands of unnecessary deaths, with few gains for ordinary citizens. How would legalized drugs affect the economy and our standard of life? We would assume there'd be strict regulation similar to that for alcohol and cigarettes, including age limits, licensing, quality control, taxes and limits on advertising. On a "strictly numbers" basis, the effect on the country's pocketbook looks promising. We'd see savings on drug-related law enforcement - FBI, police, courts and prisons - of up to $40 billion a year if all drugs were legalized, based on enforcement costs from the White House Office of National Drug Control Policy. That's before the cost of overseeing the new drug regulations. Increased productivity, as fewer people were murdered, drug offenders freed to find work and those stripped of their criminal record would find it easier to get jobs. About 1.2 million persons in prison on drug charges would be released. How many of these would turn away from crime is unknown.

Drug prices would have to fall sharply in order to squeeze out the black market. Jeffrey Miron, a senior lecturer in economics for Harvard University, calculates the $10 billion-plus U.S. marijuana market could reap $6 billion in annual taxes. The $65 billion market for all illicit drugs, he estimates, might bring in $10 billion to $15 billion in taxes. A new legal drug industry would create jobs, farm crops, retail outlets and a notch up in gross domestic product as the black market money turned clean. A 1994 study by the National Organization for the Reform of Marijuana Laws in Washington, D.C., suggested 200,000 jobs and 60,000 retail pharmacies would emerge from a legal drug industry. We'd get a shower of money for the government coffers - perhaps an initial $50 billion - and gains for business and the community.

At what cost? It all depends, mostly on how many more people would use drugs, which drugs and how much more they used. Currently, considering it can get you arrested (or kill you), drug use is surprisingly common. A 2006 federal government study said 20% of Americans 18 to 25 had taken an illicit drug in the month prior to the survey. So what if drugstores fulfilled Abbie Hoffman's wildest dreams? What if you could sit on a sofa, pick up a magazine and light up, or even shoot up, in a congenial atmosphere? Europe offers some clues. In 1976, the Netherlands decided to tolerate (though not legalize) the selling of small amounts of cannabis in licensed coffee shops. At first there was little change in usage. But between 1984 and 1992, as shops opened rapidly, smoking of the drug doubled among Dutch 18- to 20-year-olds. "In that case, it looked like changing the legal status was of minor importance, but opening commercial outlets mattered." says Mark Kleiman, the director of the Drug Policy Analysis Program at the University of California, Los Angeles.[1]

Switzerland's drug policy, administered by the Federal Council made a study on heroin assisted treatment for severely dependent heroin addicts who had failed at other treatment programs. In 1992, the Council passed an order authorizing clinical trials with the medical prescription of heroin, along with a strict scientific evaluation of the trials. The trials began in 1994 and ended on December 31, 1996. The final evaluation report was published in July 1997 and concluded that heroin assisted treatment for severely dependent heroin addicts improved their physical and/or psychic health, as well as their quality of life (in terms of housing, work and other areas). They found that participants' illegal use of heroin and cocaine decreased; the users involved in the program committed fewer crimes (the incidence of theft and property and drug trafficking offences fell sharply). The Federal Council followed the report's recommendations, and on March 8, 1999, passed the Ordinance governing the medical prescription of heroin authorizing heroin assisted treatment, setting objectives, eligibility criteria, administrative measures and providing for such treatment.

Would addiction increase? One oddity that stands out in the research is that the Dutch are still only midrange users of marijuana by European standards. By some measures, they use marijuana far less than Americans, according to a recent World Health Organization survey. It's thought that this is due to differing social norms, which raises another point. If drugs were legal in America, this could send a powerful signal to kids that drugs are O.K. Add this to the lower price, addictive effects of some drugs and easy access, and drug use could rise quite a bit. To offset this, we could run campaigns warning against the stuff. That might work. The response from marijuana reform advocates is: "So what if use increases? It's harmless anyway." As for legalizing all drugs, Harvard's Miron argues that the increase in drug abuse would likely be small. "Millions of people don't smoke cigarettes. The same is true of alcohol, because they know that too much of it is not good for you." he says. People who are prone to abuse drugs are already using them, he adds. Miron says a small rise in drug abuse would be far outweighed by the gains from reduced violent crime, freed-up police resources, a more productive citizenry and reduced illness from bad drugs and dirty needles.[2]

Former presidents of several countries, former U.N. secretary general Kofi Annan, former U.S. Secretary of State George Shultz, former U.S. Fed Chairman Paul Volcker and other luminaries will release a report calling the global "war on drugs" a failure and encouraging nations to pursue legalizing and regulating drugs as a way to put a stop the violence inherent in the illegal drug market. Former Mexican President Vicente Fox has come out in favor of legalizing drugs in an attempt to disrupt the illegal markets that have turned parts of Mexico into battlegrounds. In a proposal published on his website, Fox argued that drug addiction and drug-related violence should be treated as distinct and separate challenges. "So, drug consumption is the responsibility of the person who consumes; of the family who is responsible for educating; and of the education system and the socioeconomic context," wrote Fox, who was president from 2000 to 2006. "What we have to do is legalize the production, the sale and the distribution."[3]

Law Enforcement Against Prohibition, a group of police, prosecutors and judges who have waged the "drug war" on its front lines, is cheering these conclusions. "It's no longer a question of whether legalizing drugs is a serious topic of debate for serious people." said Neill Franklin, LEAP's executive director and a 34-year veteran police officer from Baltimore, Maryland. "These former presidents and other international leaders have placed drug legalization squarely on the table as an important solution that policymakers need to consider. As a narcotics cop on the streets, I saw how the prohibition approach not only doesn't reduce drug abuse but how it causes violence and crime that affect all citizens and taxpayers, whether they use drugs or not."

Forty years ago President Nixon declared the "war on drugs." Marking next week's somber anniversary, a group of police officers, judges and corrections officials who support legalizing drugs will join forces to detail the ongoing failures of a war the Obama administration disingenuously claims it ended two years ago. Following a press conference, the law enforcers will attempt to hand-deliver a copy of their new report to President Obama's drug czar. They will also hold a teleconference for journalists not able to attend the event in Washington. Norm Stamper, former chief of police in Seattle and a speaker for Law Enforcement Against Prohibition, said, "Since President Nixon declared 'war on drugs' four decades ago, this failed policy has led to millions of arrests, a trillion dollars spent and countless lives lost. Yet drugs today are more available than ever."

"President Obama's drug officials keep saying they've ended the 'drug war.' But our report shows that's just not true, and we'll be hand-delivering a copy to the drug czar in hopes he'll be convinced to actually end this war, or at least stop saying he already has." Obama administration drug czar Gil Kerlikowske, like Stamper, is a former Seattle chief of police. Neill Franklin, a former Baltimore narcotics cop and LEAP's executive director, said, "When President Nixon declared the 'drug war' in 1971, we arrested fewer than half a million people for drug offenses that year. Today, the number has skyrocketed to almost two million drug arrests a year. We jail more of our own citizens than any other country in the world does, including those run by the worst dictators and totalitarian regimes. Is this how President Obama thinks we can 'win the future'? Law Enforcement Against Prohibition (LEAP) represents police, prosecutors, judges, prison wardens, federal agents and others who want to legalize and regulate drugs after fighting on the front lines of the "war on drugs" and learning firsthand that prohibition only serves to worsen addiction and violence."[4]

For the first time, two American states have legalized the recreational use and sale of marijuana. Voters in Colorado, Washington State and Oregon had the opportunity to make history by voting on initiatives that would legalize the recreational use and sale of marijuana in their respective states. Only residents of Oregon rejected the move. Massachusetts voters joined 17 states and the District of Columbia in electing to allow medical use of the drug. But the victories could create a clash over states' rights since the federal government continues to consider marijuana — even for medical use — an illegal substance, and the possession, sale or distribution of marijuana a crime. Anticipating a confrontation, Colorado Governor John Hickenlooper warned celebrants not to "break out the Cheetos or Goldfish too quickly" as his administration figures out how state residents can buy and sell marijuana without running afoul of federal laws.

Joking, however, does not seem likely to stand in the way of change. The initiatives represent an increased public push for legalization; a 2011 Gallup poll found that 50% of Americans are in favor of marijuana legalization, up from just 12% in 1969. Support for medical marijuana is even higher — despite controversy over how often recreational use masquerades as medical need — and consistently averages over 70%. Three states had ballot questions on medical use; Massachusetts voters approved it, while those in Arkansas rejected the measure. Montana, which already allows such use, tightened its regulations. What would legalized recreational use mean? For one thing, Colorado and Washington don't simply lessen the penalties for users from criminal charges to fines. The states do legalize and tax sales — a step that not even countries like the Netherlands, where wholesale selling and growing is illegal but small retail sales are tolerated in licensed "coffee shops," have taken. Washington's law involves a licensing regime, to be handled by the state's liquor control board, for growers and sellers. Initiative 502 bans sales to people under 21 and sets a 25% tax on both wholesale and retail sales, which will be used to fund drug prevention, schools and health insurance.

Unlike most prior initiatives, I-502 was widely supported by state officials and mainstream media, including the state Democratic Party and local newspapers. It sets a legal limit on THC blood levels for driving (THC is the active ingredient in cannabis). It also bans growing for personal, non-medical use.

Colorado's new law is somewhat different: Amendment 64 allows personal possession and growing for one's own use or to give away. Sales, however, will require a license from the state department of revenue and will be taxed to fund school construction, at a rate of up to 15%. The Colorado Legislative Council estimates that this could bring in between $4 million and $21 million annually, after accounting for initial costs of $1.3 million and $700,000 to fund the regulatory apparatus. Both measures passed by comfortable margins — I-502 garnered an estimated 55% of support, and Amendment 64 earned 53% of the vote. Colorado's enthusiasm is especially significant given that the state already has a medical-marijuana establishment, with 204 outlets in Denver — about three times its number of Starbucks and McDonald's, combined. The federal government, however, remains a cloud that hangs over the ballot victories. Since 2009, the Obama Administration has authorized at least 170 raids on dispensaries and issued more than 61 federal indictments, according to the Huffington Post. In justifying the actions, President Obama told Rolling Stone that "I can't nullify congressional law. I can't ask the Justice Department to say, 'Ignore completely a federal law that's on the books.' What I can say is, 'Use your prosecutorial discretion and properly prioritize your resources to go after things that are really doing folks damage.' "The real question is how much damage legal marijuana sales could cause. Proponents argue that marijuana is less dangerous than alcohol or tobacco. Unlike alcohol, for example, marijuana does not often produce disinhibited behavior that triggers the risk of violence. And unlike tobacco, it does not appear to be linked with lung cancer or other common cancers; the largest and most careful studies simply have not yet found a connection, even in the heaviest smokers. THC, however, is a mild hallucinogen that also has sedative properties. Cannabis intoxication does impair memory and cognition, and marijuana addiction, as with any drug, can lead to serious impairments in judgment and result in harm. But experts agree that marijuana addiction tends to be less severe than cocaine, heroin, methamphetamine or alcohol addiction.

Whether marijuana's status as a legal or illegal drug influences how it is used remains unclear. Studies conducted in Holland, which has come the closest to full legalization of cannabis, and Portugal, which decriminalized possession of all drugs, so far do not show negative effects on either addiction rates or misuse by young people. There is also the complicated relationship between the intensity of law enforcement and the rates of marijuana use and addiction, with no clear expectation that increased enforcement will lower use or related problems. As Dr. Evan Wood, a professor of medicine at the University of British Columbia and the founder of the International Centre for Science in Drug Policy, says, "No scientific evidence demonstrates an association between the amount of money governments spend on drug law enforcement and rates of drug use. And some nations like the U.S., which spend the most, have among the highest rates of drug use." One factor that does influence drug use is price, and legal marijuana would almost certainly be cheaper than that on the black market. A study conducted while California voters considered legalization suggested that the price would drop by 80%. If that's true, and use increases, the states that now have a mandate permitting marijuana use may face another concern to public safety. Some research suggests that marijuana use substitutes for drinking, which would lower driving risks. Others studies, however, find that it is simply added on top, which makes drunk driving more dangerous. But one risk is clearly reduced by legalization: the harms related to arrest and incarceration, which are disproportionately borne by minorities. The voters have spoken. Now they're waiting for the federal government to respond.

Read more: http://healthland.time.com/2012/11/07/two-u-s-states-become-first-to-legalize-marijuana/#ixzz2dmL2IbGP

1. http://hyeforum.com/index.php?showtopic=18647

2. http://www.parl.gc.ca/Content/SEN/Committee/371/ille/library/collin1-e.htm

3. http://txconnectme.wordpress.com/2012/06/03/world-leaders-encourage-drug-legalization/

4. http://copssaylegalize.blogspot.com/

28 GUNS

I would issue an order that the Second Amendment to the Constitution, as written by our nation's founding fathers, "A well-regulated Militia, being necessary to the security of a free State, the right of the people to keep and bear Arms, shall not be infringed" means exactly what it says, and that no court or political body will have a right to interpret it other than "the people" means individual citizens.

Here is what the founders had to say about guns:

James Madison, the author of the Second Amendment, praised *"the advantage of being armed, which the Americans possess over the people of almost any nation."*

"The tree of liberty must be refreshed from time to time with the blood of patriots and tyrants." and *"The strongest reason for the people to retain the right to keep and bear arms is, as a last resort, to protect themselves against tyranny in government."* - Thomas Jefferson

"The said Constitution shall never be construed to authorize Congress to infringe the just liberty of the press, or the rights of conscience; or to prevent the people of the United States, who are peaceable citizens, from keeping their own arms." - Samuel Adams

"If circumstances should at any time oblige the government to form an army of any magnitude, that army can never be formidable to the liberties of the people while there is a large body of citizens, little if at all inferior to them in discipline and the use of arms, who stand ready to defend their rights and those of their fellow citizens." - Alexander

Hamilton

"The great object is that every man be armed. Everyone who is able may have a gun. Guard with jealous attention the public liberty. Suspect everyone who approaches that jewel." - Patrick Henry

"To disarm the people is the best and most effective way to enslave them." - George Mason

"Consider the right to keep and bear arms 'the palladium of the liberties of the republic', which enables the citizenry to deter tyranny." - Justice Joseph Story

"The advantage of being armed, the Americans possess over the people of all other nations. Notwithstanding the military establishments in the several Kingdoms of Europe, which are carried as far as the public resources will bear, the governments are afraid to trust the people with arms." - James Madison

"Before a standing army can rule, the people must be disarmed; as they are in almost every Kingdom in Europe. The supreme power in America cannot enforce unjust laws by the sword; because the whole body of the people are armed, and constitute a force superior to any band of regular troops that can be, on any pretense, raised in the United States. A military force, at the command of Congress, can execute no laws, but such as the people perceive to be just and constitutional; for they will possess the power." - Noah Webster

"Those who would give up essential liberty to purchase a little temporary safety deserve neither liberty nor safety." - Benjamin Franklin

"A militia, when properly formed, are in fact the people themselves, and include all men capable of bearing arms." - Richard Henry Lee, Senator

A look at the history of gun control confirms their insight. In 1911, Turkey established gun control; 1.5 million Armenians, unable to defend themselves, were exterminated. In 1929, the Soviet Union established gun control; more than 20 million dissidents were annihilated. In 1935, China established gun control and 20 million political dissidents were slaughtered. In 1938, Germany established gun control; 13 million Jews and others were killed. In 1956, Cambodia established gun control; 1 million people exterminated. In 1964, Guatemala established gun control; 100,000 Mayan Indians were killed. In 1970, Uganda established gun control; 300,000 Christians were slaughtered. Violent crime has increased in Australia, Canada, and Great Britain following adoption of legislation restricting firearms. Contrast this with the fact that gun ownership of U.S. citizens is at an all-time high, and "right to carry" laws have been implemented in 40 states. Violent crimes have fallen dramatically. The most flagrant exception to this trend is in Washington, D.C., the murder capital of the U.S., and New York City, where you have the most restrictive gun control laws in the country.

Here is what other prominent historic figures had to say about guns:

"If you will not fight for the right when you can easily win without bloodshed, if you will not fight when your victory can be sure and not too costly, you may come to a moment when you have to fight with all the odds against you and only a precarious chance to survive. There may be a worse case -you may have to fight when there is no hope of victory, and it will be better to perish than live in slavery." - Winston Churchill

"Political power grows out of the barrel of a gun." - Mao Tse-Tung

"If the opposition disarms, well and good. If it refuses to disarm, we shall disarm it ourselves. Ideas are more powerful than guns. We would not let our enemies have guns, why should we let them have ideas?" - Joseph Stalin

"The most foolish mistake we could make would be to allow the subject peoples to possess arms. So let's not have any talk about native militias." - Adolf Hitler

"Which gun control laws helped save Jewish lives during the Holocaust?" - Anonymous

"The whole aim of practical politics is to keep the populace alarmed (and hence clamorous to be led to safety) by menacing it with an endless series of hobgoblins, all of them imaginary." - H. L. Mencken

"Americans have the will to resist because you have weapons. If you don't have a gun, freedom of speech has no power." - Yoshumi Ishakawa, Japanese Author

"Using cross-sectional time-series data for U.S. Counties from 1977 to 1992, we find that allowing citizens to carry concealed weapons deters violent crimes and it appears to produce no increase in accidental deaths. If those states that did not have right-to-carry concealed gun provisions had adopted them in 1992, approximately 1,570 murders, 4,177 rapes, and over 60,000 aggravated assaults would have been avoided yearly." - John R Lott and David B. Mustard, School of Law, University of Chicago[1]

Prior to the Supreme Court's 2008 decision in District of Columbia vs. Heller, the courts had yet to definitively state what right the Second Amendment protected. The opposing theories, perhaps oversimplified, were (1) an "individual rights" approach, whereby the Amendment protected individuals' rights to firearm ownership, possession, and transportation; and (2) a "states' rights" approach, under which the Amendment only protected the right to keep and bear arms in connection with organized state militia units. Moreover, it was generally believed that the Amendment was only a bar to federal action, not to state or municipal restraints.

The Supreme Court has now definitively held that the Second Amendment protects an individual's right to possess a firearm unconnected with service in a militia, and to use that weapon for traditionally lawful purposes, such as self-defense within the home. Moreover, this right applies not just to the federal government, but to states and municipalities as well. In Heller, the Court held that (1) the District of Columbia's total ban on handgun possession in the home amounted to a prohibition on an entire class of "arms" that Americans overwhelmingly chose for the lawful purpose of self-defense, and thus violated the Second Amendment; and (2) the District's requirement that any lawful firearm in the home be disassembled or bound by a trigger lock also violated the Second Amendment, because the law made it impossible for citizens to use arms for the core lawful purpose of self-defense. The Court reasoned that the Amendment's prefatory clause, i.e., "a well-regulated Militia, being necessary to the security of a free State," announced the Amendment's purpose, but did not limit or expand the scope of the operative clause, i.e., "the right of the people to keep and bear Arms, shall not be infringed." Moreover, the prefatory clause's history comported with the Court's interpretation, because the prefatory clause stemmed from the Anti-Federalists' concern that the federal government would disarm the people in order to disable the citizens' militia, enabling a politicized standing army or a select militia to rule.

While everyone is distracted with budget battles and the unrest in the Middle East, the White House announced two new gun control measures. One new action attempts to close a loophole that exists related to background check and the other one prohibits the re-importation of U.S. military weapons. One new policy will end a government practice that lets military weapons, sold or donated by the U.S. to allies, be re-imported into the U.S. by private entities, where some may end up on the streets. The White House said the U.S. has approved 250,000 of those guns to be re-imported since 2005; under the new policy, only museums and a few other entities like the government will be eligible to re-import military-grade firearms. The Obama administration is also proposing a federal rule to stop those who would be ineligible to pass a background check from skirting the law by registering a gun to a corporation or trust. The new rule would require people associated with those entities, like beneficiaries and trustees, to undergo the same type of fingerprint-based background checks as individuals if they want to register guns. Vice President Joe Biden, Obama's point-man on gun control after the Newtown tragedy thrust guns into the national spotlight, was set to unveil the new actions Thursday at the White House. Here we are again. The President is using any way possible to avoid letting the people and their elected official decide what kind of gun legislation is needed. President Obama will continue to issue these executive actions until he gets what he wants. Luckily, Congress is needed in order to pass any legislation banning "assault weapons" or actions on background checks for individual sales. But why is it that the president goes about making these changes when everyone is focused on other major news stories? Apparently he just wants to hide these actions in the news cycle.

It's everyone's nightmare. An armed gunman intrudes in what had seemed a safe environment and suddenly you're in a battle zone. Even churches have been attacked by criminals and terrorists in recent years. One man, Charl Van Wyk, has not only experienced such a scenario firsthand, but shot back against terrorists and defended friends and family in his church. He makes a biblical, Christian case for individuals arming themselves, and does so persuasively. "Grenades were exploding in flashes of light. Pews shattered under the blasts, sending splinters flying through the air," he recalls of the July 25, 1993, St. James Church Massacre. "An automatic assault rifle was being fired and was fast ripping the pews -and whoever, whatever was in its trajectory -to pieces. We were being attacked!" But he was not defenseless that day. Had he been unarmed like the other congregants, the slaughter would have been much worse. "Instinctively, I knelt down behind the bench in front of me and pulled out my .38 special snub-nosed revolver that I always carried with me," he writes. "I would have felt undressed without it. Many people could not understand why I would carry a firearm into a church service, but I argued that this was a particularly dangerous time in South Africa." During that Sunday evening service, the terrorists, wielding AK-47s and grenades, killed 11 and wounded 58, but one man - Charl Van Wyk - fired back, wounding one of the attackers and driving the others away.[2]

Here is what the anti-gun people have to say about guns:

"We're going to have to take one step at a time, and the first step is necessarily, given the political realities, going to be very modest. So then we'll have to start working again to strengthen the law, and then again to strengthen the next law, and maybe again and again. Right now, though, we'd be satisfied not with half a loaf but with a slice. Our ultimate goal, total control of handguns in the United States, is going to take time. The

first problem is to slow down the increasing number of guns being produced and sold in this country. The second problem is to get handguns registered. And the final problem is to make the possession of all handguns and all handgun ammunition -except for the military, policemen, licensed security guards, licensed sporting clubs, and licensed gun collectors -totally illegal." - Pete Sheilds, Chairman, Handgun Control, Inc.

"Our main agenda is to have all guns banned. We must use whatever means possible. It does not matter if you have to distort facts or even lie." - Sarah Brady, Handgun Control, Inc.

In the words of Dr. Peter Hammond, "Just as criminals prefer unarmed victims, tyrants prefer disarmed citizens. A government that does not trust its citizens with weapons cannot be trusted with power." President Obama apparently understands this concept, and has been quietly making a few arrangements that will make it much more difficult and expensive to purchase firearms and ammunition. If you don't already own a gun and plenty of ammo, Mr. Obama's plans will likely affect you. Every year, the federal government buys massive amounts of ammunition, primarily to meet the needs of the military. For years, the government has been recouping part of its ammunition expenses by reselling the used casings for remanufacturing. The Obama administration is changing the rules on re-selling used bullet casings. From now on, they cannot be sold for remanufacturing, but rather must be liquidated at scrap value.

After the Japanese decimated our fleet in Pearl Harbor Dec 7, 1941, they could have sent their troop ships and carriers directly to California to finish what they started. The prediction from our Chief of Staff was we would not be able to stop a massive invasion until they reached the Mississippi River. We had a 2 million-man army and war ships, all in anticipation of fighting the Germans. So why did they not invade? After the war, the surviving Japanese generals and admirals were asked that question. Their answer was they know that almost every home had guns and the Americans knew how to use them. The world's largest army was America's hunters! There were over 750,000 hunters that year in the states of Pennsylvania and Michigan, making them the eighth largest army in the world. Add to that 600,000 in Wisconsin and 250,000 in West Virginia, and these states alone would compromise the largest army in the world. Hunting is not just a way to fill the freezer; it's a matter of national security. That's why all our enemies, foreign and domestic, want to see us disarmed.[3]

Norway is the land of my ancestors. They have 4,400,000 people and one of the lowest per capita crime rates in the world in all categories. The answers seem to be personal responsibility and laws to severely punish criminals. At age eighteen, all able-bodied men are required to serve 2 years active duty, followed by 20 years in the reserves. At the end of the two years, each man is given a fully automatic 9 mm rifle to take home and keep for life. When the Nazis invaded Norway in World War II, the first thing they did was go door to door and confiscate all guns. They found very few, because most had been buried. Many were badly rusted, but they allowed the resistance to kill Germans. The Nazis had a 10 for 1 edict, so when a German officer was killed, they would line up 10 Norwegian men and shoot them in front of their families. Norwegians vowed never to be occupied again, so now virtually every household has an automatic rifle. They truly understand that "the right of the people to keep and bear arms shall not be infringed."

1. http://www.press.uchicago.edu/Misc/Chicago/493636.html

2. http://caselaw.lp.findlaw.com/data/constitution/amendment02/

3. http://www.dailypaul.com/177341/can-you-guess-who-has-the-worlds-largest-army

29 UNITED NATIONS

I would issue an order to immediately move the United Nations headquarters from New York City to Babylon in Iraq. I would also issue an order that countries who vote against the U.S. in the U.N. more than 50% of the time will not receive any foreign aid. Finally, I would cut back extracurricular payments to the U.N. such as peacekeeping. The United States has the maximum assessed contribution to the United Nations regular budget - 22%. In 2009, the assessed amount is $600,000,000. The minimum assessed contribution is 0.001%. The scale of assessments for each U.N. member for the required contributions to the regular budget is determined every three years on the basis of Gross National Product. Only nine countries (starting with the largest contributor: United States, Japan, Germany, United Kingdom, France, Italy, Canada, Spain, China) contribute 75% of the entire regular budget. Cuba contributes .043% of the regular budget. Saudi Arabia contributes .0713%.

The idea of moving U.N. headquarters seems to resonate with many - those who believe that the U.S. is being manipulated by anti-American and anti-Israel elements within the U.N., as well as those who feel that the U.S. is doing the manipulation. For Americans, it would of course mean the loss of a global status symbol. However, it would also mean the reacquisition of valuable New York real estate, fewer cases of diplomatic immunity for the legal systems, and perhaps a reduction of anti-American sentiment worldwide.

Where should it go? Try Iraq. While moving the U.N. headquarters to Venezuela or Iran is probably not wise, moving it to Iraq might be a strategic coup. There is even a ready-made location for it - Saddam Hussein's 600-room palace and compound constructed over the remains of the ancient city of Babylon. Americans might even consider footing the bill for the relocation. Think about it. If the U.S. should be forced to abruptly withdraw from Iraq, a peacekeeping force - something similar to the International Security Assistance Force now in Afghanistan - would probably be deployed. Yet peacekeeping forces under temporary mandates, with all the associated communications problems, functional restrictions, and managerial arguments that so often spring from ego or nationalistic pride, generally won't work. They would be even less visible in a region like Iraq, where the threat of kidnapping and indescribable torture would keep many countries from participating. Relocating U.N. headquarters to Iraq, however, might actually be a reasonable alternative.

Former U.N. Secretary General Kofi Annan agreed with member states demands for the U.S. to leave Iraq. Yet he admitted that any force reductions would have to be planned so as not to lead to greater violence and instability. Moving the U.N. to Iraq might be the only method of insuring that a departure of U.S. forces would not leave the country and the region in chaos.

Considering the severe cutbacks in U.N. personnel within Iraq following the 2004 truck bombing of its Baghdad compound, the idea might seem ridiculous, but the mission of the U.N. is to promote and preserve peace. In order to maintain its fledgling democracy, Iraq needs international commitment, an inducement to stop factional violence, and a stable form of income not subject to the terrorists' reprisals. It is hard to imagine a more visible and binding form of commitment than a change of such magnitude. The prestige factor alone might guarantee stability. Middle East leaders may seize upon the move as recognition of the region's importance, thus stimulating their sense of self and nationalist esteem while gaining further incentive for dealing internecine conflict. It would be to the benefit of all members to ensure the security of the new headquarters. A multinational coalition under the auspices of a collocated U.N. would be perceived as a more neutral and acceptable force. Additionally, since the security of the U.N. would rest on the stability of the new Iraq regime and vice-versa, there would be a strong mutual interest in maintaining a working relationship between the multinational coalition and the security forces of Iraq.

As a model for coexistence, a resident U.N. headquarters could inspire the three factors within Iraq to forgo violence, thus reducing the need for security forces. The move might even satisfy Iran's leaders sufficiently for them to quit sending weapons into Iraq. Hugo Chavez (as a new-found friend of Iran's President Mahmud Ahmadinejad) and possibly even militant Islamic extremists (Suni or Shia) would find it hard to justify verbal or physical attacks on a U.N. headquarters in the heart of the Middle East.

New York is an expensive city, and representation at the U.N. is currently a costly endeavor. Poor countries would benefit from the move, since costs associated with membership would be drastically reduced. Representatives who may have been selected specifically because of social status or wealth might be replaced with individuals who maintain a higher commitment to the U.N. mission. The remaining big spenders should have a positive effect on the Iraqi job market and improve the overall economy of the entire region, which might in turn reduce the tendency to engage in violence. With such a large and formidable presence, fundamental human rights ranging from honor killing and female infanticide to state-imposed death sentences for children, religious converts and political dissidents (as opposed to those U.S. representatives have publicly identified as driven by "anti-Israel bias") could be more be effectively addressed.

What's in it for the United States? For those Americans disappointed with the malfeasance often associated with the U.N. leadership, the move would be a victory. It could be similarly spun for those who feel that the U.S. has not been sufficiently deferent to or reliant upon the U.N. -an implication that the U.N. could and should do what the sole superpower could not. Domestically, the move would be a win-win scenario. Globally, a move from American soil - where location might appear to indicate ownership -could reduce anti-Americanism. It might change the perception of the U.S. from that of a superpower with imperial aspirations to simply a member of a global force for peace.[1]

While America's standing in the Middle East couldn't get much lower, you wouldn't know it looking at the U.S. foreign aid budget. Of the proposed U.S. financial assistance for 2012, almost two-thirds of that amount is earmarked for Muslim nations and one-third goes to Arab countries. Yet, despite those billions in aid, opinion polls show most Arab citizens still have an unfavorable view of America, and most Muslim nations routinely vote against U.S. interests in the United Nations. "If we are giving money to countries consistently voting against our interest, we ought to cut them off," says Congressman Steve Chabot (R-OH) who sits on the House Foreign Affairs Committee. "But Congress is going to need to get some backbone here because it consistently gives Presidents the ability to waive the cut-off of that money."[2]

Here are the percentages for the times Arab countries vote against the United States at the U.N.

Kuwait 67%
Qatar 67%
Morocco 70%
United Arab Emirates 70%
Jordan 71%
Tunisia 71%
Saudi Arabia 73%
Yemen 74%
Algeria 74%
Oman 74%
Sudan 75%
Libya 76%
Egypt 79%
Lebanon 80%
India 81%
Syria 84%
Mauritania 87%

"Foreign aid might be defined as a transfer of money from poor people in rich countries to rich people in poor countries." - Douglas Casey

Here is our foreign aid to those that hate us. Egypt receives $2 Billion annually in U.S. foreign aid. Jordan receives $193 Million. Pakistan receives $1.8 Billion. India receives $150 Million. Algeria receives $80 Million. Oman receives $74 Million.

The Palestinian Territories receive $3 Billion, yet just 18% have a favorable view of the U.S. Years ago, U.N. Ambassador John Bolton proposed cutting off all aid to the 30 nations who consistently voted against the U.S. in the United Nations. Before him, President Reagan's U.N. Ambassador Jeane Kirkpatrick proposed cutting off $1 million in aid for each vote an aid recipient cast against the U.S. in the U.N. In both cases, Bolton says the State Department overruled them. "Foreign aid to a lot of countries could be readily cut, and I think it's been a mistake by the U.S. government for decades not to take U.N. voting into account." Bolton said. Some other Muslim countries show almost no friendship or allegiance to the U.S. but continue to see the State Department shower them with money.

"The U.S. has to quit being kicked around. We need to quit sending our tax dollars to countries that do not have our best interests in mind, especially in these economic times.", says Congressman Chabot. Instead, if you look at U.S. aid over time, it's largely on auto-pilot. Once a nation is on the U.S. gravy train, few are ever cut off, regardless of their loyalty, gratitude or actions. In our analysis of the numbers, of the President's 2011 foreign assistance request of $34.5 billion, 60% or $20.1 billion goes to Muslim nations, or those where a majority practice Islam. About 33% or the total budget, or $11.6 billion is awarded to Arab countries.

Countries that vote with the United States most often are Palau 98.5%, Micronesia 94%, Israel 92%, Nauru 88%, Marshall Islands 81%, Canada 75% United Kingdom 74%, Australia 73%, France 72%, Czech Republic 63%, Lithuania 63%, and Slovak Republic 83%.

1. http://onfaith.washingtonpost.com/postglobal/needtoknow/2007/04/want_middle_east_stability_mov.html

2. http://politics.blogs.foxnews.com/2011/05/24/its-all-your-money-foreign-aid-muslimarab-nations

30 ISRAEL

The reason I am including chapters on Israel and the Palestinians are that the fate of the whole world depends upon what happens there. I would issue an order that after protecting the United States from all enemies, foreign and domestic, the next most important principle of our Government policy is the support and protection of the nation of Israel. I would also issue an order doubling the size of aid to Israel from $3 Billion to $6 Billion. About 4000 years ago, God determined to call out a special people for Himself through whom He would bring blessing to all the nations. Why did He select one man (Abraham) and one tiny nation (Israel) to accomplish this? Only God knows. In Genesis 12:3, God states, "I will bless those who bless you, and I will curse him who curses you". Modern Israel is a miracle, created In November 1947, when the U.N. General Assembly voted to partition the British mandate of Palestine into two territories that were envisioned as future states -one predominantly Jewish, the other Arab.

Deuteronomy 7:6,7,8. "For you are a holy people to the LORD your God; the LORD your God has chosen you to be a people for His own possession, out of all the peoples that are on the face of the earth. It was not because you were more in number than any other people that the LORD set His love upon you and chose you, for you were the fewest of all peoples; but it is because the LORD loves you, and is keeping the oath which He swore to your fathers."

Jeremiah: 31:10, 12, 33. "Hear the word of the LORD, O nations, and declare it in the coastlands afar off; say, He who scattered Israel will gather him, and will keep him as a shepherd keeps his flock. They shall come and sing aloud on the height of Zion, and they shall be radiant over the goodness of the LORD, over the grain, the wine, and the oil, over the young of the flock and the herd; their life shall be like a watered garden, and they shall languish no more. But this is the covenant which I will make with the house of Israel after those days, says the LORD; I will put My law within them, and I will write it upon their hearts; and I will be their God, and they shall be My people."

Israel is the 100th smallest country, with less than 1/1000th of the world's population. Israel is the only liberal democracy in the Middle East. In 1984 and 1991, Israel airlifted a total of 22,000 Ethiopian Jews (Operation Solomon) at risk in Ethiopia, to safety in Israel. When Golda Meir was elected Prime Minister of Israel in 1969, she became the world's second elected female leader in modern times. Israel's $100 billion economy is larger than all of its immediate neighbors combined. Israel leads the world in the number of scientists and technicians in the workforce, with 145 per 10,000, as opposed to 85 in the U.S., 70 in Japan, and less than 60 in Germany. With over 25% of its work force employed in technical professions, Israel places first in this category as well. Israel has the highest average living standards in the Middle East. The per capita income in 2010 was over $25,500, exceeding that of the UK. Relative to its population, Israel is the largest immigrant-absorbing nation on earth. Immigrants come in search of democracy, religious freedom, and economic opportunity, with hundreds of thousands from the former Soviet Union. When the U.S. Embassy in Nairobi, Kenya was bombed in 1998, Israeli rescue teams were on the scene within a day - and saved three victims from the rubble.

The Middle East has been growing date palms for centuries. The average tree is about 18-20 feet tall and yields about 38 pounds of dates a year. Israeli date trees are now yielding 400 pounds per year and are short enough to be harvested from the ground or a short ladder. Israel is the only country in the world that entered the 21st century with a net gain in its number of trees, made more remarkable because this was achieved in an area considered mainly desert. An Israeli company was the first to develop and install a large-scale solar-powered and fully functional electricity generating plant, in southern California's Mojave Desert.

Israel has the fourth largest air force in the world (after the U.S., Russia, and China). In addition to a large variety of other aircraft, Israel's air force has an aerial arsenal of over 250 F-16's. This is the largest fleet of F-16 aircraft outside of the U.S. In proportion to its population, Israel has the largest number of startup companies in the world. In absolute terms, Israel has the largest number of startup companies than any other country in the world, except the U.S. (3,500 companies, mostly in hi-tech). With more than 3,000 high-tech companies and startups, Israel has the highest concentration of high-tech companies in the world - apart from the Silicon Valley. Israel is ranked #2 in the world for venture capital funds right behind the United States. Besides the United States and Canada, Israel has the largest number of NASDAQ listed companies. According to industry officials, Israel designed the airline industry's most impenetrable flight security. U.S. officials now look (finally) to Israel for advice on how to handle airborne security threats.

Israel has the highest percentage in the world of home computers per capita. Israel has the highest ratio of university degrees to the population in the world. Israel produces more scientific papers per capita than any other nation by a large margin - 109 per 10,000 people - as well as one of the highest per capita rates of patents filed. On a per capita basis, Israel has the largest number of biotech startups. Twenty-four per cent of Israel's workforce holds university degrees, ranking third in the industrialized world, after the United States and Holland and 12 per cent hold advanced degrees. Israel has the world's second highest per capita of new books. Israel has more museums per capita than any other country.

The cell phone was developed in Israel by Israelis working in the Israeli branch of Motorola, which has its largest development center in Israel. Most of the Windows NT and XP operating systems were developed by Microsoft-Israel. The Pentium MMX Chip technology was designed in Israel at Intel. Both the Pentium-4 microprocessor and the Centrino processor were entirely designed, developed and produced in Israel. The Pentium microprocessor in your computer was most likely made in Israel. Voice mail technology was developed in Israel. Both Microsoft and Cisco built their only research and development facilities outside the U.S. in Israel. The technology for the AOL Instant Messenger ICQ was developed in 1996 by four young Israelis. Israel was the first nation in the world to adopt the Kimberly process, an international standard that certifies diamonds as "conflict free."

Israeli scientists developed the first fully-computerized, no-radiation, diagnostic instrumentation for breast cancer. An Israeli company developed a computerized system for ensuring proper administration of medications, thus removing human error from medical treatment. Every year in U.S. hospitals 7,000 patients die from treatment mistakes. Israel's Given Imaging developed the first ingestible video camera, so small it fits inside a pill. It is used to view the small intestine from the inside for cancer and digestive disorders. Researchers in Israel developed a new device that directly helps the heart pump blood, an innovation with the potential to save lives among those with heart failure. The new device is synchronized with the camera and helps doctors diagnose the heart's mechanical operations through a sophisticated system of sensors. A new acne treatment developed in Israel, the Clear Light device, produces a high-intensity, ultraviolet-light-free, narrow-band blue light that causes acne bacteria to self-destruct - all without damaging surrounding skin or tissue.

All the above were accomplished while engaged in regular wars with an implacable enemy that seeks Israel's destruction and an economy continuously under strain by having to spend more per capita on its own protection than any other county on earth. How could they do all these things? They are God's chosen people!

31 PALESTINIANS

I would issue an order that we will support Israel in whatever peace agreement they reach with the Palestinians. I will also issue a statement that the United States does not recognize there has ever been a nation known as "Palestine" in the history of the world.

Since 1955, there have been 75 resolutions in the U.N. condemning Israel for some perceived injustice against the Palestinians, more than all other nations in the world combined. Here is one of the most egregious, during the Clinton administration. With the United States abstaining, the U.N. Security Council adopted a resolution that condemns United Nations actions that facilitated and created the state of Israel. In 1947, after extensive evaluation of the situation, the United Nations Special Committee on Palestine (UNSCOP) proposed that the territory of the British mandate west of the Jordan River be partitioned into Jewish and Arab states with Jerusalem under international control. On November 29, 1947, the U.N. adopted a partition plan. Both the United States and the Union of Soviet Socialist Republics voted in favor, while Britain abstained. Zionists reluctantly accepted the plan as the best resolution they could expect given political circumstances, but the Arab world denounced and rejected it. This new resolution condemns the actions of the United Nations in creating the state of Israel, which has resulted in injury and loss of human life. "The United States does not think it was a very good resolution, to put it mildly." U.S. Ambassador Richard Holbrooke told reporters after the vote. "Basically the resolution is saying that Israel is the reason for the violence in the Middle East, and that not for the actions of the United Nations, Israel would never have become an independent nation. But President Clinton decided in the end he did not find enough objectionable in the resolution to veto it." he said. But Nasser al-Kidwa, the Palestinian U.N. observer, said

"We think that the resolution contains an extremely important element. But for the existence of Israel there would be no violence today, and without the actions of the United Nations in 1947, the state of Israel may never have been created. Just think of the lives that could have been saved."

There is a preliminary historic fact that must be established now. There has never, I repeat never, been a civilization or a nation referred to as "Palestine", and the very notion of a "Palestinian" Arab nation having ancient attachments to the Holy Land going back to time immemorial is one of the biggest hoaxes ever perpetrated upon the world! There is not, nor has there ever been, a distinct Palestinian culture or language. Further, there has never been a Palestinian state governed by "Arab Palestinians" in history, nor was there ever a Palestinian national movement until after the 1967 Six-Day War, when Israel regained control over Judea and Samaria (the so-called "West Bank"). It was then, and only then, that a Palestinian national movement born with one primary goal: the creation of an Arab Palestinian state with which to replace Israel. It's really that simple!

Israel became a nation in 1312 B.C., two thousand years before the rise of Islam! Seven hundred and twenty-six years later in 586 B.C., these first ancient Jews were overrun and the first Jewish Temple (on Jerusalem's Old City Temple Mount) was destroyed by Nebuchadnezzar, king of ancient Babylon. Many of the Jews were killed or expelled; however many were allowed to remain. These Jews, along with their progeny and other Jews who would resettle over the next 500 years, rebuilt the nation of Israel. Thus, the claim that Jews suddenly appeared fifty years ago, right after the Holocaust, and drove out the "ancient Arab Palestinians" is preposterous. Then in 70 A.D. (nearly 2000 years ago), it was the Roman Empire's turn to march through ancient Israel and destroy the second Jewish Temple, slaughtering or driving out much of its Jewish population. Many Jews left on their own because conditions for life were made unbearable in many respects - yet thousands stayed and rebelled on for centuries in order to once again rebuild a Jewish nation in this Holy Land.

Over the next 2,000 years various Peoples, Religions and Empires marched through Jerusalem, Israel's ancient capital. None bothered, nor were in the least interested in, building a nation of their own. Included in these "invaders" were the Arabs. Thus, in the year 636 A.D., Arab marauders came to the land and uprooted even more of its Jews. However, they too did not form an Arab nation... and certainly not a "Palestinian" nation. They were simply "Arabs" who moved in a geo-political area called "Palestine!" And remember this one fact. - it was not the Jews who "usurped" (a favorite word from the Arab propagandists) the land from the

Arabs. If anything, it was the Arabs in 636 who overran and stole it from the Jews. In Conclusion, no nation, other than the ancient nation of Israel and later in 1948 the reborn nation of Israel, has ever ruled as a sovereign national entity on this land. A mighty Jewish empire extended over this entire area before the Arabs and their Islam were even born! Want to talk religion? Fine. God gave the Land of Israel to the Jewish People. And God does nothing by accident!

The term "Palestine" came from the name that the conquering Roman Empire gave the ancient Land of Israel in an attempt to once again obliterate the Jewish presence in the Holy Land. The Roman Procurator in charge of the Judean-Israel territories was so angry at the Jews for revolting that he called for his historians and asked, "Who were the worst enemies of the Jews in their past history?" The scribes said, "the Philistines." So, the Procurator declared that Land of Israel would from then on be called "Philistia" [further bastardized into "Palaistina" to dishonor the Jews and obliterate their history. Henceforth came the name "Palestine." Even 900 years later when the Ottoman Empire - Turkey - had its turn to conquer the area, the term "Palestine" was still maintained to describe one of its districts. Palestine was a place within the Ottoman Empire... and never an empire of its own. Indeed Syria did not exist, nor did Jordan or Lebanon. It was all a vast tract of the Turkish Empire loosely called "Palestine." The name "Palestine" has nothing whatsoever to do with Jews, Chinese, Cambodians, Martians and certainly not the Arabs! It was merely a term first created by the Roman Empire for their political purposes. The Arabs never give up trying to provide an historical link between the Arab "Palestinians" and the land. Some have even tried to link the name "Palastin" (which they use for "Palestine") with the ancient "Philistines!" The real ancient Philistines, however, were not Arabs, and neither was Goliath. They were a migrant "Sea Peoples" who came from the area of the Aegean Sea and the Greek Islands and settled on the southern coast of the land of Canaan. In contrast, the Arabs of "Palestine" are just that - Arabs! They have about as much historical roots to the ancient Philistines as Yasser Arafat had to the Eskimos.

The Land of Israel was never devoid of Jews, although at times, only in the tens of thousands. This was because the land was virtually uninhabitable when the Jews once again began their God-given right and duty to return en masse to the land of their forefathers (the Zionist Movement) in the 1880s. The silly rhetoric about a massive Arab presence being overrun by "invading Jews" is quickly dispelled by Mark Twain, who visited the area in 1867.

From his book, *The Innocents Abroad*:

"A desolate country whose soil is rich enough, but is given over wholly to weeds - a silent mournful expanse. A desolation. We never saw a human being on the whole route - hardly a tree or shrub anywhere. Even the olive tree and the cactus, those fast friends of a worthless soil, had almost deserted the country.

But the severest thing that has been said about Palestine was said here in Jerusalem. A pilgrim with his periodic ecstasy upon him (it usually comes in a flush of happiness after dinner) finished his apostrophe with,

'O, that I could be here at the Second Advent!'

A grave gentleman said, 'It will not occur in Palestine.'

'What?'

'The Second Advent will take place elsewhere - possibly in America.'

'Blasphemy!'

'I speak reasonably. You are in the Holy Land. You have seen the Holy Land once?'

'Yes.'

'Shall you ever want to come here again?'

'Well - no.'

'My friend, the Savior has been here once!'"

"Palestine's" early Jewish re-settlers in the 1890's were idealistic pioneers who arrived in pre-state Israel with every intention of living in peace alongside their Arab neighbors and upgrading the quality of life for all of the land's inhabitants. The vast majority of Arabs came to the area after these early Zionists pioneers began to drain the malaria-infested swamps and rebuild the land. In doing so, these Jews created the economic opportunities and medical availabilities that attracted Arabs from both surrounding territories and far-away lands. In fact, over 90% of the Arabs migrated there within the last one hundred years. So much for their unfounded claims that they have been there since "time immemorial!" Yet while the returning Jews were highly motivated to restore the land, the Arabs seethed with envy and hatred because they lacked both the leadership to inspire or motivate them, for they in fact were historical strangers to this land! Unlike the Jews, these Arabs who immigrated there had no ancient attachments or historical memories to this homeland ... this ancient Land of the Jews!

In Conclusion: There was no "Arab Palestinian" history before the Arabs created one after 1948 and especially after 1967. Archeological sites to this very day continue to yield artifacts with Hebrew writing, not some fictitious "Palestinian" or Arabic text. The so-called "Palestinian" Arabs were simply then, as they are now, Arabs no different culturally, historically or ethnically from other Arabs living in any other of the 24 Arab countries from which they came into "Palestine!" Had the Chinese come to the area, they too would be called "Palestinians!" The Arabs continue to brainwash generation upon generation into believing this historic hogwash about some "ancient" Arab Palestinian ties to the Holy Land. Most could have gotten themselves a real life by now with much less bloodshed and suffering for everyone concerned!

The Arabs have greed, pride, and envy! The Arabs of today occupy 24 nations. That is 99½% of the entire Middle East landmass while Israel has only a half of 1% speck on this same map. But that's still too much land for the Arabs to spare. They want it all, and that is ultimately what all the fighting is about today. No matter how many land concessions the Israelis might make, it will never be enough! Peace treaties between the Israeli and the Arab world are meaningless. Even the Israeli-Egyptian peace treaty is holding on by a single thread and if you were to read the Egyptian and Jordanian newspapers you'd think they were still at war with Israel! Peace is impossible - the death of compromise. There's No More Middle in the Middle East. The Arab campaign against Israel is rooted not in a negotiable grievance but in a basic opposition to the very existence of Jewish sovereignty! The intent of the Arabs is to separate out Judaism from Israel... and then to separate Israel from the face of the Earth.

The Question of Jerusalem and the Temple Mount: For over 3,300 years, Jerusalem has only been a Jewish capital - the only Jewish capital, founded by King David. Jews have always lived in Jerusalem, except when they had been massacred or driven out. There has been a nearly unbroken Jewish presence in the Jerusalem for the past 1,600 years, and at least since the early 1800s, the population of Jerusalem has been predominantly Jewish. Even when the Jordanians occupied Jerusalem from 1948-67, they (the Jordanians) never sought to change it to their capital (replacing

Amman) nor make it the capital of any "Arab Palestinian" people. In fact, Arab leaders from other Arab countries hardly ever bothered to visit Jerusalem! Only to the Jews has Jerusalem ever held special meaning! Another myth deals with the issue of Jerusalem and its Temple Mount. The myth is that Jerusalem is really an Arab city and that it is a central focus of Islam. The truth is that the Arabs expressed very limited interest in the Temple Mount before 1967. Besides, Mecca and Medina (both in Saudi Arabia) are Islam's holiest cities! One more thing about Jerusalem in general and its Temple Mount in particular: Islam's holy(?) Koran mentions Mecca (in Saudi Arabia) hundreds of times. It mentions Medina (also in Saudi Arabia) countless times. It never mentions Jerusalem and with good reason. There is no historical evidence to suggest Mohammad ever visited Jerusalem! And if he did visit Jerusalem, it could not have been until 6 years after his death. Therefore, the notion that Mohammed ascended to Heaven from a rock in Jerusalem is even more ridiculous!

From 1948 to 1967, when East Jerusalem and the Temple Mount were under Muslim (Jordanian) rule, they were ignored by the Arab world. No Arab leader ever paid a visit, not even to pray at the al-Al-Aqsa Mosque or the Dome of the Rock (both located on the Jewish Temple Mount). Arab "Palestinians" placed so low a priority on Jerusalem itself that the PLO's founding charter, the Palestinian National Covenant of 1964, made no reference to it. Only when the Jews recaptured it after the 1967 "Six Day War" did the Arab world suddenly grow very passionate about Jerusalem! In truth, the Dome of the Rock and the Al-Aqsa mosques are just but two of hundreds of thousands of Muslim mosques around the world. When a Jew prays from anywhere in the world, he faces the Temple Mount in Jerusalem. When a Moslem prays, even while IN Jerusalem, he faces Mecca (in Saudi Arabia). So in many cases, even when a Moslem is in Jerusalem, his "hind quarters" are facing these two mosques! What does this tell you? And, when Islamic suicide bombers try to take apart Jerusalem piece by piece, what does that tell you?

32 TRADE

I would issue an order that the United States will promote free trade between all nations. The only caveat will be, that the barriers of tariffs and protectionism must be reduced or eliminated by our trading partners and that currency exchange rates must be adjusted to reflect international realities, not artificially supported by a nation's government.

The Greek poet Homer, in his Odyssey, waxed poetic about the influence of trade: "For the Cyclops have no ships with crimson prows, no shipwrights there to build them good trim craft that could sail them out to foreign ports of call as most men risk the seas to trade with other men". Such artisans would have made this island also a decent place to live. The Judeo-Christian Bible warns against the pride that can come with riches, but it does not condemn international trade. In the Bible in 1 Kings, it reports that trade was part of King Solomon's splendor: "The king had a fleet of trading ships at sea along with the ships of Hiram. Once every three years it returned, carrying gold, silver and ivory, and apes and baboons." In the New Testament, in the second chapter of Matthew, we read about the famous wise men of the East, who traveled from Arabia or perhaps as far away as Persia to bring gold, frankincense, and myrrh to the baby Jesus. (Thank goodness they didn't have to contend with airport customs or the Arab boycott of Israel.) The Old Testament prophet Ezekiel does warn the citizens of Tyre, the bustling Mediterranean port city, "By your great skill in trading you have increased your wealth, and because of your wealth your heart has grown proud." Even when the Bible speaks harshly of the "merchants of the earth", it is not international trade that comes under condemnation but the intent and character of the traders. The sin is not trade but dishonest scales, greed, indulgence in luxuries, and the temptation to pride that can come from wealth. In this respect, trade is no more sinful than technological discoveries or hard work.

A number of theologians and philosophers in the first several centuries A.D. considered trade among nations a gift of God. In his 1996 book, *Against the Tide: An Intellectual History of Free Trade*, Professor Douglas Irwin of Dartmouth College describes this early view of trade that has come to be called the Doctrine of Universal Economy. That doctrine held that God had spread resources and goods unevenly throughout the world to promote commerce between different nations and regions. In the fourth century A.D., the pagan writer Libanius expanded the doctrine more fully, declaring: God did not bestow all products upon all parts of the earth, but distributed His gifts over different regions, to the end that men might cultivate a social relationship because one would have need of the help of another. And so, He called commerce into being, that all men might be able to have common enjoyment of the fruits of earth, no matter where produced. Western moral thought provides a solid foundation for pursuing a policy of economic openness. Drawing on that tradition, here are moral arguments to support free trade among nations. A man or woman engaged in honest work has a basic right to enjoy the fruits of his or her labor. It is a violation of my right to property for the government to forbid me to exchange what I produce for something produced by a fellow human being, whether the person I'm trading with lives across town or across the ocean. Protectionism is a form of stealing, a violation of the Eighth Commandment and other prohibitions against theft. Free trade meets the most elementary test of justice, giving to each person sovereign control over that which is his own. As Frederic Bastiat wrote in his 1849 essay, *Protectionism and Communism*, "Every citizen who has produced or acquired a product should have the option of applying it immediately to his own use or of transferring it to whoever on the face of the earth agrees to give him in exchange the object of his desires. To deprive him of this option when he has committed no act contrary to public order and good morals, and solely to satisfy the convenience of another citizen, is to legitimize an act of plunder and to violate the law of justice."[1]

U.S. trade policy is almost always debated in terms of economic utility: Does free trade raise or lower incomes? Does it help or hurt U.S. industry? Does it create or destroy jobs? But behind the statistics and anecdotes lie moral assumptions about human nature, the sovereignty of the individual, and the role of government in a free society. Free trade may deliver the goods and boost efficiency, but is it morally superior to protectionism? In a speech in May before the Council of the Americas, President Bush joined the moral debate, telling his audience: "Open trade is not just an economic opportunity, it is a moral imperative. Trade creates jobs for the unemployed. When we negotiate for open markets, we are providing new hope for the world's poor. And when we promote open trade, we are promoting political freedom. Societies that open to commerce across their borders will open to democracy within their borders, not always immediately, and not always smoothly, but in good time." Friends of free trade should not shrink from making moral arguments for their cause; those arguments have deep roots in our culture. To promote economic growth, the Administration should advance more free trade agreements and lead negotiations at the World Trade Organization to eliminate agricultural subsidies, antidumping measures, and other protectionist policies that benefit a very small group of Americans at the expense of most other citizens. In addition, instead of threatening to impose barriers against inexpensive imports, the Administration should lower the tax and regulatory burden on U.S. companies so that they can be more competitive. Moving toward greater, not less, economic freedom benefits all Americans.[2]

Free trade is again under attack, despite having been, for over a century, the basis of America's wealth. Some groups in the United States blame free trade for the loss of manufacturing jobs, while others blame it for exposing some U.S. producers to foreign competition. Free trade, however, is good for America, and for a very simple reason: It allows American workers to specialize in goods and services that they produce more efficiently than the rest of the world and then to exchange them for goods and services that other countries produce at higher quality and lower cost. Specialization and free trade allow the U.S. to become more competitive and innovative. Innovation constantly provides new technologies that allow Americans to produce more, cure more diseases, pollute less, improve education, and choose from a greater range of investment opportunities. The resulting economic growth generates better-paying jobs, higher standards of living, and a greater appreciation of the benefits of living in a peaceful society. New technologies bring about change, which, as U.S. economic history shows, benefits society as a whole. In the process, however, some sectors suffer until they can adapt to the new changes and begin to benefit from them. Today, Americans are experiencing some of that "suffering" because new technologies are challenging old methods of production. This change is especially visible in the manufacturing sector, just as it was in the agricultural sector 100 years ago. But in the same way that it adapted then to a new, more industry-based society, America will adapt again to a new, more knowledge-based society. American Administrations should support free trade by all means at its disposal. Keeping America free of protectionism and special favors helps to generate opportunities and fosters economic growth. Economic growth is of particular importance today because eliminating the large federal budget deficit requires either growth to generate tax revenues or something even harder to come by - the political will to cut spending.

For over a century, free trade has been one of the most important determinants of America's wealth and strength. There are several important reasons for continuing to support free trade. The most compelling reason is that society as a whole benefits from it. Free trade improves people's living standards because it allows them to consume higher quality goods at less expensive prices. In the 19th century, British economist David Ricardo said that any nation that focuses on producing goods in which it has a comparative advantage will be able to get cheaper and better goods from other countries in return. As a result of the exchange, both trading parties gain from producing more efficiently and consuming higher quality goods and services at lower prices. Trade between nations is the same as trade between people. Consider what the quality of life would be if each person had to produce absolutely everything that he or she consumed, such as food, clothing, cars, or home repairs. Compare that picture with life as it is now as individuals dedicate themselves to working on just one thing to earn a salary. It simply makes sense for each person to work at what he or she does best and buy the rest. As a nation, the United States exports in order to purchase imports which other nations produce more skillfully and inexpensively. Therefore, the fewer barriers erected against trade with other nations, the more access people will have to the best, least expensive goods and services in the world "supermarket." Producers benefit as well. In the absence of trade barriers, producers face greater competition from foreign producers, and this increased competition gives them an incentive to improve the quality of their products or services while keeping prices low.

With new technologies evolving continuously at home and abroad, open economies are constantly challenged to change the way they do business. In the process of adapting to change, some sectors suffer until they can adapt to the new changes and begin to benefit from them. During the Industrial Revolution, workers in the agricultural sector had to adapt to the "new industrial economy", competing with machines that could do the same work more efficiently. Eventually, the agricultural workers trained themselves to use machinery and seized the opportunity to be part of the new industrial economy. Today, America again faces major economic changes. The U.S. economy is moving from an industry-based to a knowledge-based model. For example, the U.S. textile industry gradually disappeared during the past two decades because it became increasingly less competitive vis-à-vis the lower cost of labor in foreign countries. As a result, many U.S. textile factories shut down their operations. South Carolina was one of the states most affected by the shutdown of textile factories. South Carolinians, however, did not become permanently unemployed, because other industries moved to the state to take advantage of a trained labor force. In 2000, BMW leased a research facility at Clemson University's automotive research campus to train engineers to sustain BMW's growth. IBM and Microsoft each contributed to this project with the idea of creating high-paying jobs tied to knowledge. Through this project, BMW "invested $2.5 billion at the plant, and now employs 4,700 people, with most production workers making $24 per hour." BMW's investment illustrates the process of adjustment in an economically open society. In order to remain competitive and benefit from the economic evolution brought about by the new knowledge-based technological change, South Carolina's workers trained themselves to seize the higher-paid job opportunities. The adjustment brought better-paying jobs and, with them, the possibility of raising the living standard of all those involved in the process of change.[3]

America is perhaps the world's best example of how competition fosters innovation. Although at times the United States has become somewhat protectionist, its economy has been built primarily on the principles of a free market, private enterprise, and competition. In such a competitive environment, new technologies, from computers to medicines to machinery, have helped the economy to become increasingly more productive per unit of labor and machinery employed in the production process. Since 1948, according to the Bureau of Labor Statistics, multifactor productivity - a ratio of output to combined inputs - in the U.S. private business sector has more than doubled. Productivity has fostered economic growth and, by lowering production costs, has given ordinary Americans the opportunity to raise their standard of living The U.S. economy is replete with illustrations of how competition fosters innovation. For example, in the 1980s, personal computers were very expensive, few people owned them, and those they did own handled only word texts and a few calculations. Due to increased competition, by 2002, 65.9 percent of people living in the United States owned a personal computer that handled text, calculations, graphics, media, Internet access, and many other functions. In 1975, the airline industry carried about 200 million passengers. Now, due to competition and lower costs, it carries almost 600 million passengers a year. In 1987, only 0.3 percent of Americans owned mobile phones. By 2002, 50 percent owned one. Similarly, in 1975, only 37.3 percent of people had a telephone mainline. Now, 64.6 percent have one. The percentage of people who own a television set soared from 48.6 percent in 1975 to 93.8 percent in 2001. These are just a few examples of the millions of products and services made available to increasing numbers of people, thanks to the opening of trade and to the freedom of the U.S. economy. America's ability to compete and innovate derives from its open markets and from the continual search for new markets through the expansion of free trade. Goods and services flowing across borders foster new ideas and allow U.S. producers to learn about the market through the failure and success of traded products. As they learn more, they are able to innovate to remain competitive.[4]

1. http://www.libertarianism.org/publications/essays/seven-moral-arguments-free-trade

2. http://www.cato.org/publications/commentary/seven-moral-arguments-free-trade

3. http://www.heritage.org/research/reports/2004/05/why-america-needs-to-support-free-trade

4. http://www.cato.org/publications/commentary/logic-trade

33 MEDIA

I would issue no order concerning the fourth estate (the press). The First Amendment (Amendment 1) of the U.S. Constitution -part of the Bill of Rights - is explicit in protecting the rights of free speech and the press. The amendment prohibits the making of any law "respecting an establishment of religion" impeding the free exercise of religion, abridging the freedom of speech, infringing on the freedom of the press, interfering with the right to peaceably assemble or prohibiting the petitioning for a governmental redress of grievances. For decades, a majority of the mainstream media in all venues has had a distain for Christianity, the U.S. Constitution, United States military power, free enterprise, conservative Republican philosophy, our relations with Israel, and envy of wealth by private individuals and corporations. Many are environmental and income redistribution zealots who believe government has the answer to most problems. With the rise of the Internet, talk radio, and a 24/7 cable news cycle, the 6 o'clock evening news is no longer the source of information for the American public. Many major newspapers are in decline and financial trouble, and cable channels such as MSNBC are losing viewership in droves. It is not because of competition from other news sources, it is because of political correctness and liberal or "progressive" bias and ideology. In this chapter I will document some representative examples.

This is how today's mainstream press and the Democrats would report D-Day, 1944. "Roosevelt, with his poodle Churchill, has escalated the war in Europe. Rather than finding work for them, Roosevelt has sent thousands of underprivileged Americans to their certain death. In a last letter before he was killed, Private Jose Alvarez told how unsafe he felt going into battle against the far superior Nazi Panthers in his thinly armored Sherman deathtrap. His father said, "Roosevelt is getting rich by sending barrio kids off to die." Roosevelt exaggerated U.S. military strength before the invasion. Mistakes lead to hundreds of unnecessary American deaths on Omaha beach. This is much too high a price to pay. Bring the troops home now! After the "Day of Infamy", Roosevelt still hasn't invaded Japan. He is now fighting German forces (Germany has not attacked the U.S.) in France. U.S. soldiers desecrated a French church by killing a sniper in the church tower. D-Day protestors in New York are chanting, "No blood for Brie!" The League of Nations say that sanctions would have worked. That idiot Roosevelt should have used billions wasted on the illegal war in Europe for domestic priorities, such as raising teacher's salaries."

Here is a classic liberal offensive rant by Bill Moyers in November, 2002, immediately after the 2002 elections. "Way back in the 1950's when I first tasted politics and journalism, Republicans briefly controlled the White house and Congress. With the exception of Joseph McCarthy and his vicious ilk, they were a reasonable lot, presided over by that giant war hero, Dwight Eisenhower, who was conservative by temperament and moderate in the use of power. That brand of Republican is gone. And for the first time in the memory of anyone alive, the entire federal government -the Congress, the Executive, the Judiciary -is united behind a right-wing agenda for which George W. Bush believes he now has a mandate. That mandate includes the power to force pregnant women to give up control over their own lives. It includes using the taxing power to transfer wealth from working people to the rich. It includes giving corporations a free hand to eviscerate the environment and control the regulatory agencies meant to hold them accountable. And it includes secrecy on a scale you cannot imagine. Above all, it means judges with a political agenda appointed for life. If you like the Supreme Court that put George W. Bush in the White House, you will swoon over what is coming. And if you like God in government, get ready for the Rapture. These folks don't even mind you referring to the GOP as the party of God. Why else would the new House Majority Leader say that the Almighty is using him to promote a Biblical worldview in American politics? So it is a heady time in Washington -a heady time for piety, profits, and military power, all joined at the hip by ideology and money. Don't forget the money. It came pouring in this election, to both parties, from corporate America and others who expect the payback. Republicans out-raised Democrats by $184 million dollars. And came up with the big prize -monopoly control of the American government, and the power of the state to turn their ideology into the law of the land. Quite a bargain at any price."[1]

In World War II, the media repeatedly referred to our enemies, the

Germans and Japanese, with ethnic slurs and derogatory terms. The Obama administration is now creating revisionist history to even try and sanitize that period. Framed 60-year-old front-page newspaper headlines reading "Japs Surrender" are being removed from halls of VA hospitals. The Islamic terrorists of the Bush era are gone. Now there are violent extremists or man-caused disasters in a purge of the government's political lexicon. In the Pentagon's Quadrennial Defense Review, the words "Muslim" or "Islam" are not used. The Taliban and al Queda are called "non-state actors" and terrorist networks. The Obama administration wants to stop using the words "Illegal Alien", and replace them with "undocumented worker" or "undocumented immigrant", because both convey the same information without the powerful emotional and psychological inferences It seems the only group not immune from Justice Department political correctness is organized crime. In a news conference on January 20, 2011, Attorney General Eric Holder liberally used the words la Cosa Nostra, mafia, and mob. If they became "Illegal Aliens", "Islamic terrorists", or World War II enemies, they could avoid being labeled. With political correctness, drug dealers will soon be "unlicensed Pharmacists".[2]

Bill Keller's column for the New York Times's Sunday magazine, "Asking Candidates Tougher Questions About Faith," raised familiar liberal paranoia about the conservative religious views of Republican presidential candidates Mitt Romney, Michele Bachmann, and Rick Perry. The official headline for the print edition: "Not Just Between Them and Their God." Keller had no time for respectful criticism: "Mitt Romney and Jon Huntsman are Mormons, a faith that many conservative Christians have been taught is a 'cult' and that many others think is just weird." Keller, the outgoing executive editor for the Times, got off on the wrong foot by mockingly comparing the candidates' Christian beliefs to belief in space aliens. Then he made the latest in his impressive string of column factual errors, identifying the Catholic politician Rick Santorum as an evangelical Christian.

Linda Greenhouse, former Supreme Court reporter for the New York Times, posted her twice-monthly column Wednesday evening, on the dangers of today's conservative Supreme Court going "Over the Cliff" in defending...the right to free speech. You read that correctly: A liberal Times reporter is faulting a conservative Supreme Court for being on a "dangerous path" and showing "arid absolutism" by expanding the First Amendment's protections to corporations.

Greenhouse jump-started the discussion with a rarely-cited 1978 Court decision, First National Bank of Boston v. Bellotti.[3]

NBC Today previewed an upcoming Dateline interview with Dick Cheney about his new memoir and labeled the former Vice President "controversial" three times in less than a minute. Co-host Ann Curry proclaimed him to be "one of the most controversial figures of our time." Turning to correspondent Jamie Gangel, who conducted the interview, Curry noted: "I understand that you asked the former Vice President, in a wide-ranging conversation, about one of the biggest controversies of his time in office and that's the so-called enhanced interrogation techniques?" Gangel described how Cheney's book was "filled with revelations and he does not back down on those controversial programs he championed that made him such a lightning rod for criticism after 9/11." Referencing Dick Cheney's revelation in his new memoir that he urged President Bush to bomb a Syrian nuclear reactor in 2007, CNN's Kyra Phillips posed this obnoxious question to her panel: "Was Cheney even more of a hawk than we gave him credit for?" The upcoming release of Cheney's memoir, "In My Time," should re-ignite the media's decade-long war on the former Vice President, as he himself has predicted that the book will have "heads exploding" in Washington. In the book he detailed a meeting in 2007 where he was the only one the room supporting the bombing of the Syrian nuclear reactor. President Bush declined to take that approach, and Israel bombed the site months later.[4]

What Would You Do?, an ABC News hidden camera program that often engineers scenarios to expose the supposed bigotry of Americans, was asked on Wednesday to stop filming by the town of Greenwich, Connecticut. The ABC program uses a hidden camera to see how people react. On February 4, 2011, host John Quinones explained how the show hired an actor to play a security guard and pretend to harass Mexicans. The piece, billed as an investigation of Arizona's immigration law, featured the faux-security guard spewing, "If they're not legal citizens, they shouldn't be here. They should be deported. They look Mexican."

Another week, another new Obama scandal. Whatever that scandal is, you can bet the American mainstream media will be playing catch up and not having the glory of breaking the story. Over the past couple years, four major scandals have broken over the Obama administration, and it is a very sad (and frightening) truth that our pathetic, American, lapdog mainstream media are not responsible for breaking even a single one. Verizon? Nope, not our guys. That was the Brits over at The Guardian. IRS? Nope, not our guys. The IRS broke their own scandal with a planted question. The Justice Department's seizure of Associated Press phone records? Nope, not our guys. Believe it or not, the Associated Press didn't even break that story.

Like the IRS, we only found out because the Justice Department outed itself in a letter notifying the AP of what it had done. Benghazi? Are you kidding. With a couple of rare exceptions (Jake Tapper, Sharyl Attkisson) the media have spent the last eight months attacking those seeking the truth (Congress, Fox News)--not seeking the truth. It was the GOP congress that demanded the email exchanges concerning the shaping of the talking points, not the media. Left up to the media, we wouldn't know anything about Libya. All of the media's energy was collectively poured into ensuring the truth was never discovered. And do you want to know what makes this realization especially pathetic? In three of the four scandals (the AP being the exception), had our media been less interested in protecting the Obama administration and more interested in holding them accountable, these huge, career-making stories were right there for the taking. For over a year now, conservative Tea Party groups have been complaining about IRS harassment. But because Obama told them to, the media hate the Tea Party. So in the face of these complaints and even a few Congressional inquiries, the media either ignored the harassment reports or openly sided with the IRS. Obviously, you can say the same about Libya. All the dots were there to connect, with security failures, two weeks of lies, and the midnight arrest of some hapless filmmaker. But rather than do this, the media played goalie for Obama against Fox News and Darrell Issa. There are still plenty of dots to connect about Libya, but the new line is overreach, and already the lapdogs are in goalie formation. Politico missed the four biggest scoops of the Obama administration, and they have plenty of lazy, lapdog, sycophant company in that department. Our media are not only biased; it is an utter and complete failure and embarrassment. And although there are plenty of remaining table scraps to make meals out of, the media are already losing interest in the IRS, Libya, and AP scandals, but for only one reason - they are absolutely terrified of where they might lead. Get down on your knees and thank God for the conservative news media, Roger Ailes, and for the few true liberals left in the media, like Glenn Greenwald - who works for the Brits.

In the latest in a series of snipes from reporter Ashley Parker directed at Republican candidate Mitt Romney, a brief "Caucus" item in the New York Times, "Romney Stands By Corporations Remarks," suggested Romney's remark to a heckler that "corporations are people, my friend" made him look like "an out-of-touch millionaire." But isn't Romney right? (Parker's article first appeared in a different form online Wednesday afternoon.) The print version opened: Former Gov. Mitt Romney of Massachusetts stirred a bit of a tempest when he said on the campaign trail in Iowa that "corporations are people, my friend." Some called the remark tone deaf, saying it fed into the perception of him as an out-of-touch millionaire.

On the Today Show, Matt Lauer interviewed one of the wives of one of the Navy Seals killed in Afghanistan. He asked her what she would say to her children about their dad and how she would want them to remember him...She said, and I quote, "His love for Christ" and then continued with a few other things... This man loved his country and loved his God and gave his life for both, On the MSN homepage, when the story was replayed they edited out the "Love of Christ" part...Why? Because saying the name Christ might offend someone, and as Christians we are asked to tread lightly so as not to offend someone of another religion.

The "progressive" elite media don't seem to understand what would happen to them if the United States were ever conquered by some foreign force with the same hostility for American values that they have. They would probably be the first ones jailed and/or killed. In Egypt, Libya, Yemen, Syria, and Bahrain during the "Arab Spring" that American liberals loved so much, the first persons arrested (with some tortured and raped) were journalists and reporters. We should remember the famous words of Martin Niemoeller (1892-1984). "In Germany, they came first for the Communists, and I didn't speak up because I wasn't a Communist. Then they came for the Jews, and I didn't speak up because I wasn't a Jew. Then they came for the trade unionists, and I didn't speak up because I wasn't a trade unionist. Then they came for the Catholics, and I didn't speak up because I was a Protestant. Then they came for me, and by that time no one was left to speak up."

1. http://www.commondreams.org/views02/1109-02.htm

2. http://www.stabroeknews.com/2010/archives/02/20/islam-terror-and-political-correctness/

3. http://www.nytimes.com/2011/08/28/magazine/asking-candidates-tougher-questions-about-faith.html?_r=3

4. http://newsbusters.org/blogs/kyle-drennen/2011/08/25/nbc-dick-cheney-one-most-controversial-figures-our-time-did-we-mention

ABOUT THE AUTHOR

Marlin Thompson was born on a farm near Brocket, North Dakota on October 1, 1934. He graduated as a Mechanical Engineer from the University of North Dakota in 1957. He was an editor for two years on The Dakota Engineer, an in-school magazine.

After graduation, he worked for Bendix Missile Division, in Mishawaka, Indiana. He worked nine years on the Talos and Typhon anti-aircraft missile programs for the U.S. Navy. He was the co-author of BxM-5000, a book on missile workmanship. During this time, he was active in Republican politics, working on the Barry Goldwater campaign in 1964. Marlin is an ultra-conservative constitutionalist.

He joined M-D Pneumatics in Springfield, Missouri as a project manager designing and building lobe pumps for the wastewater and meat packing market. He wrote articles published in several national design magazines, including a fluid viscosity cross-reference chart that has become a standard for industry.

Marlin holds 6 patents on pumps, electric motors, pneumatic cylinders, and material handling equipment. He is now a semi-retired owner of small company designing and building custom automation machinery. During this time, he authored a booklet on Engineering Documentation Systems, with an emphasis on an organized system for information retrieval.

Marlin has submitted about 300 Letters to the Editor from a conservative perspective to local newspapers in Springfield, MO, and Roanoke, VA, for 35 years (with most published). Also, since 2006, he has submitted about 90 articles, on topics of current cultural and political interest, to an international website - PA Pundits International - that were all published.

Marlin has written seven Christian articles on major scriptural subjects such as The Pre-incarnate Christ, Life After Life, The Origin of Evil, and God's Chosen People.

He is presently working on a book about the history of Norwegian immigrant homesteaders in North Dakota and growing up to see the last of the old West before 1949, when the area he lived in got electricity, roads, and running water. He also continues to submit articles regularly to PA Pundits about topics of current cultural and political interest from a conservative perspective.

54041585R00119

Made in the USA
Middletown, DE
12 July 2019